# NOT IN VAIN

# NOT IN VAIN A Rifleman

Remembers

World War II

## LEON C. STANDIFER

Louisiana State University Press     Baton Rouge and London

Copyright © 1992 by Louisiana State University Press
All rights reserved
Manufactured in the United States of America
First printing
01  00  99  98  97  96  95  94  93  92     5  4  3  2  1

Designer: Amanda McDonald Key
Typeface: Bembo
Typesetter: G&S Typesetters, Inc.
Printer and binder: Thomson–Shore, Inc.

Library of Congress Cataloging-in-Publication Data

Standifer, Leon C.
    Not in vain : a rifleman remembers World War II / Leon C.
Standifer.
        p.   cm.
    Includes bibliographical references.
    ISBN 0-8071-1703-X (cloth : alk. paper)
    1. Standifer, Leon C. 2. World War, 1939–1945—Personal
narratives, American. 3. Soldiers—United States—Biography.
4. United States. Army—Biography. I. Title.
D811.S763   1992
940.54'8173—dc20                                            91-23154
                                                                CIP

Bill Mauldin Drawings Copyright 1944 By United Feature Syndicate, Inc.
Copyright 1945 By Henry Holt and Company, Inc.

For King Company, 301st Infantry Regiment
of the Ninety-fourth Division
*Men who were girt for the combat,*
*Men who were grit to the core.*


And for Dale Proctor
*Greater love hath no man than this,*
*that he lay down his life for his friends.*

"Not in vain" may be the pride of those who survived and the epitaph of those who fell.

—Winston Churchill

# Contents

x    Contents

# Illustrations

# Preface

During the tragedy of Vietnam, I was listening while a student explored the problems of ethics, patriotism, loyalty, and courage. He was opposed to our country's role in Vietnam and horrified by what he saw on television. He wanted to be a loyal citizen but could not serve the military or take a job that would release someone else to fight. He would not retreat to Canada, and accepting an educational deferment was only another form of retreat. He wasn't asking me for advice. I represented only an outlet and a source of sympathy and concern. After a long pause he asked, "Why did you fight?" The question surprised me. For years I had spun semifactual yarns of my war, but none were based on any reason for fighting. Had it simply been the thing for boys of my generation to do?

In my best professorial manner I reached for my pipe, filled it with tobacco, tamped it, lit the tobacco, and drew a long puff of smoke. That procedure usually gave me enough time to think of a reasonable answer, but it didn't work. I remembered the ridiculous propaganda film that we saw during basic training: *Why We Fight*. It had become a joke among the trainees. I remembered rumors about the concentration camps, and newsreels on the bombing of London. I remembered the military parades, passing in review to the music of "Stars and Stripes Forever." I remembered "On my honor I will do my best to do my duty" and I remembered "Meine Ehre heisst Treue"—"Loyalty Is the Foundation of My Honor." I couldn't make any of the fragments fit together.

Finally I said, "It was a different war and a different time." That was no answer; there are no different wars, and young men go to war because the community sends them. His question continued to cling. It brought back old scars: the eerie feeling of watching an early morning mist clear and wondering if a monster would step out; the vague chill of dread on moonlight nights. I could remember the sick, dirty feeling while I walked through clean white snow on a dark night. I could tie those thoughts to "the war," but I didn't know where they fitted or why they lingered. I needed to unravel that mess and find— well, why I fought.

Now, after our fifth major war of the century, I am attempting to address his question again and realizing that there were several questions. Why must young men die to atone for the sins of their country and of other countries? At age eighteen, what do we owe the society that has loved, fed, sheltered, and taught us? Who should fight in the infantry? Should the most intelligent, confident, and capable boys be sacrificed as cannon fodder when they could serve better in more technical positions? Must the illiterate bear the cross alone and all the rest go free? Those are more than World War II, Korea, Vietnam, and Persian Gulf questions. They are fundamental: Johnny, get your gun— make your daddy glad to have had such a lad.

All wars have common threads of fear, boredom, horror, pride, and excitement. The underprivileged and poorly educated were not as badly overrepresented in Kuwait, but body bags came home, just as they did from Vietnam; in World War II we used mattress covers. Again, brave men and cowards broke under stress and all enemy soldiers were perceived as animals. War correspondents reworked stories to make war more exciting and convert ordinary men into gallant warriors.

I dug into letters my mother had saved, visited with old friends, visited with new friends who were sociologists, psychologists, historians, and a climatologist. I read books on the war and on war. Now, having written this account, I am more at peace with myself, the army, and my community but I have not answered the questions. I have only addressed them, helped to define problems that young men have faced after every war, including the Persian Gulf. For me, the Boy Scout Oath is a starting point: "On my honor I will do my best to do my duty." But there is more, and deeper, imprinting involved. I can demonstrate it by asking the reader to go with a young, idealistic, religious boy as he is slowly forced to look war directly in the face, and as he tries to rationalize what he sees there.

Although most people who have been in combat will identify with some of the scenes I describe, there is no typical battle or soldier. I offer this account through my experiences simply because that is what I know; I was there. I was in no important battles and received no citations for bravery. My experiences were unusual only in that I was in combat as a rifleman for over three months—but that was largely because our fighting was seldom intense. What a nineteen-year-old boy saw or believed was happening is accurate only in the sense that it was his perception. Where this remembered perception differs from the objectively factual, I have tried to add a broader viewpoint. In some instances, I have changed or omitted names where I see no reason for causing embarrassment and the story can be told as well without it. I have sometimes used quotations to re-create the images and emotions that I remember, without meaning that the conversation is verbatim. I have occasionally shifted events, particularly those on the patrols, into different time frames; life in combat is often painfully dull, and that must be noted, but there is no need to emphasize it. With these qualifications, the account is as accurate as I have been able to make it.

This story is largely about courage, dedication, and loyalty. It's about dedication to principles taught by the community. But it is primarily an appeal for tolerance. It questions a society that feels that it must hate in order to justify killing and that there is no honor for brave German or Iraqi soldiers who died in ways their families and communities regarded as dutiful and even heroic. It's about the simplicity of a bumper sticker that says: "Hate War, Not the Warrior."

# NOT IN VAIN

# 1 That's What Soldiers Are Made Of

Sept. Beats me, 15?, 1944
Somewhere in France

Dear Folks,

I know you have been worried, and am sorry that I couldn't write. The Army has a policy saying that there must be a ten-day delay in reporting troop movements. When we got to France we could no longer mark letters as Somewhere in England—or Somewhere in France. So we couldn't write.

We are now officially in France and in combat—but it's more like "at combat." Nobody has been hurt and we aren't doing much. Ed and I went on one short patrol, George didn't go. If anything had happened I couldn't tell about it—but it didn't. We captured one German—a scared boy about my age. He was shaking like a leaf. I'm not sure "captured" is the right word. He had deserted and was trying to find some Americans.

I can't say much more, or even comment on the war. They say it is still going on but we don't get any newspapers and our company radio is stored somewhere.

The foregoing is from the first letter I wrote during combat. My guess at the date was badly off. It was probably between the eighteenth and the twenty-first of September, but we had lost our sense of time. Life was dull, but it didn't stay that way. Within a week, one of my friends had been killed and another had lost a hand. About a week after that, we had our first real combat patrol.

•   •   •

I led off in front of the patrol—point scout in front of the whole army. The next people in front of me were Krauts. I was careful but relaxed. The rifle felt good in my hands. My rifle belt was heavy and biting into my hips. I wasn't accustomed to having it full of ammunition. Maybe I should start wearing the harness of a combat pack. I cocked the helmet to the side of my head so I could hear better. Ed was about twenty-five yards behind me and off to the side. His primary job was to keep contact between me and the patrol. Just past Cap Kerdudal, a creek ran under the road. The patrol formed a line along some brush beside the road. Ed and I began the trip up the valley. It wasn't quite a valley, just a long draw feeding into the creek. I walked very carefully, stopping when something looked strange. Everything looked strange; I had learned that the beautiful rolling hills could explode into chaos. I was going up the draw like a scout in a war movie, one of those exciting scenes in which there is background music until you see that the enemy is ready to attack. Then there is deadly silence.

I realized that the countryside was absolutely quiet. I strained to hear any sound. A bird was singing.

I stopped and looked back at Ed, who just shrugged his shoulders. Either he didn't see anything wrong or it was too late for us to confer. If this was a trap I already had gone too far into it. The patrol was still safe, but Ed and I were in a bad place. There was a shed on the ridge at the head of the draw, a perfect machine-gun position. A board had been pulled off to make a hole to fire through. The gunner was watching me, waiting. Without looking back, I knew what the squad was doing. George was cool, calm, his BAR aiming directly at the shed. His finger was resting lightly on the trigger. If I were shot, the German gunner would die within two seconds. Westmoreland was twitching his chin and breathing hard. Ray was cursing me for being too slow. Prado and Peewee were relaxed and bored.

My mind was running through options. If I turned around to walk back, the gunner would fire. Flanking was impossible. "Yea, though I walk through the valley of the shadow of death, I will fear no evil." My muscles were tense, my hands were sweaty—the rifle felt slippery. I slid the safety lock off and walked straight at the gun, boldly and aggressively but very carefully.

At thirty yards I stopped and dropped to one knee. The gunner would open up somewhere between here and ten yards. I couldn't see a thing. Where would the enemy riflemen be? There was no cover close to the shed. Rifles would be along that hedgerow.

I thought, Leon, you're stalling. The squad is watching. I came up to a crouch, rifle ready to fire from the hip. Cut every thought out of your mind. Depend on instinct. Fire at any sound or motion, anywhere.

Thinking back over forty-five years, I still remember the excitement: aggression, caution, but no fear. We had an expression: "This isn't the kind of work Mama raised her little boy to do." I hadn't joined the army for the honor of leading an infantry rifle squad into combat. When, how did I become an animal, ready to kill or die—and why?

Young men have developed their potential for becoming soldiers long before their eighteenth birthdays. I don't believe any community raises its children "a soldier for to be," but the interactions of family, community, and personality are primary determinants in how well each of us will "soldier." Looking back to World War II, I see evidence that almost any kind of protective community will produce good soldiers, but for this account I can only describe my own community and the way it sent me off to battle.

The Standifers came from Scotland. We are told that the name was originally Standiever, or roughly, "Stand fast." I don't know when the family left Scotland, but it was in Georgia long before the Civil War (Standifers rode with Forrest's cavalry in that war). My father grew up in Oxford, Mississippi, playing with John and Bill Falkner. Bill later took on strange airs, added a *u* to make the name Faulkner, and wrote some novels that won him a Nobel Prize. My father got along with John but didn't really like either of the brothers.

Because Daddy moved to the southern part of the state as a young man, I grew up with no close ties with the north Mississippi Standifers. I was better known for my mother's family: throughout central and south Mississippi I was "Tom Moore's grandson," a magic phrase that would always establish me as the right kind of people. Thomas Jefferson Moore had been a pioneer Baptist minister, establishing churches in rough logging camps that gradually became small towns. Mother grew up in Carthage, Purvis, Prentiss, Richton, Bay Springs,

Eastabuchie, and Eden. The Moores were originally from southern Ireland but had been in Mississippi since way back. Moores also fought in the Civil War. One of them deserted at Vicksburg. Another refused to be reconstructed; this one had to spend a few years in Texas after he killed a former slave for an allegedly disrespectful remark.

All in all, I come from sturdy Scotch-Irish stock, with a little mixing of some Anglo-Saxon English and very likely a bit of Muskhogean Choctaw. But I no longer believe that a person's genetic heritage is important; culturally, the Deep South, east to Georgia and west beyond Texas, was Celtic, with a lot of African seasoning. The Celts were a proud, colorful warrior culture that spread across western Europe and into what is now England, Wales, Scotland, and Ireland. The well-organized Roman army defeated the Celts in France and England, but only held them at bay in Wales, Scotland, and Ireland. The legends of King Arthur's knights tell of the defeat of proud, heroic, individualistic Romano-Celtic warriors by the barbaric, better-organized Anglo-Saxons—again in England, but not in Wales, Scotland, and Ireland.

The earliest Celtic migrations to America took them largely into the mid-South, where the newcomers retained their warrior tradition of courageous charges accompanied by wild, high-pitched screams (which eventually became the Rebel yell); their clannish tradition of fighting well only as individuals or small groups; and their unfortunate tradition of being soundly whipped by well-organized barbaric armies. But the Celts brought much more from the old lands: love of art, beautiful ballads, the oral tradition of a well-spun yarn, a devotion to the God of our fathers, the customs of calling the clan together with a flaming cross and of wearing the white robes of the ancient Druid priests. I grew up in a Celtic culture, and it is still the foundation of my personality. I am proud of some of the principles that it instilled in me. Others are embarrassing, but they are as deeply imprinted as those that I admire. I am a Scotch-Irish, Celtic, redneck, Good Ole Boy.

Although my deep roots are Celtic, the sustaining feeder roots draw from a small college town in central Mississippi. Clinton was located on the old Natchez Trace about ten miles from Jackson. During the eighteenth and early nineteenth centuries, frontiersmen sold their furs in Natchez and traveled the Trace back to Nashville and civilization. Clinton developed as a "stand," or hotel, with a small artesian well beside the Trace. Because the water supposedly had medicinal value, the place eventually gained a minor reputation as a health spa. Early in the nineteenth century a men's college was established, which the state Baptists later purchased and named Mississippi College. Its primary purpose was to train ministers, but a strong emphasis on academics made MC the first choice of young men from the wealthier Baptist families. A Baptist family then established Hillman College as a parallel institution for women.

In 1932 Clinton was a town of perhaps 1,500 people. Like much of the country, it was under serious stress from the Great Depression. The Roaring Twenties, speakeasies, bootlegging, and gangland rule in the cities had frightened rural communities with what the future might bring if they didn't cling to the old values. Everyone's memory of his hometown is highly subjective, and I probably could not present a documentary view of Clinton if I tried; what follows is simply the way I remember the place and its culture from boyhood. Fundamentally, Clinton was a typical isolated community. Except for obvious points of cultural and religious emphasis, it was very much like Bruno, Nebraska; Mount Sterling, Ohio; Spartanburg, South Carolina; or a Jewish neighborhood in Brooklyn. Clinton did differ from many small towns in that about 75 percent of the families were economically dependent on the two colleges. Some of the remaining 25 percent were employed by the Mississippi Baptist Convention. Clinton was a popular retirement town for Baptist ministers and missionaries. Most of the town's elected officials were also employed by the college. The mayor was the Mississippi College chemistry teacher.

Clinton was bounded by U.S. Route 80 on the north and extended five blocks south to the Illinois Central railroad tracks. Hillman College backed on the railroad east of the depot. West of the depot, a silted-up artesian spring and the barely visible foundations of an old hotel showed where "downtown" Clinton once had been. The town's center had since moved two blocks north toward Mississippi College, which occupied a ridge north of the highway. The quiet little Clinton streets were made of red bricks with tar poured between the cracks. In summer the tar would melt and bubble up. We would dig it out and chew it. It tasted terrible but was said to be good for your teeth; I don't remember why we were so concerned with keeping our teeth clean. The streets had no names that we knew. When you know who lives in every house, street names have no meaning. Things happen "in the lot by the Jenkins house" or "in front of Dees's store." We knew everybody in town and they knew us. If we did anything, good or bad, the news often reached home before we did.

For the time, Mississippi College was probably a very good liberal arts college. Students from influential families often took their B.A.'s from MC before going to medical or law school. If they were going into business or law, they would try to put in about two years at MC and transfer to Ole Miss. Academically, MC was probably superior to Ole Miss. The comparison is difficult because MC offered hardly any professional courses, but certainly MC had the advantage of much stronger discipline than was possible at the state colleges. Students with poor grades were "campused"—allowed off campus only for church services—with no social activities. If the low grades continued, the student was encouraged to leave or to enroll in the prep school until he was ready for college. The college was strong in English, history, chemistry, biology, and classical languages. A department usually consisted of one very good man and one or two younger assistants.

Besides the academic advantages, MC was a good place to make political associations with people who would become influential in the state. I think it was a rather expensive school, but grants and scholarships were given by influential alumni for deserving students. Children of ministers and those who had shown promise of active Christian leadership could usually find some kind of financial aid. The father of my closest friend, Bob Canzoneri, entered MC with a total of fifty cents in savings. The grants and scholarships usually required some kind of work, so in effect the students were working their way through college.

The depression had a much larger influence on MC than we children realized. The college was funded entirely by the Mississippi Baptist Convention, but that had been substantially reduced by the depression. The shortfall was partly made up by increased support from alumni who were lawyers, doctors, and lumbermen. These men also had been hurt by the depression, but they wanted MC to continue. The price for their support was that they wanted to see the college run in a businesslike manner. The board of trustees began to watch expenses more closely. The old president retired and was replaced by a businesslike young man. The prep school and a lot of the discretionary money disappeared. The faculty had to be more careful about their opinions than they had been earlier. This last point was not so much a matter of losing academic freedom as of expressing opinions only within one's own area of authority.

Charles Deevers was the botanist, with a Ph.D. from the University of Chicago. I discussed the issue of academic restriction with him after the war. Charles taught all aspects of botany, pretty much as the spirit moved him. If he thought some students ought to have a plant physiology course, he taught it. His only essential duty was conveying the botanical part of biology. Neither he nor the zoologist had any problems teaching evolution—so long as they avoided the human aspect of it. "Most of the Holy Joes weren't upset about evolution, and those who would have been didn't understand what we were saying." Deevers had to be very careful, however, not to express opinions on any theological question.

Dr. Michael O'Rourke Patterson was a brilliant scholar, specializing in Old Testament. His father had believed that all boys should attend school until they were twelve. They then owed him nine years of farm work. When Dr. Patterson arrived at MC, he was twenty-one, with a sixth-grade education and no money. He enrolled in the college's prep school and graduated from MC six years later. He was such an outstanding scholar that people held him a bit in awe. No one except his wife called him "M. O."; he was Dr. Patterson to everyone else. His son Joe was my age and a close friend. After Joe was about twelve, Dr. Patterson would take him into the study regularly for short lectures and reading assignments from deep books. Joe didn't know what his faher was trying to show him, but felt it was something Dr. Patterson didn't want to teach openly. If so, it wasn't a very good approach because Joe kept revealing the secrets to us. Joe still isn't sure what his father wanted him to know; it may have been nothing more mysterious than his ideas about the roots of the Jewish faith. There was a school of thought that said Abraham came from the Indo-European culture; a necessary assumption was that Abraham and possibly Sarah were Hittites, whereas the tribe that served him was Semitic.

I think the situations of the rest of the faculty lay somewhere between those of Dr. Deevers and Dr. Patterson. It wasn't a very restrictive place. When you accepted a position at MC, you knew it was a Baptist college and that you were expected to be a Christian example to the students and the community.

Hillman College had once been called Central Female Institute, and the girls were still called "Stute girls." The school was located on the other side of town from MC, about five blocks away. It was privately owned but precisely the sister college, with the same standards and requirements as MC. Insofar as possible, the two schools were sexually segregated. Although Stute girls could take courses at MC if they showed a special need, most of the girls' courses were taught on the Hillman campus. We didn't know the Stute girls as well as we did the college boys. The girls weren't allowed off campus alone. If they wanted to go downtown to the drugstore (two blocks from campus) they needed a group of five girls. To go to classes at MC or to church, they walked in an orderly double line with a chaperon. This was called the "Stute line." When the Stute line marched back from Sunday night church, the girls' boyfriends could walk along with them.

The two schools created an atmosphere of intellectual inquiry. As children, we enjoyed living in a college town. We had authorities to go to with our questions on biology, chemistry, or history. It seemed to me that half the adults had doctoral degrees. The degree was a social title in Clinton, but as far as I could see it was not a matter of prestige. Some people were called "Doctor" or "Professor," and others were called "Mister." From our perception, Mister was just as good as Doctor. The college students always had time to tease us and play with us. Our high school footbal heroes didn't go off to college, they just started playing for MC. At the time, we didn't realize that the better players wanted to go to the big Southeastern Conference schools but had to stay in Clinton so Daddy could keep his job. Two afternoons a week in the fall, the college band practiced marching on the Clinton streets. Townspeople sat on their porches waiting for them to come by. We kids gathered at the band hall to fall in behind the musicians and strut all over town marching to Sousa music. The band played a lot of military music because it was a military band. To be in the band at MC, you had to join the National Guard. Then you were given a uniform, an instrument, and a small check when you went to summer camp. In a sense, you had a music scholarship. When the war started, the entire band was called out to become part of the Thirty-first Infantry Division.

I was eight years old when we moved to Clinton, but there was no problem of acceptance. I already belonged: my father had graduated from MC and my mother from Hillman. Mrs. Canzoneri came to visit and brought her son Bob, who was just my age. Bob's father was a preacher and a marvelous singer. He was out of town a lot, leading the singing at revivals. Mr. Canzoneri had lived in Purvis and had been baptized by my grandfather, who also helped him get financial aid to go to MC. Mrs. Canzoneri was a Barnett and had been at Hillman with my mother. Her cousin Ross Barnett was a criminal lawyer who was a bit of an embarrassment to the family. From the stories I heard of Mr. Ross back then, nothing would have suggested that he might become governor. Joe Patterson lived across the street from us. Atley Kitchings' father had been at MC with my father. Dr. Kitchings preached at two rural churches on Sundays, but during the week he taught modern languages at MC.

There were difficult aspects of living in a church town, but our parents helped to soften them. Because the church was opposed to the wild life-styles shown in movies, Clinton didn't have a theater. But cowboy movies were generally considered to be a good, healthy influence, and almost every Saturday some parent would take us to Jackson to watch Tom Mix and our other heroes. Most parents would even let us buy popcorn and coke.

Some facets of churchly influence were simply part of life. A few years ago I was talking with Anna White Eager, a friend who had been an Episcopalian in Clinton—every Sunday her family drove to Jackson for church. She remembered that each fall and spring, the Baptist church had a revival week during which a visiting minister preached every morning at eleven o'clock. Each day at ten thirty, all children in the Clinton public school's elementary classes were marched to church for the sermon. (High school students had the option of going to study hall instead of to church.) I asked Anna White what she had thought of having to go to the revivals. "The same thing you did. When revivals came, we all went to the Baptist church. It was part of going to school."

Throughout the week our life was built around church activities. On Monday afternoon the boys went to R.A.'s (Royal Ambassadors; we are strangers to this world, sent here as ambassadors for our King) and the girls to G.A.'s (Girls Auxiliary). Our task in these groups was mainly to study the lives of missionaries. You answered roll call by giving a Bible verse. You weren't allowed to use one that someone else had quoted. The first person always snapped up "Jesus wept" because it was the shortest verse in the Bible. One day Snerd Goodrich tried 1 Sam. 25:22, but the leader stopped him before he got to the funny part where David threatens to kill "any that pisseth against the wall."

Even the more glorious verses from the Old Testament were not quite acceptable—we were New Testament Christians. Still, I enjoyed a lot of David's poetry. His eulogy on the deaths of Jonathan and Saul was beautiful. "How the mighty are fallen in the midst of battle! O Jonathan, thou was slain in thine high places." I remembered the eulogy years later when a close friend was slain while he saved a patrol from annihilation. His high place was a little French farming village in Brittany.

We also answered roll call with Bible verses in elementary school. A few teachers didn't like the practice because some students didn't know many verses. In the fourth grade, Mrs. Lassiter gave each pupil a verse that began with the first letter of his or her first name. Mine was "Let your light so shine before men."

On Wednesday nights we had Prayer Meeting. It was adult-oriented, but children old enough to stay awake at night were expected to go. Having homework wasn't an excuse because Wednesday afternoon was study time.

Sundays started at 9:30 A.M. with Sunday school, devoted to Bible study. The younger children (Beginners' Department) learned Bible stories and children's songs:

> Jesus loves me, this I know,
> For the Bible tells me so.
> Little ones to Him belong.
> They are weak but He is strong.

In the Junior Department (ages eight through twelve), we began learning all about the Bible. We learned the names of all the books of the Bible and many, many quotations. You needed to know them to do well in Sword Drill. The name came from the idea that the Bible is the sword of the spirit of God, so that your sword in the fight against evil is to know the Bible well. We would line up holding our Bibles. I think the command was "Draw swords." Then the leader would give a Bible reference and order, "Charge!" The first person to find the reference won a point and was allowed to read it. If you knew the reference well, you could fudge a bit by pretending to find it quickly and then quoting from memory. This tactic was risky because if you found the reference too quickly, you would be asked to read not only it, but also the verse that followed it. The best people at Sword Drill got to represent the church in regional and state contests. I was never that good.

Sunday school was segregated into boys' classes and girls' classes (in the 1930s, segregation didn't refer only to race). The morning church service, at eleven o'clock, was segregated in a different way: children sat with their parents. The Sunday morning sermons were pompous and dull; we lasted through them by dreaming of Sunday night and BYPU.

# 2 But the Bible Says

BYPU stood for Baptist Young People's Union: "Training for Church Leadership." We had a manual that scheduled topics for discussion and outlined points to be considered. About once a year we studied the theme "Our Baptist Heritage." We learned that Baptists were advocating individual religious freedom long before the Reformation. In that sense we were not Protestants. In early America, Baptists were active in promoting the separation of church and state and in seeing that the Bill of Rights contained a clause about freedom of worship by the individual.

Because Baptists believe that each person is responsible for his own interpretation of God's word, it was considered essential that we develop a good understanding of the Bible as it related to our lives. This was one aspect of the doctrine of the "Priesthood of Believers," which we were told represented the fundamental difference between Baptists and Catholics. In the Catholic church, supposedly, only the priest was allowed to study the Bible; he then told the church members what to believe. But each Baptist believed that he himself was a priest in the eyes of God, and therefore was responsible for his own interpretation.

Although this doctrine was the cause of many arguments within our congregation and other congregations, the adult leaders were fairly tolerant of different scriptural interpretations. They were a little less tolerant about what we children believed, but every Sunday night we were allowed "semiadult" discussions of the Bible.

BYPU was the only program in which boys and girls met together. Because it began at an age in which we were trying to understand sex, we developed new insights into the topics being studied. David took another man's wife. Abraham "knew" his servant, who then had a baby. We snickered over the price David paid for his first wife (the foreskins of two hundred Philistines). The girls giggled and the boys shuddered at the imagery of Deut. 33:11 concerning smiting through the loins of the enemies of the Lord. (Some translations use "break the back," which probably has less meaning to adolescents than to senior citizens.)

BYPU was essentially a weekly seminar in Christian living, and because we attended it for six years, beginning at age twelve, it was roughly equivalent to twenty semester-long seminars. The weekly topic in the manual was divided into about five or six subtopics. These were assigned among the group, and each of us was expected to lead a short discussion on his portion. The leader reserved the last ten minutes to summarize or to explain what our proper attitude should be.

"But he, willing to justify himself, said unto Jesus, And who is my neighbour?" (Luke 10:29). The story of the Good Samaritan is simple: your neighbor is anyone who needs your help. One night when the discussion was plodding along, Joe Patterson said: "Jesus has another lesson hidden under that one. The Jew in need was passed up by other Jews and was helped by a man from a race that the Jews wouldn't associate with. I wonder what the Samaritan thought of the man who would accept his help but wouldn't invite him into his home."

We knew exactly what Joe was saying because it was a topic that his mother emphasized. Mrs. Patterson, from a wealthy, influential south Mississippi family, was a leader in state-wide efforts for increased understanding of social problems. If our BYPU leader had realized what Joe meant, she would have guided us away from it as quickly as from the Song of Solomon. Before she knew it, we had gotten into the race question. We had grown up with and accepted separation of the races, so that wasn't the issue. But Jesus meant for us to treat blacks as we would our neighbors. Finally, the leader had her ten minutes to explain the proper attitude: the Samaritan wasn't black, he was as white as the Jews. The blacks were all descendants of Ham, and God had ordained that they should always be servants of the whites. "But because they are our servants, God expects us to love them and help them. We love them as neighbors who are different from us and would rather be with their own kind."

If the leader didn't push too hard on the "children of Ham" theme, we usually dropped the subject. Genesis wasn't an easy book to defend. There was the question of whom Adam's children married in the land of Nod. And Noah's curse wasn't on Ham, but on Ham's son Canaan, who must have been white because the Canaanites were white. But there were plenty of other reasons for the leader to avoid the topic of race.

The infamous Clinton race riot of September 5, 6, and 7, 1875, was an embarrassing bit of local history that people only mentioned vaguely and in hushed tones. The occasion for the riot was a Republican-Democrat debate about the first postwar gubernatorial election, to be held that November. The predominantly black Republican party sponsored the debate and accompanying barbecue, which were held at the Moss Hill plantation, about a quarter-mile north of town. An estimated one thousand black Republicans attended, along with a handful of whites. Some drunk whites from the nearby town of Raymond began arguing with blacks, a shot was fired, and all hell broke loose. Blacks and whites ran in all directions, shooting as they went. Judge Cabiness sent a telegram to a loosely organized white militia in Vicksburg, the Modocs. (The name originally belonged to a small but fierce Indian tribe.) The Modocs boarded a train and arrived in Clinton that night.

The next day was Saturday, and throughout the daylight hours and into the night, the Modocs established peace by killing every black man they found. Fortunately, they found only about twenty or thirty, the rest having gone to Jackson for protection. On Sunday morning the white women of Clinton served breakfast (biscuits and coffee) to the Modocs on the campus of the Central Female Institute and congratulated the militiamen on a job well done.

Even sixty years after the riot, it remained something of a dark family secret in Clinton, and to some degree it still is; in writing this account, I had to get the facts from a historical journal. At the time, the town's whites argued that the riot was caused by outside agitators (those drunks from Raymond), although of course the blacks themselves were largely to blame because they had become so arrogant. The "outside agitator" excuse lost some of its weight when the local black leader, Charles Caldwell, returned to Clinton in December and was shot while walking down the street. As he lay dying from fifteen bullet wounds, he reportedly said, "You may fire as many shots as you please, but you shall not say that I did not die like a brave man."

Despite this bloody bit of history and our BYPU leader's concern, in the 1930s racism in Clinton lacked the suffocating importance that it had in many other places in the South, perhaps largely because the local economy did not depend on labor. The town had a cotton gin and a grist mill, both serving a small farm population that was probably about 50 percent black. About 30 percent of the town's white families had black maids, who on the average worked about two days a week. Mississippi College had a black construction crew, and several stores had black workers. There seemed to be no worries about blacks' taking white jobs or about black discontent. The term *black*, of course, was not used then. We always spoke of "colored people." *Negro* was not a polite term, and *nigger* meant you needed to have your mouth washed out with soap—it was a word trashy people used. We had a few trashy people in town. I wasn't allowed to play with their children.

Colored people should be loved and helped because they were so unfortunate. Their schools were run down and the teachers weren't very good. Without education, they couldn't get good jobs. There were trashy colored who got drunk, fought, and were always stealing, but there were a lot of nice, clean colored families too. When I was little, Mother let me go over and play with Veenie's children: "Be sure to mind Veenie." Once, I tried to get Mr. Dees to hire me in place of his delivery boy, Amos, who was always making mistakes. I succeeded only in getting Mr. Dees mad at me. Amos was a poor little colored boy, but he could read; he made delivery mistakes because he didn't half try. Mr. Dees preferred to overlook the mistakes: "His home life is bad and his family needs the money." I sometimes heard women say that maids with a little white blood in them were more reliable. I didn't understand that or how the maids got white blood. Later, I couldn't understand why they were still colored when they were three-quarters white.

This is a condensed description of attitudes I personally witnessed, but I don't know what the community actually believed. The town marshal was cruel to blacks, and one of the leading merchants owned a farm where he punished his field hands with a bullwhip. Perhaps we rationalized such actions through paternalism, the most insidious and degrading form of racism. The "better people" of the community loved their poor, incompetent colored, who shouldn't be allowed to vote because they could be so easily swayed by politicians. I would like to say that things have improved, but legislation doesn't change condescending attitudes toward blacks, Jews, Catholics, or rednecks.

In BYPU we had long discussions on salvation. The Baptist church was evangelical and described salvation in simple terms: "By grace are you saved, not by works, lest any man should boast." Yes, but how do you know if you are saved? "If you aren't sure, you aren't saved. It's a lot like trying to go to sleep—if you try too hard, you can't. Just relax." I worried about this before coming to the conclusion that salvation came with baptism; because I had been baptized, I was saved. The Baptist church taught eternal salvation. At the time of accepting salvation you are forgiven for any sins you might ever commit. Other churches believed a person could fall from grace if he continued to sin. For me, eternal salvation took all of the fear from religion. I wasn't going to hell; why worry about it? After being saved, I should have worried about others who were going to hell. I suppose I must have done so to some degree, but I wasn't personally evangelical.

"With salvation, you have no fear of death." Perhaps, but having no fear of death became a complex matter when we studied it carefully. Revival preachers described heaven in such glowing terms that we were in a hurry to get there. "Why not die now and go to heaven?" We are on earth to serve until God calls you to heaven. "Do some people commit suicide to go to heaven sooner?" That was a tough question, but real Christians don't commit suicide. The question did bring out the point that none of us was ready to die. You can want not to die and still not be afraid of death. I drew comfort from "Yea, though I walk through the valley of the shadow of death, I will fear no evil." It meant both that God would protect me in times of danger and that death wasn't something to fear. When we got into the war, there were stories of this or that man who would have been killed except that he was carrying a Bible in his breast pocket, and the Bible stopped the bullet. There were even Bibles with metal covers to protect and comfort soldiers in combat. I carried a small New Testament with Psalms in my jacket pocket during combat, but I didn't think it would protect me. I depended on "Yea, though I walk through the valley."

The Civil War permeated Clinton. There was a memorial to the Mississippi College Rifles, and old buildings that had housed wounded soldiers. The United Daughters of the Confederacy held a beautiful service every Confederate Memorial Day. Because Mrs. Patterson was usually on the program committee, things were done with great dignity. We would gather at the church and march to the cemetery, where the graves of Confederate dead were decorated. I remember one Memorial Day at which Joe decided we should also decorate the graves of the few Union soldiers. We learned that love for our fellow man did not extend to enemy dead.

Nobody spoke of "Rebel" soldiers. Ole Miss used the word as a name for its mascot, but that was wrong. Let the North pretend that the Civil War had been a rebellion. The South had not rebelled; it had seceded legally. On the other hand, the argument had been over slavery, which was morally wrong; therefore, secession had been an awful mistake. Our politicians had led the entire South up Fool's Hill, but the fault didn't lie with the soldiers. The boys in gray had served with honor. On Memorial Day, after an inspiring speech and the laying of a wreath, someone would read from Lee's writings or from "The Conquered Banner," by Abraham J. Ryan. Lee's letter accepting the presidency of Washington College was good: "I think it the duty of every citizen, in the present condition of the Country, to do all in his power to aid in the restoration of peace and harmony and in no way to oppose the policy of the State or General Government directed to that object." I preferred Father Ryan's "Conquered Banner":

> Furl that Banner! True, 'tis gory.
> Yet 'tis wreathed around with glory,
> and 'twill live in song and story.

It ended with:

> Furl that Banner, softly, slowly!
> Treat it gently—it is holy—
> For it droops above the dead;
> Touch it not    unfold it never,
> Let it droop there, furled forever,
> For its people's hopes are dead!

I loved those ceremonies. They treated the war with dignity and honor. We were Americans and always had been. We still hated the Yankees, who had been so awful during Reconstruction, but they weren't America. We were one nation, indivisible. In the 1950s I fumed at trashy people who waved "Rebel battle flags" and screamed "Dixie." Furl that Banner! Touch it not—unfold it never.

The final Mississippi Confederate Veterans reunion was held in Clinton when I was about ten. The thin gray line, marching behind the Mississippi College band, quietly carried the Banner, furled. After the parade I sat and listened to the old men tell about fighting the Yankees. They had funny tales of the awful noise and how scared they had been, but there were no stories of glory and courage. I was disappointed to learn that most of the men reliving the battles had been ten-to-fifteen-year-old drummer boys. The war had been over for seventy years.

BYPU taught us courage based on integrity and sense of duty. You did the right thing because that's what Jesus would have done. Somehow, this kind of courage usually involved refusing to smoke, drink, dance, or play cards. It was at its maximum if you were the only one in a group who did the right thing. Once, our study guide said that fear is a necessary part of both courage and cowardice. Being afraid is not cowardly, but letting fear decide your action is. Courage is doing what is right in spite of fear. If there is nothing to be afraid of, or you don't see the danger, doing right doesn't require courage. Occasionally, we drifted into physical courage on the football field. This was generally a matter of continuing to play when you were hurt or of tackling the big guy who was going to break your collarbone. Fundamentally, physical courage was exactly like real courage: you did what had to be done, regardless of fear.

Until the early 1940s, "Thou shalt not kill" was a very simple commandment for us. No one should be killed under any circumstances, except for criminals convicted by courts. Wartime killing was not discussed. Because our parents were products of World War I, we were all cynical about the "war to end wars." War was a horrible, brutal activity that accomplished nothing. Hitler was on the rise in the mid 1930s, and he was terrible, but the United States was through fighting in European wars. When France fell in 1939, we began to wonder how we could resist Hitler if England were beaten. There were stories that Argentina and Brazil were supporting Hitler. England was barely hanging on, and Russia was falling rapidly. Then came Pearl Harbor. Joe's brother, a West Point graduate, was stationed there. Wake Island and Bataan fell. The National Guard was called up. The MC band made its farewell parade around town. This time they weren't dressed in colorful football-game uniforms. They were dressed as soldiers. We marched along behind them, but it wasn't as much fun. The band came on strong, blaring out defiance in the loud parts of "Stars and Stripes Forever." Somehow, they weren't very convincing. They were going to war because we were getting whipped everywhere.

"Thou shalt not kill" became less clear. We started learning about justified killing. It came on slowly until Pearl Harbor. After that, "Kill the dirty Japs" was a popular sentiment. A store in Jackson displayed the skull of a Japanese soldier killed on Guadalcanal. That, at least, overstepped the bounds; the skull was soon removed. But support for "justified killing" became stronger. "Praise the Lord and Pass the Ammunition" was about a chaplain manning an antiaircraft gun, an act contrary to the Geneva Convention; the song was highly popular. BYPU became an interesting forum. Killing still was justified only when it was absolutely necessary, but we could find places in the Old Testament where God told his servants to kill every man, woman, and child in a town. Evidently, that was absolutely necessary, although for reasons we couldn't understand. In a modern war, killing enemy soldiers was justified.

At the time, I thought we had it all worked out. I had visions of charging a machine gun with my rifle blazing while I destroyed the enemies of democracy. I couldn't imagine looking at a terrified German kid who had surrendered, but you were on a patrol and shouldn't risk trying to take him back to your lines. We didn't discuss the blood seeping into your wool gloves after you had grabbed a kid and cut his throat.

At the end of our long discussions, the adult leader would set us straight with the ultimate answer: "Live as Jesus would." I suppose we each developed individual ideas of Jesus. I saw him as a distinct loner. He was always brave and usually chose the most difficult path to prove his courage. In our studies on Jesus, he was described as "the man for others." Jesus loved everyone and went to an undeserved death because of that love. There is a spiritual that says, "Jesus walked this lonesome valley / Had to walk it by himself," and "I must go and stand my trial / Got to stand it by myself." The Baptist church didn't use many spirituals, but that one seemed to describe part of my image of Jesus.

I learned concepts of applied religion in BYPU, although only a little at a time. Most of the programs were dull and useless. Even so, nobody wanted to miss BYPU. At the Sunday night preaching service, you could sit in the balcony with your girl. You could write notes, look at song titles, and giggle. After church you could walk your girl home and sit on the porch. Actually, you didn't have to come straight home. Parents offered a lot of tolerance for nice Christian couples walking back from church.

I don't remember the logic, but it wasn't proper to walk your girl *to* BYPU. You met her there by accident. On Saturday night, though, you could have a real date. You could go to the girl's house, walk her to the church social, and walk her home again. Church socials were frequent because otherwise Saturday nights were pretty empty. If you can't dance, play cards, or go to movies, there aren't many options left. On the few Saturdays when there wasn't some sort of church social, we could go to a girl's house and make candy.

I don't think we felt the church was binding us tightly on the matter of sex. From our point of view, the girls set the standards much more than did the church. Holding hands on the walk home was acceptable. A hug while sitting on the porch swing was a great concession. The goodnight kiss was an occasional thing, and then only with couples who were in love. In love or not, nothing else was acceptable. Your body was the Temple of God and anything more than a kiss before marriage was wrong. Of course, we had learned this at church, but the enforcement was among ourselves. The boys would have liked to do a little exploring, but we knew that nice girls didn't allow that sort of thing.

In Clinton we had very little personal freedom and probably felt a little rebellious, but rebellion was difficult because the rules, strict as they were, were not very clearly defined. The Bible said, "Thou shalt not"; Clinton said, "Nice people don't do that." We couldn't play cards because it led to gambling. But what if you only played games that didn't involve gambling? "Well, our kind of people don't do that." We knew the rules were there and that we would be in serious trouble if we broke them, but they were always cushioned by warm love. That's just the way life was in Clinton. The entire town seemed to accept the social creed of the church, so we did too. Coach Robbie would throw boys off the college football team for drinking or smoking, and suspend them for two weeks for swearing. Stute girls never even tried to slip out for a date. Our science authorities in botany, zoology, and astronomy all believed that every word of the Bible was literally true. It was easy for us to build a dichotomy of thought. Topics other than religious ones were always open to question and had to be proved. Scriptural questions had to be taken on faith.

Actually, not quite the *entire* town felt this way. We knew of people who didn't accept everything the church and college said. "Silk Stocking Street" was made up almost entirely of people whose fathers worked in Jackson. They weren't trashy, but they weren't our kind of people. We knew that they smoked and played cards, and that some of the parents drank. The better people in town didn't do that. We were very much an ethnocentric community. We knew the right way to live, and Mississippi College was one of the best academic institutions in the country.

Until we became teenagers, the fall and spring revivals were pure pleasure. We got time out of school and had no homework for the entire week. Because of the strong emphasis on salvation, most of us had joined the church during a revival, usually at about ten or eleven years of age, just as we were beginning to think of careers. The outstanding aspiration was to be called of God for full-time Christian ministry. This didn't mean that just anyone could decide to become a preacher: only those with good personalities and good speaking voices were called. Neither I nor anyone else in town believed that quiet, shy little Leon might become a preacher; I dreamed of being an agricultural or medical missionary instead.

Revivals were fun for teenagers, except on the night set aside "especially for the youth." That evening always entailed a sermon on sex or drinking. Most of the sex sermons used the edicts of Paul, and for the rest of the week we were afraid to speak to a girl.

A few of the ministers tempered their exhortations with discussions of Christian love. Sermons of this kind usually began with a careful explanation, which we had heard many times, of the three Greek words for love. (Anytime a preacher began using the "true original meaning" of a scriptural word, we were in for a boring night.) *Agapē* refers to pure, giving love. God loves us simply because we have needs. He expects nothing in return and needs nothing that we can offer. We can show this love by helping someone who cannot possibly repay us for a kindness. Missionaries on foreign fields were showing *agapē* to heathens who had done nothing to deserve it and could not help anyone. *Philia* is the friendship of two people, but this kind of love is based on the fact that each of us needs friends—or help in working toward a common goal. A football team is an example of friends working together. Finally, there is *erōs,* the root of all evil. This is love purely for self-gratification, wanting to use another body for your own purposes.

Occasionally, a preacher would say that love between a boy and a girl is partly *erōs,* but softened by the deep friendship of *philia.* One man quoted the Sermon on the Mount passage in which Jesus says that if you look on a woman with lust, you have already committed adultery. This point made teenage boys (and girls) uncomfortable, but the speaker qualified it a bit with an interesting approach to Jesus' admonition that if your right hand offends you, it should be cut off: "If you were to go to the doctor with a badly infected hand, he might be able to lance it—or he might have to amputate before the infection spread over the entire body." He went on to say that sex is a normal, healthy part of life, but only a part. Don't let it dominate your life. Simply thinking about sex is one thing, but when you let sex become the most important part of your life, that is lust. I suppose this explanation helped, although we wondered what would need to be amputated if sex became too important.

Sermons on the evil of drink were uniformly awful. The Baptist church was both strongly opposed to drinking alcohol in any form and firmly dedicated to scriptural support for all doctrines. But good antialcohol references are hard to come by. The standard scriptural text was Prov. 20:1, "Wine is a mocker, strong drink is raging; and whosoever is deceived thereby is not wise." Beyond that, 1 Tim. 3:3

describes a potential deacon as "not given to wine" and 1 Pet. 4:3 has a fairly serviceable reference to "excess of wine." In general, however, the preacher had a hard time pushing the biblical condemnation of strong drink. He never used 1 Tim. 5:23, "Drink no longer water, but use a little wine for thy stomach's sake and thine often infirmities." On Golgotha, the Romans tried to get Jesus to drink wine mixed with myrrh, but he refused it (Mark 15:23). We knew these references from way back, and the preacher knew that we knew. But he would get into the swing of the oratory and rail against demon rum. "Your friends will say that one little drink won't matter, but—THE BIBLE SAYS . . ." When you know the argument isn't strong, yell like the dickens.

The BYPU leader must have dreaded those sermons because in discussing them we would always bring up the obvious objections: "But the Bible mentions wine frequently, and most of the time it says that drinking is good. Jesus drank wine regularly. At the wedding he changed water into wine." The standard answer was: "Well, it was different back then. Water wasn't safe, and they couldn't make lemonade or iced tea." The same defense was raised if someone pointed out that the Bible doesn't really say that smoking, gambling, and dancing are sins. "Things were different back then. Today we see that those things lead to a wasted life and destroy your health." We knew that, and we knew that our kind of people didn't do such evil things. Why didn't the preachers say that, rather than lying about what the Bible said?

For a rural town in the 1930s, Clinton had some cultural advantages. The Mississippi College–Hillman College drama group was rather good. There was a small admission charge for adults; children were admitted free. I remember the plays only broadly, but I enjoyed them. I was very impressed with *Only the Valiant,* which took its theme from Shakespeare's *Julius Caesar:* "Cowards die many times before their deaths; / The valiant never taste of death but once." We already knew that. Courage is facing the fact that you might die, and living as a coward is worse than dying quickly and bravely.

There was no college orchestra, but the MC band gave concerts and Hillman gave choral presentations. The spring graduation exercises were the social highlight of the year. An outstanding minister was invited to give the baccalaureate sermon on the Sunday before graduation. The theme was always something like "The Great Challenge Before You," and for some reason the sermoners tended to rely on the same few scriptural passages. My favorite was when a minister chose Josh. 14:12, "Now therefore give me this mountain whereof the Lord spake." Said the preacher: "Good old Caleb, now there was a real man. He didn't take the easy route—'give me the mountain!'" The baccalaureate address itself was really just another sermon, albeit one urging the graduates to undertake great adventures. It was delivered under the giant oaks on campus. Then the band played the alma mater: "Clear gleams thy beacon of virtue and truth." Truth and Virtue was the MC motto. I grew up with it as the creed of life. "Be absolutely honest and do what you think is right." The motto would haunt me when the civil rights movement developed fifteen years later. I loved Clinton and tried to live by Truth and Virtue.

Not surprisingly, the prime cultural attraction was sermons. Clinton was on the chautauqua circuit for touring preachers. I suppose one reason was that the ministerial students took a course in *homiletics,* the art of preaching a sermon. We called it "Ecclesiastical Jargon 101." Every Sunday night the students in the course went to church with notebooks so they could jot down the sermon outline and comments on the preaching techniques. After church we could go to the Owl Cafe and listen to the ministerial students critique the sermon. They had long discussions on the structure, delivery, timing, and anecdotes: "That was a good tale, but I heard Brother Roberts give it at Huspuckena. I think his timing was much better." And they picked up choice phrases for later use. "He rose up like the wrath of God!" I liked that. It had speed, power, vengeance, and determination in it, although it wasn't easy to bring it into daily conversation. The words would come back to me bitterly at Nennig, a small town just inside Germany.

Early on, I realized that the ministerial students were discussing structure and technique, jargon rather than content. Did they ever listen to what the preacher said? The preacher was usually the local pastor, but sometimes a famous visiting minister came and delivered his favorite sermon. These outstanding preachers enjoyed the honor, the chance to repeat a good sermon (they couldn't do that at home), and the political advantage of preaching to young men who would later help direct the Mississippi Baptist Convention. The road to success in the ministry is paved with political favors. This situation also made the post of Clinton pastor a prime step for an ambitious preacher. The man who was pastor while I was growing up became general secretary of the Southern Baptist Convention.

I enjoyed hearing a new preacher. He put on his best act, polished for the Clinton audience. Some men were pompous and spent most of the time telling how they had enjoyed being students at MC. Some had marvelous dramatic scenes that they brought to life with high professional skill. Most of these pieces were from the standard repertoire of classic sermons. I could see them coming. One was the chess game tale. It was designed to parallel a plea for sinners to "make the move" of accepting eternal salvation. A chess champion was asked to comment on a painting depicting a chess game in which one player seemed certain to be checkmated. The champion studied the painting for nearly an hour. The observers were tense to hear his comment. Finally, he saw a possibility for the player to escape his predicament. Then he worked out what should happen next, and found a chance to win. Quietly he whispered, "Make that move." Then he shouted, "MAKE THAT MOVE!" There were real dramatic possibilities in that.

One minister gave a sermon on prayer. He said that revival preachers seemed to emphasize what God would do for you if you accepted him. "They have it turned wrongside out. God is not in heaven to serve you here. You are here to serve him. You are the servant of God. If you serve God well, your community will be better, your church will be better, and you will live a fuller, happier life. But you must serve God through love and loyalty. Don't try to make bargains with God—'I will serve you if you will do this for me.' When you pray, don't ask God to help you make an *A* on the test. Don't ask for a new bicycle. God doesn't deal in bicycles. God deals in strength, courage, and perseverance. When you pray, follow the model of Jesus at Gethsemane: 'Father, all things are possible unto thee; take away this cup from me; nevertheless, not what I will, but what thou wilt.'"

That was one of the stronger sermons. Many—most—of them were good, simple philosophy of life. The actor George Burns reminds me of those warm, confident old visiting preachers. There was usually a touch of humor, and a deep insight into human problems. The jokes and anecdotes were classics of timing. All of us learned to spin yarns from listening at the feet of those old masters. But we also became dreamers and wanted to dare great deeds.

The Baptists were a singing church. What we lacked in quality we compensated for through volume. There was no youth choir and no voice training; we just sang. The Bible says, "Make a joyful noise unto the Lord, all ye lands." We were scriptural, if not musical. Most of the songs were evangelical, built around repentance and salvation through joining the church. The themes were courage, love, and sacrifice. "'Are you able,' said the Master, / 'to be crucified with Me?'" We sang "Onward Christian Soldiers" and "Am I a Soldier of the Cross?" We asked, "Must Jesus bear the cross alone, / And all the world go free?" and answered, "No; there's a cross for every one, / And there's a cross for me."

The revival songs were invitations for sinners to join the happy Christians. "Oh, who will come and go with me? / I am bound for the promised land." The revival preacher would say: "That was beautiful. It's getting late and time to leave"—it had been time to leave thirty minutes ago—"but I can sense someone out there who is almost persuaded to come forward and accept eternal life. Let's sing one more verse just for him." And we would sing a verse, and often a few more, feeling content that we were saved and enjoying the knowledge that we were leading someone else to Jesus.

In Clinton the church was so strong that the influence of the high school seemed weak, but in fact the two institutions were interlocked. Like the college faculty, most of the high school teachers were active in the church. As for secular pursuits, although the town was enthusiastic about our football and basketball teams, almost everyone placed academics above athletics. The townspeople gossiped continuously about who was doing well in school and who might have to drop out. You needed good grades and a good reputation to win any kind of scholarship at MC. "Study to shew thyself approved unto God, a workman that needeth not to be ashamed" (2 Tim. 2:15). "A good name is rather to be chosen than great riches" (Prov. 22:1). Despite all that, I don't remember any tight competition for grades. Grading followed an absolute scale, not a curve, so we could all do well. We argued with the teachers even more than we did in BYPU, but they always won. The teacher was the authority on the topic and was probably right. We were arguing more for the experience than because we expected to win.

I was disappointed that the Boy Scouts didn't fare well in Clinton. When I was in the seventh grade, Daddy was temporarily transferred to Hattiesburg, and I joined the Scouts there. The Scout Laws were a challenge to be the best you could. I particularly admired the Scout Oath: "On my honor I will do my best to do my duty to God and My Country." That, in one brief statement, was everything the church and community taught. In Clinton the high school coach was the scoutmaster. The troop gathered every Tuesday night at the high school gym and played basketball while the coach watched. We must have had some sort of regular meeting, but I can't remember any. In good weather we would plan a Friday night camping trip out in the woods. It wasn't very exciting; we just stayed up all night telling stories while the coach slept. I was an occasional member for about a year. It's oversimplified to say that Scouts could not compete with the Clinton church. A good Scout troop would have fitted in well, but we didn't have a leader.

The Mississippi College teams were known as the Choctaws; our Clinton High teams were the Arrows. The football team wasn't very good while I was in high school. The coach had been a good player at Mississippi College and was a deacon in the church, so he was obviously a good influence on us. He taught the team all kinds of tricks that walked right on the edge of ethics. Well, some of them stepped way over the line. We enjoyed trying to discuss the subtleties of his philosophy in BYPU. In the ninth or tenth grade all the boys had to try out for football, because there were only twenty-five to thirty students in each class. The entire senior high school had about eighty students, with around forty being boys. More than half that number were needed just to field first and second teams. I lasted about three weeks and proved I was too skinny and not nearly aggressive enough. I had known that all along, but I had to make the effort. Actually, if I had tried harder I could have made the second team, but I wasn't second team material. I was accustomed to being at the top of the class and wasn't willing to be second team to boys I had always helped through math. Because I wasn't good at football or at fighting, I avoided them both.

Not having to practice football in the afternoons gave me time to wander in the woods or to stay at home and read. My father had a book of Robert Service's poems. He had bought it for the World War I poems. I preferred the Yukon pieces:

> Send not your foolish and feeble; send me
>     your strong and sane—
> Strong for the red rage of battle; sane, for I
>     harry them sore;
> Send me men girt for the combat, men who are
>     grit to the core;
> Swift as the panther in triumph, fierce as the
>     bear in defeat,
> Sired of a bulldog parent, steeled in the furnace
>     heat
>
> .   .   .   .   .   .   .   .   .   .   .   .
>
> Ye would send me the spawn of your gutters—
>     Go! take back your spawn again.

In a few years, General George Marshall would say the same thing to our army about its infantry.

I memorized "The Shooting of Dan McGrew" and "The Cremation of Sam McGee," plus bits of many other works. The school library had stories of King Arthur, Sir Lancelot, and Sir Galahad. *Sir Gawain and the Green Knight* was an interesting tale. Before meeting a challenge of courage, Sir Gawain has to pass three tests put to him by the beautiful wife of a nobleman. The first is to reject her enticements to make love to her. The next is to refuse to accept her ring, which would have obligated him to her. He fails the last test by accepting a talisman that will protect him from harm in combat. A knight cannot prove his courage if he is protected from all harm. I had already learned that in BYPU.

In the eleventh grade we got a new English teacher. To give us a broader literature base, Miss Williams set up a schedule for writing book reports at two-week intervals and memorizing poems on alternate weeks. We had trouble with the new books she assigned, but she was impressed with how well we learned poetry. We had been memorizing hymns and biblical passages since we were six-year-old Sunbeams (the children's equivalent of R.A.'s and G.A.'s). We also had learned to look for the spirit of biblical passages with no great concern over specific words. I asked her about including "The Cremation of Sam McGee" in the required poems, but that suggestion didn't go over well at all.

I liked the Richard Lovelace poem about war, "To Lucasta, Going to the Wars": "And with a stronger faith embrace / A sword, a horse, a shield." It ended with the classic lines, "I could not love thee, Dear, so much, / Loved I not honor more." The poem glowed with courage and dignity. I couldn't imagine the pain its subject would bring to me. What is honor, and what is courage?

# 3 Pride of America

When the United States entered World War I in 1917, we had not fought in a full-scale war for over fifty years. Many boys had died of disease in the Spanish-American War, and Teddy Roosevelt had led the charge up San Juan Hill, but those events had not involved the whole country. The boys who remembered Gettysburg and Shiloh were seventy-year-old grandfathers. Nobody was quite sure how the world war had started, but suddenly it was time to whip those atrocity-committing Huns. Patriotism swept the country like wildfire; recruiting offices were swamped with volunteers. Men who wouldn't volunteer and seemed to be evading the draft might find their homes smeared with yellow paint. Men who were in the service but worked at safe desk jobs might receive letters with no message but that of a white feather. Conscientious objectors, "yellow-bellied cowards," were sent to jail to rot. The last of them were released in 1933 under Franklin Roosevelt.

When the men who had fought in the trenches came back home, we relearned the ageless lesson. Some of my earliest memories are of visiting the McCann family, who lived at the Veterans' Hospital in Gulfport. Dr. McCann, a college friend of my father, loved to take us over the spacious grounds with its massive live oaks and magnificent view of the Gulf coast. We would stop to visit with the physically crippled men who navigated their wheelchairs along the sidewalks, but there were also clusters of shell-shocked men who simply gazed out at the water. Their bodies were sound but they had no minds. The most severely shocked men were kept in a large building with barred windows. Dr. McCann said that when they became violent, they were calmed down with electric shock or alternating hot and cold baths. These mentally crippled veterans both frightened and shamed me; they were the brave men who had fought so that kids like me would never have to go to war.

Now Pearl Harbor had been bombed, and more American boys would die. But this war wouldn't be like the old trench warfare. Germany's blitzkrieg had shown that we were in a technological war. In Europe we would defeat Germany by bombing the factories and railroads. The final invasion would simply be a massive tank assault. In Japan, the navy would bombard islands to rubble before the marines went in to take over.

Immediately after Pearl Harbor there had been a surge of enlistments, but it slowed as we realized that boys should remain in college until they were needed. The point at which this need arose was usually defined by the draft board; a classification of 1-A meant that you should volunteer for something immediately. Clinton would not tolerate a man who took a war-essential job just for draft deferment; people no longer resorted to yellow paint, but social snubs were serious. Because ministerial students usually were deferred, the town made snide remarks about boys who were suddenly called into the Lord's service a few months ahead of being called by the president.

Until 1942, I was only a quiet observer. The war would have to last four years before I could be drafted at age twenty-one. But fighting in both the Pacific and European areas drained the manpower pool, and there was talk of lowering the draft age. Bob Canzoneri, Atley Kitchings, and I began taking extra courses so that we could graduate early and get some college training before going into the service.

When they started drafting eighteen-year-olds, life at high school became more exciting. Most of the football team wanted to become marines or fighter pilots. I thought maybe I would like to fly a bomber, but found that I wouldn't be able to pass the Army Air Corps physical; I was badly underweight for my six-foot-one height. That wasn't any great disappointment; I could join the Signal Corps or maybe become a medical technician—I thought I might want to go into medicine after the war anyhow.

Girls were fascinated with the whole war. They seemed to want us all to become fighter pilots, marines, or at the very least, paratroopers.

I couldn't quite understand why they were so patriotic about "pouring it to those dirty Japs." The church was almost as excited; everyone seemed pleased to see the brave boys going off in the service of our country. Ministerial students began volunteering as chaplain's assistants. Mother seemed to be always worried about my going; she knew much more about shell shock than I did. Daddy worried too, but during World War I he had been deferred—working for the railroad, married, and the sole support of his widowed mother—and although he never talked about the ostracism he had suffered, he said that if I didn't have a service record, there could be problems after the war.

Personally, I was eager to be in uniform. I wanted to come home on leave, have everyone brag about me, and be able to date any girl in town. I was tired of food rationing. The war was a just one; we were fighting to free an enslaved world. After watching war movies, I knew I didn't want to fight. I wanted to serve and I wasn't afraid to die for my country, but the fighting and killing weren't very appealing. There were a lot of army jobs that helped the war effort without killing people.

I graduated from high school in the summer of 1942 and entered Mississippi College that fall, taking math, chemistry, biology, history, and English composition. Our history book was *History for the Citizen Soldier,* primarily about United States foreign policy between the wars. I don't remember much about the course, except that I learned the meaning of jingoism. Our instructor would assign a chapter from the book plus other references giving different viewpoints. I was shocked to learn that history is subject to personal interpretation, and that some people believed Roosevelt was a warmonger.

In January, 1943, the college circulated a notice about special training programs that were being started by the army and navy. There was a classification that people said would draw on the top 5 percent of high school graduates. These boys could choose to get two years of college training by volunteering for either the Army Specialized Training Program (ASTP) or the navy's V-5 and V-12 programs. The V-5 training involved naval aviation; the V-12 had something to do with ships. The precise nature of the ASTP was even less clear. All we knew was that it involved two years of "specialized training." Bob, Atley, and I qualified for these programs. We were not the upper 5 percent of our class. We were the upper 25 percent of the twelve boys in our class.

At the time, we thought that meant a Clinton education was much better than anywhere else in the country.

Now we had it made. The war would certainly be over before our two years' training was completed. We would do our bit and get an education too. Atley wasn't completely happy—he really wanted to be in a combat unit, although he didn't want to turn down the honor of being among the academic select. Bob and I were willing to forego the thrill of combat. Naturally, Atley ended up as a naval officer in Pensacola, Bob became a tail gunner in a B-24 fighting over French Indochina, and I went into the infantry.

Bob and Atley chose the navy. I can't remember why I decided to go into the army instead. It had something to do with not wanting to fight from a ship. At any rate, we all signed up for the programs in the spring of 1943. The week after school was out, Bob and Atley were told to report to the navy V-5 program at Mississippi College. We had known that the college was to get a navy program, but we hadn't thought local boys would be allowed to stay in Clinton. I had heard nothing from the army. Soon Bob and Atley were wearing uniforms and tossing around naval terms like *deck, bulkhead,* and just plain *head.* I was tagging along. When we went to Jackson, they could have gone to the USO Club if I hadn't been with them. They didn't feel as awkward about the situation as I did; still, they were navy and I was nothing.

Some of the townspeople were becoming a little suspicious of me, asking why I wasn't in the service. I told them I had decided to wait for the draft. That was a shocker. Nobody waited to get drafted. The patriotic thing was to volunteer as Bob and Atley had. Volunteers could choose the kind of training they would receive.

"If you wait to be drafted," people informed me, "you might get put anywhere."

I would put on my innocent expression and say, "Well, I want to serve where they need me the most."

"That's why you should volunteer. This way, you'll wind up in the infantry."

"The army knows where I can do the most good."

"They'll put you in the infantry. Just wait—you'll see what kind of people are in the infantry."

This kind of chat was just a game. I knew that real patriots volunteered, and I was tired of explaining that I didn't know why the army wasn't taking me. Technically, I hadn't volunteered. I had accepted an offer to join the ASTP, and my instructions were to go into the army through the Selective Service System.

I decided to go to Ridgecrest for a two–week session. Ridgecrest was the summer assembly area for the Southern Baptist Convention. It was a large, beautiful place set in the mountains of North Carolina. Throughout the summer there were one- and two-week programs for the various parts of the church: BYPU, Sunday school, adult Sunday school, and others (the session I attended was for college students). The housing and food at Ridgecrest were very reasonable because most of the buildings represented donations, primarily from the wills of wealthy Baptists. Ridgecrest was one of the fringe benefits of being a Baptist.

The program I attended offered several study courses, which met every morning. The afternoons were for individual study and for rec-reation: hiking, swimming, canoeing, or reading. Every night there was an inspirational sermon followed by close fellowship between the boys and girls. For my morning activity I chose a survey of the Old Testament. It was an intensive study with two hours of lecture fol-lowed by about an hour of discussion. I spent about half of every after-noon reading the assigned reference material.

The real theme of Ridgecrest that year was war. Most of the boys were soon to be in the service. The church was preparing us to fight. "You are the Army of the Lord. This is a holy war to free an enslaved world." The lectures on the Old Testament had a strong emphasis on the men of Israel killing the enemies of the Lord. (The lecturers went easy on the sections where all the men, women, and children were killed after the town had surrendered.) We were being given a crash course in courage and sacrifice. The night sermons were in the "give me the mountain" mold. "Old Caleb was a real man. He chose the hardest task." The songs were martial too. "Stand Up, Stand Up for Jesus" addressed "ye soldiers of the cross":

> Stand up, stand up for Jesus,
> The trumpet call obey;
> Forth to the mighty conflict,
> In this His glorious day;

> Ye that are men, now serve Him,
> Against unnumbered foes;
> Your courage rise with danger,
> And strength to strength oppose.
>
> .   .   .   .   .   .   .   .   .   .
>
> Put on the gospel armor,
> And, watching unto prayer,
> Where duty calls or danger,
> Be never wanting there.

It was a wonderful time to be a young man ready to serve God and Country. The close fellowships after the evening sermons were better than walking home after church in Clinton. There were a lot more girls than boys, and they wanted to send us to war happy. Well, it wasn't quite that good. Most of the girls were older than the seventeen- and eighteen-year-old boys who hadn't been drafted. I was eighteen but looked about fifteen. Daddy had given me a razor for my birthday and had shown me how to use it. I hadn't needed it yet. The younger girls quickly were taken by the good-looking boys. The older girls weren't very happy dating kids, but I enjoyed it. Kipling has a poem about going with an older woman who wasn't much to look at, but "I learned about women from 'er." I got some practice spinning yarns I had heard from the boys at Mississippi College. I wasn't very good at building up drama, but most of my Mississippi stories were new to girls from other states. It all was good for my ego.

The sermon on the last night was a beautiful way to leave for war. "Soon you will be defending us throughout the world. Our prayers go with you. We will suffer with you. You are the pride of America." As we walked to the front of the auditorium to rededicate our lives, the crowd was singing "America the Beautiful":

> O beautiful for heroes proved
> In liberating strife,
> Who more than self their country loved,
> And mercy more than life.

When I got back to Clinton, I was ready to fight. But the army wasn't ready for me. All though July, I could hardly wait for the mail to come, hoping each day would be the one. Finally, in early August, I got the form letter: "Greetings from the President of the United States." I took my physical, passed it, and received instructions to report to the bus station in Jackson at eight thirty on Monday morning. Daddy drove me over there before he went to work. The bus deposited me at Camp Shelby just in time for lunch—good food, and plenty of it: mashed potatoes, beef hash, beans, a dessert, and iced tea. I was so impressed that I wrote home about it; I was going to get fat in the army. After eating, we chose bunks in the barracks, then went to a building where we took off all our civilian clothes and put them in bags to be sent home. We had a short physical, got some shots, and started drawing clothes. According to the old joke, the army has only two sizes—too big and too small—but my clothes fitted better than the ones I had at home. In the army's wide range of sizes were shirts that accommodated both my skinny neck and my long (thirty-four-inch) arms. The pants were just right too: twenty-nine-inch waist, thirty-four-inch length. Then came the fatigue uniform: cotton, herringbone twill. Even I knew that fatigues were the primary wear of the army. The other clothes were for parades and inspection. Fatigues didn't come in many sizes; the pants were thirty-one waist, thirty-two length. The man said it wouldn't matter because I could tighten my belt and leggings would hide the length. The jackets were sorted only by chest size. The size that fit my chest had sleeves that reached just beyond my elbows. I finally settled on a compromise: too big in the chest, but with sleeves that came within a couple of inches of my wrists. We were told we needed only one fatigue set because in a few days we would be sent to a permanent assignment and issued more. (I got my second set two months later.)

This was fun. I had never before had so many new clothes, a complete wardrobe. The next stop was the barracks again, to wait for a man to check our gear. The sergeant said: "Dump everything on your bunk. When I name an item, pick it up, hold it high, and put it in your barracks bag." It seemed a waste of time. We had moved along a line being issued everything in order, then listened to a man read from the list of what we were supposed to have. But the army was right. About a fourth of the people were missing something: clothes, leggings, coat. How could you walk right past a station and not know it?

Finally, we sat on our bunks waiting for supper and going through the ritual, "What's your name, where are you from, and what did you do?" The group was surprised that I had graduated from high school and attended college. One man said: "I went to the sixth grade, but it got boring and I started sawmillin'. It sure beat going to school." Then he gave us the old sawmill story. A preacher hears that a stranger is in the local jail, and goes to visit him.

"What do you do?" the preacher asks.

"Sawmillin'."

The preacher says, "I used to work in a sawmill."

"You ever been in jail?"

The smug preacher replies, "No, can't say that I have."

"Beats hell out of sawmillin'."

It was a classic tale, but he ruined it. His timing was bad and he added no embellishment at all. He would have been booed at the Owl Cafe. I sat and listened to accounts of jobs: what these young men did and how good they were at it. Most had been "public working" all their lives. I didn't know the term. It meant not having a profession or skill, but finding a job that served the public in some way, such as driving a truck for the county, working part-time in a store, or hauling cement for brickmasons. I was surprised at how proud some of the fellows were of public working, although in a depression any job was good. As I listened I felt a little like one of Chaucer's pilgrims hearing the others' strange tales. The talk was mostly lies, but some were told with color and skill.

Most of these men were much older than I, in their twenties. Those my age were farmers. I was the only one who had gone to school beyond the eighth grade. It had been a mistake to mention college: I was now College Boy. I kept quiet and listened.

One boy my age said: "Daddy started taking me to town for supplies when I was fifteen. It sort of scared me at first, but I learned. Now I can turn on a light or operate a telephone as well as anyone." I sat there dumfounded and thought, Leon, these aren't your kind of people. Don't get involved with them, and try to stay out of trouble. How did I get here? Everybody who could read and write must have had enough sense to volunteer for something else before being drafted. Except me.

The next morning we all took the Army General Classification Test

(AGCT). It was generally accepted as being equivalent to an IQ test (studies made after the war showed that it was actually heavily weighted in favor of self-confidence, mathematical ability, and experience at taking tests). We had forty minutes to answer 150 multiple-choice questions, largely comprehension. Even the math portion required only a little background; it mainly tested recognition of patterns and sequences.

Afterward we sat outside, waiting to be sent somewhere. One man said: "Man, that was awful. Do you suppose those questions really had answers? Hey, College Boy, how did you do?"

"I don't know. It's pretty rough."

The next day we reported for our results. "Standifer, you made 130, and it only takes 110 to qualify for OCS. You can pretty well choose your assignment."

"Well, I have this letter assigning me to ASTP."

"Why don't you forget it and go to the Signal Corps?"

"I want the college training."

"Okay, but you'll have to wait until we get enough for a shipment."

When I got back to the barracks, it seemed to me that half of the men already had left for the Special Training Unit school. It was only half a mile away; people assigned to it were told to take their gear and go on over. "Special Training Unit" sounds impressive, but it was basically a literacy school and I don't think 50 percent of my group were illiterate. Maybe they just did very poorly on the AGCT.

The rest of us fell out for formation the next morning after breakfast and listened to the shipping list. "If your name wasn't called, grab a sack lunch and get on this truck." The army was building a lake to use for practicing assault landings. German POWs were to clear the brush, but we were to clear lanes for the guards to watch them. This was a wet bottomland that probably had been in corn before the army bought it and left it idle. Now it was grown up in oak, sweet gum, and wax myrtle about six to eight feet tall. We were given bush hooks and told to go to it. By noon I had blisters on both hands and was completely exhausted. That night I was almost too tired to move. I showered, put on my uniform, and walked over to the service club. I found a book and sat, half-reading and watching the people. Rayford Rogers walked in. He had been a ministerial student at MC and was now a chaplain's assistant. "Leon! I thought you had joined the V-12 program at MC."

"No, I'm going to ASTP."

"Yeah, I heard about a boy who aced the AGCT but didn't want to go to the Signal Corps." (My 130 wasn't even close to aceing that test; it was the bottom score for a Class I grade.) "But Leon, the ASTP shipment left last week; you're going to be here at least a month. What are you doing?"

"Today I cut brush—look at my hands."

"You've got to get out of that. Can you type?"

"I passed the typing course with just barely thirty words a minute. I believe I'd rather cut brush."

"Look around and find something you want to do. There are good openings for anybody with a high school education."

The next morning we went back to the brush. I burst my blisters in the first hour. During the ten-minute break, I noticed an officer running a transit and trying to signal to his rodman, who didn't understand what he wanted. That was my chance. At MC I had taken surveying under Professor Hitt. He was the professor of mathematics but had once been a surveyor and enjoyed teaching it. I wandered over to the officer and asked some leading questions. The poor rodman knew nothing about surveying, and the officer knew just a little more. He had been given an army manual and told to learn it. He was having a lot of trouble calculating elevations.

The man in charge of my detail yelled, "Hey, you, get back over here cutting brush."

"Leave him here, Sergeant. I'm going to teach him about surveying." After the first day, Lieutenant Roberts let me get firsthand experience in running the transit and in calculating the cuts and fills. After the first week, I saw him at the end of each day when I gave him the data to file.

The work wasn't bad, but the army was—always being yelled at, pulling details designed only to keep us busy. The barracks were tarpaper huts: rough lumber put together crudely and covered with tar paper to keep the wind out. I think my biggest problem was loneliness. I stayed in the same barracks for a month. Every four or five days it would empty, then refill with a new group of civilians just like the ones who had left. There were interesting boys, but they always left before I really knew them. There was a pretty good library, but only permanent party people could check out books, because we inductees might leave any day. I asked if I could just sit there and read. "No, you have to check out a book to read it. Go over to the service club; they have books." Yes, some detective stories and joke books. I couldn't go to the movie because I didn't have any money left and wouldn't get paid until I reached a permanent assignment.

Finally, at morning formation, the sergeant said: "Standifer, Leonidas C., Jr. Fall out and report to the office." There I got my orders: "Report to the train depot at 1300 hours." In one month, Camp Shelby had accumulated enough ASTP candidates for a shipment: Billy Manning and me. He was made acting corporal and put in charge of the detail because his name came before mine.

# 4 Benning School for Boys

At the Columbus, Georgia, train station there was a sign: Report Here for The Infantry School. (The capital *T* in the word *The* was no accident; that was the way The Infantry School thought of itself.) I said, "Billy, we're going to ASTP, not the infantry." But the subheading listed ASTP trainees. Comfortable army buses took us to Fort Benning; it was more like entering a college campus than an army camp. Boy, this was my kind of army.

The driver gave us a commentary as we rode through the grounds. The Infantry School headquarters occupied a massive brick building with immaculate grounds. The school's insignia, an upright Roman sword with the motto Follow Me, graced a large raised pillar. The primary purpose of The Infantry School was to give advanced training to officers. West Point graduates who had chosen the infantry were sent here for preliminary instruction before going to permanent posts, and returned every few years. The demonstration troops, a regiment of infantry, were housed in brick dormitories with freshly mowed lawns. These men were veterans of combat from all the theaters of war. The Infantry School also conducted Officer Candidate School for enlisted men who had shown leadership ability; the candidates received three months of training and were given wartime commissions. OCS was located in the Sand Hill area, adjacent to the ASTP, which was in the Harmony Church area. Just up the Cusseta road from us was The Paratrooper School, which we soon were calling "jump school." It was a unit of The Infantry School.

Fort Benning was a big place. We rode among rolling hills and large pine trees and came to a group of two-story barracks that were painted white with green trim. This outlying area wasn't kept as pristine as the Main Post, but the grass was mowed and the walkways were gravel. This was the Ninth Company, Fourth Training Regiment, ASTP, Basic Training Center. The sergeant called off names for each platoon. It was an alphabetical list, with Fourth Platoon including men whose last names started with *S* through *Z*. We were quartered in barracks by platoons, lined in 1, 2, 3, 4 order.

Billy and I walked together down a gravel walkway shaded by pines. The company training field had bleachers to sit on while we watched demonstrations. Fourth Platoon was the last building. After the tar-paper huts, this was like a palace, spacious and open with plenty of windows. I walked between rows of double-deck bunks to the far end, where a group of boys were talking. I don't remember who they were, but the discussion was impressive. They were deep into an analysis on the authorship of Shakespeare's plays. I kept quiet because I thought Shakespeare had written them. The group wore that topic out and switched to new concepts in chemistry.

I began to think maybe I had gotten into a program that was over my head. I had read some of Shakespeare's plays and knew a few sonnets. He had come from a town called Stratford. I also had taken inorganic chemistry at MC, but we hadn't discussed anything like what I was hearing now. Maybe I should apply for a transfer before I flunked out. Maybe—maybe this was mostly bluff. Gradually I realized that this was a standard session of new kids establishing a pecking order. It was "look how smart I am" instead of "I played quarterback." I ended low on the pecking order with either approach, but it really didn't matter. The army very quickly taught us that none of us knew much about our new situation.

That situation was run by Sergeant Cohen, a stocky bull of a man who never changed his expression. Well, he changed from glum, to mad, to very mad. Cohen had been platoon sergeant in an armored infantry company, from which he was selected for OCS. He had almost completed the course when he got in an argument with one of the instructors and was washed out. He would have made a good officer. He was confident, forceful, and extremely good at handling men. He sometimes had problems in dealing with teenagers who weren't particularly interested in becoming men—at least not in the near future.

In the barracks Cohen let us harass him up to a limit. In the field we had to soldier. It was like having an extremely good teacher in high school. We always knew that the teacher was in charge, but he liked us, and before the class started he would let us play. Fourth Platoon had about 120 boys in it, 60 upstairs and 60 down. I didn't know the upstairs group very well. Downstairs we began developing little subgroups. Bob Souder, in the lower bunk beside me, was from Pittsburgh and a big fan of the Pitt Panthers. He was the only one in our group who would get into philosophical discussions (arguments) with me. We didn't agree very often, but the discussions were fun. Dick Sovish, just above him, was the local clown—the slapstick clown. Bill Summey, from Mount Holley, North Carolina, was down the row from us. Summey was the only musician in the group; he had a harmonica with which he could play almost any tune, or rather almost play any tune. Bill Smith (Smitty) was from Dayton, Ohio. He had been in the band and could play a saxophone, but that wasn't as useful as a harmonica. I was impressed that he knew all the words to "Stars and Stripes Forever." I hadn't even known it had words.

We had another group downstairs who were college boys—they had a year of college and had joined fraternities. There were so few of them that none belonged to the same fraternity so they all became fraternity brothers *pro tem* To them I wasn't really a college boy because MC hadn't allowed fraternities. And there was a jock group who did push-ups and deep-knee-bends on one leg at a time. One boy did rifle exercises every night. We adopted the army system of calling everyone by his last name—except for me. I became 'Sippi, the boy from Mis'Sippi.

I got heavy doses of racism in Ninth Company. I suppose they all thought a southerner was by definition a bigot. "Hey, 'Sippi, did you know Second Platoon has a nigger?" I decided to go over and visit the poor colored boy to offer him a little friendship. He was from New York, very sharp and polished. He was lonely, but not enough to put up with a "cracker." (I had never heard the term until he used it.) I don't remember his name because he was quickly shipped out; the reason was that there might have been trouble if he went to town with white boys. I also learned how bad Jews were, that they were clannish and would never help anyone who wasn't Jewish. And I heard all about Pollacks and blockhead Swedes and dumb rednecks. How could every group be so much better than every other group?

The first morning our platoon leader, Lieutenant Donaldson, came by for an informal talk. Training wasn't to begin for several days, but he wanted to start us off right. He had just received his commission and wasn't quite accustomed to his new role. He was probably about twenty-two and wasn't nearly the leader that Sergeant Cohen was. But he was competent, and there was no real need for him to be outstanding. Cohen handled the platoon, and The Infantry School's instructors gave the training lectures.

The company commander, Captain Rawl, was a character who performed once a day from up on a platform. We never really understood what he was like. While the lieutenant was talking to us that first day, Rawl screamed from company headquarters, "Lieutenant Donaldson!" Donaldson slapped his swagger stick against a post and said, "Holy Mary, Mother of God!" At the time I was shocked at the sacrilege, but I came to sympathize with the emotion expressed. We didn't see this screaming menace until the next morning at our first formation. He was a small, sharp-featured man with a high-pitched rasping voice. That's about all we ever knew of him. He would stand on the command platform and posture as blatantly as Mussolini. My entire image of him consists of those postures and his screaming speeches about how tough the training was going to be. His favorite phrase was, "This week we will see what you are made of!" He worked at the image of a tough, aggressive, macho man.

Sergeant Cohen managed his informal talks at night while we were cleaning equipment and getting ready for the next day. I can't remember anything Donaldson told us, but Cohen's talk made sense. He realized that we wouldn't ever fight as infantry, but that the basic infantry training was more important than simply how we would fight. Infantry training was tough and demanding, a good foundation for any young man. In high school football we had learned the value of personal and team discipline. The infantry would teach that and more. We would learn how tough we really were and that team success depended on absolute obedience. "You may also learn to hate my guts, and that I don't care what you think of me." It never really got that bad, but Sergeant Cohen made sure that we knew it could.

We weren't what The Infantry School had expected. We were just a bunch of high school and early college kids selected for elite training in a setting much like a college campus. This was so obvious that we came to call the ASTP program "Benning School for Boys." We didn't invent the nickname; it had been applied to The Infantry School itself long before the ASTP was created. I suppose West Point cadets originated it. But the program did have some of the trappings of an exclusive boys school. The faculty always reminded us that we were the "cream of the crop," the best there was, and they expected us to learn more than ordinary recruits. We had a school insignia to sew on our blazers: a golden lamp of knowledge superimposed on the Roman sword of The Infantry School. We even had a school paper, the *Pine Burr*. It was run by the faculty, but they let us write articles for it. I read some of these old pieces recently. Forty years ago they were fascinating, but now they sound like something from a high school paper.

After a week of marching and learning to salute, we were issued rifles: Eddystone Enfields, which America's Eddystone Arsenal had made for the British army during World War I. They were the last word in useless: big, heavy, and poorly balanced. The army protected its rifles for storage by dipping them in a hot grease called "cosmolene." We dipped our rifles in kerosene to get most of the thick grease off, then took them apart under a hot shower, dried the parts, and removed the rest of the grease with toothpicks, cotton patches, and gun oil. That took all afternoon and well into the night. Part of the delay was that we would stop and play soldier with our rifles. Boys who had taken ROTC showed us how to do the manual of arms. One boy could do the Queen Anne Salute, twirling the rifle like a light stick and kneeling to hold it upright. We marched, sang, and practiced bayonet thrusts.

Ben Sokol was a quiet boy who usually played with us, but I noticed that he was just sitting on his bunk, looking at the rifle. I walked down to see what was wrong. He said: "Leon, I know it doesn't make sense, but my mother has always been terrified of firearms. This thing frightens me. Do you know Wilfred Owen's poems?" I didn't. Ben said that Owen was a British poet and soldier who was killed in combat seven days before World War I ended. To my surprise, he began quoting Wilfred Owen's "Arms and the Boy," a finely crafted World War I poem that is almost erotic and absolutely horrible. It tells of a boy caressing his bayonet and stroking bullets designed to "nuzzle" the heart of another boy. It concludes with the implication that the boy with such arms has no need for claws, talons, or horns such as animals use; rifle and bayonet make him a far more effective killer.

That wasn't the sort of poem we had learned in Clinton. I was shocked but knew that Sokol wanted a comment. "Ben, rifles are part of soldiering, but it doesn't mean we will kill anyone. We're going to become officers in some technical branch. Try to look on the rifle as part of your uniform." I believe that worked—he seemed to adjust. Throughout basic training, though, he wrote his mother twice a week and never even hinted that we were using rifles.

The ASTP program tended to select a bright, scholarly person who was willing to fight, but not eager for the glory of combat. This contrasts with the Marine Corps and the army paratroop programs, which promoted the idea of macho boys who were eager to get into the thick of the fight. No selection system is perfect: ASTP got some aggressive combat glory people, and the paratroops had some gentle, sensitive soldiers.

The Infantry School began immediately to make proud infantrymen out of us. The indoctrination lectures explained that the infantry was the fundamental unit of the armed forces. The primary purpose of all combat operations was to place the infantry in a position to defeat the enemy. The infantry was the Queen of Battle. All other troops were support forces. Infantry soldiers wore light blue braid on their caps and crossed rifles on their lapels. There were signs scattered around: Look Sharp: You Are Infantry. I think we tried to believe, but it was hard. Infantry wasn't something you joined. You joined the marines, the Air Corps, or ASTP. You got into the infantry by mistake. As soon as you proved that you could read and write, they transferred you out.

"Sir, what is the origin of the term *infantry*? It seems to be based on *infant.*" The officer said: "Infantry refers to the basic soldier of the army. Its origin is entirely different from infant." That exchange was from one of our indoctrination lectures, and it provoked a long discussion in the barracks that night. The name did seem to be based on infant, but how did that relate to soldiering? The next Sunday, Souder and I went to the library on the main post to look it up. We came back glowing. The word *infantry* goes back to medieval days, when lords fought as knights on horseback. A lord's serfs accompanied him as his foot soldiers, fighting with swords and pikes to clear the way for him to ride in and win the battle. The serfs were referred to as his "infants" or "children"—and with the social customs of the times, many of them may have been.

We had fun with the idea of wearing baby blue braid and being the little children of the army. We told Sergeant Cohen we were his sweet little children, but he didn't see the humor in it. He didn't see the humor in our jokes about army terminology, either. You couldn't be a good soldier unless you talked like one. It sounded foolish to us, but the system works. I had felt like an outsider with Bob and Atley almost as soon as they learned a few naval terms. Most of the army names were ones we had used at summer camp, such as *mess hall, latrine, bunk,* and *post exchange.* Cohen got mad when we argued that *barracks* was plural, and that we lived in the Fourth Platoon barrack. But he won: Fourth Platoon barracks. A smoothbore weapon was a *gun,* one with rifling was a *rifle.* Shotguns were guns, but we had rifles. A machine gun was really a rifle, but that didn't matter—all of the artillery "guns" were rifles too.

One night when Souder and I were discussing army "logic," he said: "'Sippi, you never bitch about the army. You seem to have found a home here."

"Well, there are a lot of foolish rules I don't like, but I didn't like all the rules in Clinton either. The army isn't nearly as rough as I had expected. I'm in better physical condition than ever before. I like the group of boys we run with. Yeah, I like the army here." As I thought about it later, I saw that I enjoyed the orderliness of the army. The rules were spelled out clearly, and if you conformed to them, everything went well. The army had rituals that were boring and seemed meaningless, but were in fact very important for reasons we couldn't understand. (Clinton had rituals too, but the army's were worse— more boring.) Even though I was homesick occasionally, I didn't want to be back in Clinton. All of my friends were in the service now. I was content. The ASTP wasn't quite the Army of the Lord, but I wasn't eager to be needed there.

"When I was a child, I spake as a child." Life was so simple when you had only to obey the rules and everything would work out right. (This formulation assumes that the people who devise the rules are intelligent, unselfish, and ethical.) Following orders, even in the face of danger, doesn't require nearly as much courage as disregarding stupid, cruel orders. How can you be sure that you are right and your superior is a fool? Should you be loyal to your ethics or to your army?

Each week The Infantry School posted a training program for us that we called "the curriculum." We had to take detailed notes at all lectures because every Friday afternoon we had a quiz on the material covered that week. It was pure chaos. Instructors who had never heard of a tests and measurements course were writing quizzes for kids whose greatest talent was passing tests. Some questions had three correct answers, others had none at all. That's not the way the instructors intended it. We finally learned that you could pass the Friday quizzes only by thinking dumb.

Looking back, I think that our basic training was simply a modification of The Infantry School's OCS program. If we were to be commissioned immediately after our college training, this would be our only exposure to officer training. It had a review of fundamentals that officer candidates learned in basic training, but it was heavy on tactics and philosophy of warfare. Bright kids like us were supposed to pick up marching, rifle cleaning, and standing guard with no problems. This optimism ignored the fact that most of us were poorly coordinated and all thumbs. I think I was close to the bottom in physical prowess. Doing the manual of arms was my first big problem. Standing at attention, you lift the heavy rifle and hold it at high port in front of you. Then, by some sort of magic, you flip it to your right shoulder. That was hard enough, but to go back to high port, you had to lever the rifle off your shoulder with a tiny wrist movement. I could make it work if I gave the Enfield a little momentum with a slight shoulder push, which I hoped nobody would notice. The instructors wanted us to run the obstacle course as fast as the paratroopers did. I always managed to clear every obstacle, but not very fast. Climbing over those big board walls with a pack and rifle was particularly hard. Sergeant Cohen would stand there and shout: "All right, Standifer, move it. Show me some speed." My skill on the obstacle course earned me the nickname "Lightning."

One night the program called for a tactical problem from 2100 hours until 0100 (nine at night to one o'clock in the morning). It was really just an army version of capture the flag. Three-man patrols would crawl slowly through the woods, trying not to be shot at (with blanks) by enemy machine gunners or riflemen. Right after supper it started raining, one of those hard, cold October rains of south Georgia. We stood at the barracks door and reached a decision. "Tomorrow night would be much nicer. It would be clear with a full moon. Let's ask Sergeant Cohen to postpone it."

Three skinny eighteen-year-old boys knocked on his door and said, "Sergeant Cohen, it's raining outside and we would like to postpone tonight's game until tomorrow."

We waited quietly for the explosion, but it didn't come. "The Japs love to fight at night in the rain," Cohen replied matter of factly.

"There aren't any Japs at Fort Benning. Surely you don't want to send your sweet little children out in such horrid weather. We could catch our death."

That worked; according to my letter home the explosion lasted twenty-five minutes by actual timing. It was the longest curse we had ever generated. "Sweet little children" always worked, but we tried to save it for special occasions. Another sure-fire phrase was our answer to Captain Rawl's, "This week we will see what you are made of." The reply, of course, was: "Frogs and snails and puppydog tails, that's what little boys are made of"—but we said that in ranks, and very quietly. When Sergeant Cohen heard it, we could count on cleaning the barracks on Saturday night. We cleaned the barracks every Saturday night during the first few weeks of training. I don't remember much bickering about who had screwed up. We must have realized that group punishment was designed to make us think as a unit; anything one person did affected us all. Because Sergeant Cohen didn't stay to watch over us, we played a lot and made up little songs:

> We are hopeless, this we know,
> For the sergeant tells us so.
> Our little butts to him belong.
> He is right and we are wrong.

I was always the squad's first scout on the patrol problems. This was because of my height, rather than a matter of superior skill. Lieutenant Donaldson had arranged our positions in the squad so that the tallest were in front, tapering off to the shortest at the rear. By army protocol, the squad leader was first in line, followed by the first scout. I became scout because I was the second tallest in our squad. Most of us enjoyed night problems because it was one thing at which we were good, and the rain didn't matter much once we got wet. The trick on tactical problems was to lie still until a machine gunner got nervous and fired. That way, we could spot him and crawl forward while his ears were still ringing from the shots. It took a long time; but we had to stay out there until one o'clock regardless of how fast we went.

There was one night problem that we went through easily. The night compass course called for a three-man patrol to walk through enemy territory with only a sequence of directions and distances to follow. The first direction might be "ten degrees east of north for three hundred yards." You would read the compass and line up on some object and pace off three hundred yards. Then one man would crawl under a couple of raincoats with a flashlight, read what the next direction was to be, and take that compass direction. Our version of the game was to follow the first direction, crawl under the raincoat, and use trigonometric functions to reduce the whole problem to a single distance and direction. It worked once, but Sergeant Cohen saw what we were doing. Lieutenant Donaldson was amused. Captain Rawl was furious. We repeated the problem with a corporal waiting to check us off at each compass station.

Most of the training was fun. At first we were afraid of being washed out of the program, but soon we realized that almost nobody had been. We still felt lucky to be in it. Most of The Infantry School instructors were very good. We knew that their lectures were much better than we would have gotten in standard basic training.

The lectures on "Spirit of the Bayonet" were interesting. We learned that the bayonet is a tactical anachronism and a psychological gem. Use it to scare people, but don't try to kill anybody with it. It can easily get stuck between bones; brace your foot against the body and pull hard. Sometimes firing the rifle will jar the blade loose.

"One day when we were clearing a town in Italy, I came around a corner and met a giant of a German soldier who had a bayonet on his rifle too. He grinned and went into the on guard position, ready for a bayonet duel. I grinned, crouched into position, and pulled the trigger. The poor German was shocked at my ethics, but I won the duel." That was the sergeant who instructed us. "As long as you have ammunition, don't consider using a bayonet. If you run out of ammunition, you should first consider running. Always put the bayonet on when you guard prisoners. It scares hell out of them." Sokol had our whole group helping to compose his letters home for that week. It was hard to avoid letting his mother know we had to use rifles for bayonet training.

During the break after the lecture, we gathered around the instructor to learn more about combat. The stress of clearing towns day after day seemed awful. The sergeant said: "You don't do it day after day. Combat is like the rest of army life: you spend most of your time waiting. You clean your rifle, oil your ammunition, and try to rest. The worst part of combat is trying to get warm, dry, or cool. When you are clearing a town or on patrol, you are tense and scared. You begin to think nothing is going to happen; then it flares up for a few minutes and somebody is killed. Then nothing happens for a week."

Bayonet lab—we called it a "lab"; the army called it "field training"—wasn't as interesting as the lecture. In fact, it was physical torture. Our Enfield rifles had foot-long bayonets on the end of them. It was easy to crouch on guard, pointing the bayonet up at the throat of the enemy, but when we made a long thrust with it and held the position until everyone had it right, we got top-heavy. Skinny, boyish arms weren't designed for that sort of thing. Bayonet attacks didn't go over well with the sweet little children. In the squad attack practice, we would individually get up, run forward, hit the ground, roll, and then get up again. Finally we formed a line near the enemy position and were all to jump up together and charge with fixed bayonets so that the enemy would surrender in terror. "When you attack, come up a'growlin'." But growlin' was hard on eighteen-year-old boys whose voices were changing. Sometimes the growl would come out as a squeak. "Not enough noise. Try it again—and growl!" Then Smitty would simper, "Now, let's fight fiercely, fellows." He was convinced that the army looked on the bayonet as a phallic symbol: "Long thrust and hold, move!"

We weren't always acting like kids. We were adolescents, trying to be men yet also trying to hold on to high school. If we had been integrated with older men, as was the case in most programs, peer pressure would have made us try harder. The whole setup encouraged a Benning School for Boys attitude. But it was a lot more fun than basic training was supposed to be, and we probably learned to soldier just as well.

The labs on hand-to-hand combat made better sense than bayonet practice, but for more of us they were reminiscent of football practice: we got all torn up trying to do something we weren't very good at. "Assault on a Defended Village" was more enjoyable. It was a lot like cowboy shoot-outs—although we soon realized that Tom Mix wasn't really a very good fighter. He fired without aiming and never considered fire cover from the cowboys with him. We also realized that the old blitzkrieg pictures of the Germans capturing French villages showed that they were only marginally better at it than Tom Mix. They bunched up badly and didn't support one another well. A platoon of the sweet little children could have short-circuited the blitzkrieg. The key to house-to-house fighting is to know what the rest of your squad is going to do. You take turns running out into the street, hoping nobody shoots at you. But you know that the squad is standing back away from windows, watching and ready. Anybody who does shoot at you is going to be killed—you hope he misses with the first shot. It was interesting to watch the demonstration squad in action. They never made a sound and exchanged only a few hand signals, but if a shot was taken at them, every window in the area blazed with rifle fire.

There were several good lectures on tactics and psychology of infantry warfare. We learned that killing the enemy was poor psychology; it made his friends mad. By only wounding him, you put three men out of action: the wounded person and the two others who must carry him back to the aid station. We liked that idea, but then they came up with the rest of it: Never think of the enemy as human. If you hesitate before shooting, you may become the one who dies for his country.

In one of the psychology lectures the officer got into the question, "Are you willing to kill?" Since most men believe they will kill in certain situations, the question can be refined: "Under what circumstances are you willing to kill?" Then there is the interesting parallel,

"For what or whom are you willing to die?" You won't have time to decide those things in combat. If you hesitate in combat you may die, not because you decided to kill or not kill, but because you didn't decide.

The lecturer's intended conclusion was that you kill because you are ordered to and because your squad may die if you don't follow orders. Actually, the officer didn't handle his topic well—it was as if he were using notes someone else had given him—but his lecture started a lot of discussions. It hadn't occurred to me that killing was a decision for a rifleman. You were there to fight, so you did. Our best sources of information were the demonstration troops. Some of the combat veterans from the Italian campaign said that they hadn't killed anyone and had tried not to. They had fought, fired rifles, attacked, gotten wounded, and been willing to die. Some had shot to wound, but not to kill. All of that was considered reasonable; what was contemptible were the eight balls who simply wouldn't fight. This wasn't a matter of integrity, but of simple cowardice: when you fire your rifle, it attracts attention and you get shot at. The men who wouldn't fire were a complete drag, without the courage to fight or to refuse. If you won't fire your rifle, you are useless. Even if you fire and never hit a thing, it keeps pressure on the enemy. Marksmanship is seldom very important in combat, but noise is.

Those questions of not being willing to kill got a lot of attention that night. Summey said that he thought most of the soldiers who didn't fire were afraid, and were only pretending to be unwilling to kill. If you read the Old Testament in context, it really says "Thou shalt not kill another Jew." The Old Testament heroes were always killing enemies of the Lord. Our society, Summey claimed, praised the killing of Indians, Yankees, and Germans—just don't kill Americans (he apparently didn't look on Yankees—or Indians—as Americans). I knew Summey was wrong, but I couldn't find a good refutation. After a lot of worrying, I decided that it is cheating to make your buddies carry the load of killing. Nobody wants to kill, but if you aren't willing to become a conscientious objector, you are committed to killing. That's what people do in the army. When you put on the uniform, you say that you are willing to kill. But that didn't answer the whole question. From BYPU, I knew that Jesus would kill only if necessary. "Absolutely necessary" is a case-by-case decision, and you won't have time for it in combat. As for whom I would die for, I got nowhere with that either. I would die for some of my friends, but not for others.

Some of the dullest lectures concerned foot discipline. "The two most important weapons of a rifleman are his rifle and his feet." We learned that we should wear two pairs of socks on hikes, even in the summer. The inner sock was cotton to absorb sweat. The wool outer sock had a cushioning effect that reduced the possibility of getting blisters. After each hike we had to take off our shoes and lie on the bunks with our feet sticking over the end. The platoon leader would walk through to make sure that nobody had blisters. The foot discipline lectures harped endlessly on taking care of our feet in cold, wet weather when we were in foxholes and couldn't get much exercise. Every few hours, we should take off the shoes and socks, wring out the water, and rub our feet until the feeling came back, then put the wet shoes and socks back on and hope for a chance to walk around soon. The lectures made sense. The main cause of trench foot in World War I was poor blood circulation. But why did they have to keep repeating the lectures? It seemed that any fool would know how to take care of his feet. (In Europe during the winter of 1944–1945, the army lost almost 45,000 men as "foot casualties"—the equivalent of all the riflemen in seven divisions.)

We began to understand how military discipline differed from what we had known in high school. Fundamentally, the idea is that unified effort, even with a stupid plan, is superior to intelligent anarchy. One objective of basic training is to impart the army way of doing things. We learned that there was "the right way, the wrong way, and the army way." If you thought you knew a better way, you could forget it. The army didn't pretend that its way was better, more efficient, or more economical. You just did it the army way or you did it over.

The logic of the army way is that in a combat situation, the officer in charge doesn't have time to weigh all options and choose the best. He often acts on instinct—but even a poor plan can work if everybody obeys it. So part of our training was to accept discipline without question. Unfortunately, that never quite worked with us. We could accept discipline, but we always questioned and complained. High school discipline was the only life we knew, and we always wanted to argue for a better way. The Benning School for Boys eventually wore us down on this point of philosophy, but never really won.

There was another aspect of this emphasis on unified action that I didn't understand at the time. Throughout the army there was the advice, "Never volunteer for anything." This wisdom reflected the general belief that whenever the sergeant asked for volunteers for what sounded like a good job, it would turn out to be a dirty, useless job. But what we actually were being taught was that the army succeeds through unified action. Individuals looking for glory or easy jobs just cause problems. The army wants soldiers, not heroes. This is a principle that goes back at least to the Roman legions. And it's why the Celts were beaten by the Romans, the Greeks, the Germanic tribes, the Anglo-Saxons, and the Yankees.

# 5  Why We Fight

The Infantry School gave excellent lectures and demonstrations on night fighting. The logic was that fighting at night required training, organization, and careful planning. You could usually expect that the enemy wasn't good at it. You had a distinct edge if you were. Night fighting involved patrolling much more than fighting. You almost never used a rifle at night because you couldn't see to aim. Our instructor, Sergeant Schmidt, said: "On night operations don't carry a rifle, ammunition, or a helmet. Carry a knife you can throw away if you are captured. Make a garrote from fine wire with sticks tied at each end." He showed us how to sneak up behind a person and break his neck—but it doesn't work if the man has a thick neck and you are a skinny little kid. Schmidt said: "The knife always works. Grab his chin, throw your knee in his back, and cut his throat. The only sound will be the gurgle of blood."

The garrote is just as good as the knife and less messy. You flip the loop over the enemy's head, throw the knee, and jerk. The hazard is that the loop might catch on his helmet or cap. If it does catch, run—he is going to yell. Never try to capture someone behind his lines. Don't get softhearted and try to choke him or knock him out—kill! Why do you kill? Occasionally to get past a person, although if you can slip up that close, you usually can slip past him. The principal reason for one-on-one night killing is to gain information on new units, morale, and so on. You kill, then steal everything in the dead man's pockets. Bring it back for interpretation. Assault troops (paratroopers) sometimes fought with knives and fists during night attacks, but nobody considered ASTP as a potential assault organization.

Although killing wasn't the primary reason for night patrols, it was the topic of long barracks discussions. There is a horror of learning to kill silently with a knife. Smitty had picked up on the Owen poems that Sokol knew. He quoted the ending of what I feel is Wilfred Owen's most lyric and revulsive poem, "Has Your Soul Sipped?" The poem describes the beauty of a sunrise, moonlight, a rose, and a nightingale's song before extolling the "sweet" emotion of cutting a boy's throat. As the "life-tide leaps" from his slashed throat, there is a faint smile that holds "no threat" on the boy's lips; his entire life is condensed in that final smile.

That poem ended the night's discussion. "My God, Smitty, why did you have to say that?" But we weren't really worried. We would never have to do that sort of thing. We were going to college.

The fun part of night patrols was locating machine guns, company headquarters, artillery, and similar objectives. It took hours to move a few hundred yards. You would slip by demonstration teams and listen to them discussing tactics, guns, and so on. We were a bit concerned that the problem assumed the enemy would speak English while they made small talk; of course, the teams weren't supposed to be talking on line at all. But it was a fun game. "If you think you are discovered on patrol, drop your knife and garrote, and die. Don't move even if they kick you. If they release the safeties on their rifles, come to life and surrender." If you are captured unarmed, pretend that you've come over to surrender—although it probably won't work.

Saturday was a big day at the Benning School for Boys. Every Saturday morning the entire battalion went to see a Hollywood movie. This was a twelve-part serial *Why We Fight*. It was just like the Saturday movies back home except that there were no cowboys and no popcorn. The plot was just as logical and honest as a good Tom Mix show. This series is now described as a classic of positive propaganda, made by the great director Frank Capra and using actual newsreels to tell history as it happened. Maybe so. It played well with the paratroopers and OCS men, but not with our group. To us, it was simply unrealistic to believe that everything the Germans and Japanese did was wrong and that we were always right.

The Saturday night discussions of *Why We Fight* were a revelation to me. Although I knew that history was a matter of interpretation, I hadn't realized there were so many facets to the causes of the war. For example, one group argued that Germany was largely justified in her territorial demands. The Versailles Treaty had been grossly unfair in giving the Saarland to France, and in placing German-speaking people under Polish rule. The Austrians had voted in free elections to join Germany, and the Sudetenland of Czechoslovakia was logically a part of Austria because it consisted almost entirely of Austrians who had lived there for generations. Yes, Hitler had become a dictator who was trying to conquer the world, but that would not have happened if we had treated the Germans fairly. As for the Japanese, unfair economic policies had forced them to fight. This "Roosevelt is a warmonger" group said that the president had gotten us into the war because he liked the English and because rich capitalists needed a war to end the depression. One or two boys claimed that Roosevelt was really a Jew named Rosenfeld, and that we were in the war because Hitler hated Jews.

I enjoyed listening to all the arguments but wasn't swayed by any of them. Roosevelt was our president, doing what he felt was best for the country. I knew very little about our relationships with Japan, but I assumed that we probably had made the blunders I kept hearing about. But those were discussions on the causes of the war; "why we fight" was an entirely different, and more personal, matter. The *Pine Burr* ran an interview feature, asking trainees why they were fighting. Most of the answers were prefaced with, "If I were to be assigned to a combat zone . . ." We didn't expect to actually fight; we were considering an abstraction. The answers were idealistic and tribal: "to defend the American way of life"; "I am Polish, and I know what the Nazis are doing to my people"; "I'm Jewish." That sort of thinking bothered me. Should I fight only if Scottish people were being mistreated? Even the boys who were most fervent about capitalist warmongers believed that we had to win the war now that we were in it. "Hitler must be stopped" sounded good, but it was secondary to the fundamental motivation. We were ready to fight (in the abstract) because our country was in trouble. Win the war first, and then see that this sort of thing never happens again.

On Saturday afternoons each company marched to the battalion parade ground. As we followed the winding road through the pines, the other companies would join us carrying their flags. It looked like a gathering of the clans in Scotland. Fourth Platoon had a little parody of "Why Don't You Do Right?" that we liked to sing on the outings:

> We know how to soldier and we're looking fine,
> Poor Third Platoon's rotting on the vine.
> Why don't they do right, like the Fourth Platoon do?
> You stand there wonderin' what it's all about;
> If you don't learn to soldier they will wash you out.

At the parade ground the band played marches to help us keep in step as we lined up in a company front. (Actually, we had a live band only on special days; more often, the music was recorded.) Each platoon had columns extending back to what should have been a depth of twelve men, although in training platoons it was far more. When the whole mass had lined up, the band would stop and the Lord God Battalion Commander would step up to a loudspeaker and shout, "Infantry, pass in review." That was followed by a wild confusion of commands that would have made no sense if we hadn't already known what to do. We were going to march by in four-row platoon units. The company commander would shout, "Ninth Company—" and pause. The leader of First Platoon would interject, "First Platoon, forward," but our leader would say, "Fourth Platoon, stand fast." The company commander would then complete his command: "March!" The band would boom out "Stars and Stripes Forever" as the platoons swung out one by one. Fourth Platoon would "stand fast," shaking with excitement, until we heard, "Fourth Platoon, forward—march," and stepped off smartly as a proud unit. I was back in Clinton marching behind the Mississippi College band. It was the high point of the week. The Cream of the Crop was polished and shining. The Infantry School was proud of us, and Sousa had written that march especially for such as we. It really was an excellent march for ASTP, brash, proud, and cocky—so cocky that it was all ham and noise:

> Sing out for liberty and light,
> Sing out for freedom and the right,
> Sing out for union and its might,
> O patriotic sons.

After marching past the reviewing stand, the Cream of the Crop marched back to eat supper. Then we cleaned the barracks for Sergeant Cohen. He was never quite as proud of us as The Infantry School was.

The Infantry School was big on music and songs. The theory was that a singing soldier was a happy soldier. We were supposed to sing old infantry songs as we marched back at the end of an all-day hike. We called ourselves the "BSB a cappella choir." The preferred songs dated back to World War I and even the Indian wars. One rousing line was: "The infantry, the infantry, with dirt behind their ears, / Can lick their weight in wildcats and drink their weight in beers." Another said that in the infantry, "You sweat till you get there the hard way." The officers and instructors could forgive eighteen-year-olds for not having booming bass voices, but they couldn't understand why we didn't like their songs. We had parodies of most of the old marching lyrics: "We're infantry, we're infantry, still wet behind the ears. / We'd rather have some Ovaltine, we hate the taste of beers." Summey had one based on "The Bonnie Blue Flag": "Hurrah, hurrah, the infantry, hurrah. / Hurrah for the bonnie blue braid, that sends us off to war." We liked a few of the approved songs. "The Yellow Rose of Texas" went over well. Sergeant Cohen didn't like our "God Bless America" parody: "God bless our infantry, Queen of the War." The paratroops had a little song we liked: "Gory, gory, what a helluva way to die." It was about a trooper who was killed while hanging in his parachute. "His intestines were hanging from his paratrooper boots. / They had to pour him in his grave." The paratroopers thought we were cheating to sing that song, since we would never have to fight. Most of our marching songs were from the radio "Hit Parade": "Pistol Packin' Mama" and "Deep in the Heart of Texas." The tunes weren't really much good for marching, but we liked to sing them.

Two years later I saw what The Infantry School had wanted us to be. We had finished the war in Czechoslovakia, and the division was ordered to send a unit to Prague for some sort of victory-friendship parade with the Russian army. We formed a composite battalion made up of riflemen who had gone overseas with the division. We wore our freshly pressed dress uniforms, our medals, and our polished helmets. The Russians had no dress uniforms. They wore their tattletale gray cotton jumpers with a black belt around the waist. We swung into Wenceslaus Square with the band playing a Sousa march. Then we got into position and stood at attention while the nondescript Russians marched by with no band at all. But, boy, could they sing! Great booming voices that reverberated over the square. We suspected it was really a selected choir, but we felt very sheepish marching out to another Sousa march. The Infantry School would have loved it.

One of my psychologist friends says The Infantry School had a good foundation for the emphasis on music and singing. Martial music and the marching songs are based on the "One, two, three, four" rhythm. It worked long before psychologists knew about hypnotic imprinting, but it is an excellent example of that phenomenon. You are continually imprinted with the pride of working as a unit. In training exercises, the unit never loses. Infantry is Queen of Battle, and you are in the best infantry unit. This sense of oneness is reinforced with "Hut, tup, thrup, fourp" or "You had a wife and twenty-two kids and you left, you're right" or "Infantry, pass in review." The infantry attacks in the Civil War show the hypnotic effect of the drumbeat. Men marched in straight lines directly at an enemy who was firing on them. When the man in front fell, the next stepped into his place. The hypnotic drumbeat and sense of unity kept otherwise-ordinary men marching into the certainty of a wound and the probability of death. Was that courage?

The imprinting is extremely effective. After forty years, I still tingle at "Stars and Stripes Forever." On our first day in France, our platoon leader would use that imprinting to get us past a difficult situation.

In our part of Fort Benning we had two groups of neighbors. The officer candidates were getting training similar to ours, but we didn't relate well with them. They were all old men, about twenty-two to twenty-eight. And they took their training so seriously. There was a very good reason: each week they were graded, and those who didn't pass were washed out. We were graded and were threatened with washing-out, but it didn't happen—at least not for military performance.

Early in our training, however, we did have to take the mind-boggling, three-hour Officer Candidate Test–2. It tested mental ability in order to screen out marginal students, and measured acquired knowledge in order to determine the training we would take in college. A rather large number of boys failed the OCT–2, and were to be reassigned after our basic training was completed. Even intelligent boys who lacked good engineering, language, or medical-education backgrounds from high school were washed out in this process.

Our other neighbors were paratroopers. Actually, they were in jump school, training to be paratroopers. They weren't washed out but were continually harassed with "quit slips." The ominous reminder was that "any time you aren't man enough to take it, you can sign a quit slip and leave the next day." Our main tie to the paratroopers was that they were our age peers. Several people in our platoon had high school friends in jump school who would come over to visit and tell us how rough it was. Being a paratrooper was a lot harder than training to be straight-leg infantry. The paratroopers liked to call us "straight-legs" because they wore jump boots with their dress uniforms and bloused their pant legs out of the boot tops. The highly polished boots were a lot more impressive than our ordinary shoes, and we envied them.

We enjoyed the paratroopers' visits. They weren't exactly our kind of people, but we knew them well. We all had high school friends who were paratroop material. They were aggressive, usually good physical specimens, and very tough. In high school they had been the strong, dependable linemen of the football team; we had been noisy cheerleaders. They thought *Why We Fight* was a great movie: "Everybody at home should see it." We liked the parachuters. We teased, fought, and harassed each other, but we always knew how far we could go. Paratroopers did weird things, like running instead of marching. And they sang the good old army songs as they ran. They also jumped off the back of trucks running at thirty miles an hour—or so they told us. Discipline was different at jump school. Well, discipline was the same—like us, they were expected to obey stupid orders. But punishment was different. They had to do fifty push-ups when they did something wrong; we had to dig foxholes or clean up the barracks on Saturday night. We couldn't have done fifty push-ups. The troopers couldn't have cleaned the barracks on Saturday night because that was when they had to go to town to drink and fight. I think that was part of the training. Troopers who didn't have bruises and black eyes on Sunday morning weren't good paratroopers.

After we got the really important elements of soldiering behind us, The Infantry School started teaching us how to fire a rifle. The ASTP was the cream of the crop, but we weren't first in line for equipment. We were still training with World War I rifles. The paratroopers and OCS had the new M-1, the finest infantry rifle in the world. At about the sixth week, we received a series of lectures on how the M-1 worked and how to dismantle it. The rifle was an outstanding innovation. At the time, the standard infantry rifle throughout the world was based on the Mauser action. This mechanism, invented in the 1870s by Peter Paul Mauser of Germany, was a bolt action that ejected an empty cartridge and in the return stroke inserted a new one. The M-1 was an American improvement that fundamentally used the Mauser action but added a small gas port near the end of the rifle barrel. As a bullet was driven out of the barrel, some of the expanding gas went through the gas port and into a cylinder, forcing a piston backward. This action ejected the empty cartridge and inserted a new one.

The M-1 was called a "semiautomatic" because each time the trigger was pulled a shot was fired and a new cartridge automatically fed into place. A rifleman could fire the entire clip of eight cartridges as fast as he could pull the trigger. This rapidity of fire gave us both a functional and a psychological advantage over soldiers using the slower Mauser action. The functional advantage was that we could fire about three shots while the enemy was firing one. The psychological edge was that after you fired the first round, the enemy tended to think that you would have to work the bolt before you could fire again. We were taught to fire the first shot from the hip without aiming, then put the rifle to the shoulder to aim. The speed of the second, aimed shot was a surprise. In the excitement of combat, of course, we usually forgot to aim from the shoulder—we just emptied a clip from the hip. In close fighting, aiming didn't matter much anyhow. Noise was important.

The M-1 wasn't nearly as accurate as the Mauser rifle—I think this flaw had to do with the gas port. But accuracy is a comparative term. At five hundred yards, the Mauser was better. At two hundred yards, the Mauser was a little better. But we usually fought in the range of twenty to one hundred yards. At those distances the M-1 was as accurate as any Mauser, and much faster.

Obviously, it was very important to know exactly how your rifle worked and to be able to take it apart and reassemble it quickly. The

ASTP issued an M-1 to each fourth person and had us practice taking it apart every night. Ultimately, we had to be able to take it apart and reassemble it blindfolded. That wasn't as hard as it sounds. The key was to remember exactly where you had put each part.

The method by which we learned to shoot was incredibly slow and tedious—just this side of pointing our fingers and saying "Bang." We began by working as partners. One man aimed at a small target and—although the rifle had no ammunition—pulled the trigger. As he did so, the partner gave a sharp whack on the bolt to simulate the recoil of actual firing. First we did it lying prone on the ground, then sitting, then standing. After days of that drudgery we went on the rifle-range bivouac, a week of living in tents, firing our rifles (for real, finally), and conducting patrol exercises. While we were waiting to load onto trucks for the bivouac, Smitty gave his Saint Crispin's oration:

> We few, we happy few, we band of brothers;
> For he to-day that sheds his blood with me
> Shall be my brother; be he ne'er so vile,
> This day shall gentle his condition.

Smitty's quotations added to the spirit of the band of brothers, and I would remember this one a year later when a friend and I were preparing for an attack in which we stood an excellent chance of shedding our blood together.

At first, I dreaded going to the rifle range. Back home, I had enjoyed hunting quail and squirrels, except for one small difficulty—gunshot noise terrified me. Soon, however, I found that shooting on the range was so much fun that I could ignore the sounds. Lie flat, put your arm directly under the stock, line up the sight picture precisely, stretch, take a deep breath, let it out, relax, disconnect your ears so the sound won't matter, and squeeze the trigger. Roll back with the recoil and you will fall back on target.

I loved it—it was the first army procedure that I was good at. I had problems on the obstacle course and was always sloppy trying to do the manual of arms, but I could make a rifle talk. Shot after shot went directly into the bull's eye in a tight little group. I particularly liked the rapid-fire test. You put a clip in the rifle and stand at a crouch. The range officer calls: "Ready on the right? Ready on the left? Ready on the firing line? The flag is up, the flag is waving, the flag is down. Targets up!" You throw yourself on the ground, line up the target, stretch, relax, squeeze, roll, squeeze, your mind focused only on the target. The empty clip springs out with a *ping,* and you relax. "Okay, Standifer, you got a tight group in the lower left of the bull."

I could do almost as well from a sitting position, but the standing position ruined my record. I just couldn't hold that big rifle steady. My system was to aim high and pull the trigger as the sight drifted past the bull. The army recognized three levels of competence—expert, sharpshooter, and marksman. I always made expert at the prone and sitting positions, but only marksman at standing. It averaged out to sharpshooter. That embarrassed me, because I loved firing the rifle.

Basic training wasn't all fun and games. It varied from interesting to dull to harsh—but high school had been like that too. You could enjoy it if you tried. My little group in Fourth Platoon worked at enjoying life. They taught me to laugh—at myself and at life. That group, in that part of the program, is the one I remember as an example of teenagers learning to soldier. I particularly remember a time when we were all on KP. We had peeled the potatoes, served the meals, and washed the pots. Then we had to mop the mess hall. We were working on a new parody for marching:

> Sergeant loves the little children,
> All the little children under him.
> 'Sippi, Souder, Smith, and Sipe,
> We are precious in his sight—

Smitty started giggling. He couldn't mop, he could hardly stand up. Then we all giggled, standing around watching Smitty. I looked up and saw the mess sergeant coming over, but I couldn't stop laughing. He wasn't mad—just amazed. "You kids can make a game out of mopping the floor," he said, shaking his head. We could and we did. But we got the floor mopped. Smitty, Sovish, Souder, Staton, Stevie, and Stumph were all good soldiers and a lot of fun. I don't remember any of them as being close friends in the sense that I later had friends in the rifle company. We were a close group, which is what The Infantry School intended. I don't know what became of them. They completed basic in the group ahead of me and were in college when the program collapsed.

Somewhere along the tenth or eleventh week, I went on sick call with a light fever and headache. I wanted to get some APC—aspirin, phenacetin, caffeine—pills and go back to training. That was the customary thing, but a new order had come down to put everybody with a fever in an isolation barracks because there was a lot of flu in camp. I don't think I had flu when I went there, but the next morning I had it. I missed a little over a week of training, which meant that I had to transfer to the battalion that was two weeks behind my group. When I went back to the company to get my equipment, they were all out on a three-day combat problem. The weather was bitterly cold with drizzling rain, so I was sent over to the mess hall to help get a hot meal ready for the boys when they returned. There was a transportation mix-up, and they ended up out in the rain waiting for trucks until nearly midnight.

Seeing my platoon come in from that problem was my first big shock in the army. Part of it was that I had been in a clean, warm hospital and had begun to forget the old ways where you expect to be wet, cold, and muddy. But they were in bad shape. They had been wet, cold, and muddy for three days, with almost no sleep. They were tired and hungry and had a drab, hollow look in their eyes. They just wanted to sit and breathe the steam from the coffee. Then Captain Rawl strutted in to make a speech. He had been on the problem but had come in early to shower, shave, and change clothes. He couldn't understand how ridiculous he looked, so warm, dry, and clean, trying to give a lecture on how rough war is: "You just think you are tired, hungry, and cold. You have had only one lick from the lollipop of war."

I wanted to laugh, but I was the only one alert enough to see what he was saying. Having lived through Nennig, I can look back and understand him, or rather what he thought. He hadn't seen war, and he thought mud, cold, and exhaustion were the bad part. In fact, that may be the good part of war. If you are tired and cold enough, your mind doesn't register the really bad things. They begin to hurt later.

# 6   The School Solution Won't Work

I was sent to Fifth Company of the Fifth Regiment, where it became evident that The Infantry School was beginning to lose faith in its Benning School for Boys adjunct. My new group had started only two weeks behind the old one, but they were quartered in tar-paper hutments—small twenty-man buildings with a coal stove at each end. Because the sergeant lived in an NCO barracks, nobody was in charge at night, and the ten o'clock lights-out meant nothing. I realized that I had enjoyed the orderly routine that Sergeant Cohen imposed on us. Sergeant Swords was a strong leader, but not the man that Cohen was. He didn't tolerate much foolishness because he was afraid of losing control. We had to do our teasing in subtler ways.

I was an outsider. I couldn't find a group to join, or rather, didn't like the groups I found. The crowd in my hut was vulgar and loud. Boys in Clinton had told dirty jokes and cussed; I didn't, but it hadn't bothered me. My group at Ninth Company hadn't cussed much, but it wasn't a matter of piety—I was the only Bible boy in the bunch; it was just that we hadn't talked that way at school, so why change? Smitty collected dirty poems and knew some good ones Robert Burns had written, and I liked his jokes and poems well enough. But these new boys were just crude. There had been a few like that in Ninth Company, but I didn't have to associate with them because there were plenty of other groups to choose from—for one thing, the entire 120-man platoon had been in one barracks instead of having twenty men cramped in a small hut. The new set-up was almost as bad as the reception center. It wasn't my kind of army.

Several nights a week, I would follow a trail over a large wooded ridge back to Ninth Company. Too steep for barracks and too small for practice assaults, the ridge was crosshatched with rambling paths worn by soldiers who needed occasional bits of solitude. I enjoyed sitting in the grove of large pines on the crest. Below I could see the barracks and hear faint sounds that seemed to emphasize rather than disrupt the isolation. Occasionally I could hear an officer candidate practicing his "voice of command"; in last Saturday's critique he had been told that his orders lacked authority and must show improvement during the coming week. Every night he was drilling a ghost platoon: "By the right flank, harch!" I had been in the army about five months and was already sick of it—but not frightened like the officer candidate. The Infantry School had given me a lot of confidence, more than Clinton had ever tried to; back there I was just a bright, shy, clumsy kid. I wished I were in the navy with Bob, or at least back in Ninth Company.

Sometimes I would only sit in the woods without even going to Ninth Company. The woods was my escape, but not a solution. I remembered the Robert Frost poem:

> The woods are lovely, dark and deep,
> But I have promises to keep,
> And miles to go before I sleep.

I had joined the army with promises to God, Country, and Clinton. "On my honor I will do my best to do my duty." Rumors were developing that the ASTP was going to be canceled and we would all go to combat units. My biggest problem was that I hated being in Fifth Company. But basic training wouldn't last forever, and afterward I would serve where I was needed. Could I soldier in the infantry? Hell, yes—with any outfit—I was grit to the core, swift as a panther in triumph.

Training had reached the stage where they were hardening us up with twenty-mile hikes. The assignment was to walk on dusty roads all day long carrying eighty pounds of equipment, come in singing "The Yellow Rose of Texas," and do twenty push-ups to prove that you could have gone longer. Oh, yes, there was one other trick. At the end, you had to pour a splash out of your canteen to show that you could save water. If you couldn't, on the next hike you carried a canteen full of sand. The long hikes weren't very difficult but could be boring unless you had someone interesting to walk alongside. We had some choice of partners, so the hikes often became day-long cultural dialogues. I enjoyed my walks with Abe Goldstein, from Brooklyn. Our primary topic was how religion had dominated our family and community lives.

"If you weren't active in the Clinton church, your social life was dead," I remember telling him.

Abe understood. "That's what an Orthodox Jewish community is like; they live the rules from the Torah and the Talmud."

"Yeah, I know. We had preachers who would twist the Bible in all directions to make a point. You could get mixed up if you didn't know the Bible."

Abe understood that too. "Well, the Bible, Old and New Testaments, is full of contradictions. I didn't know any Baptists in Brooklyn."

"It's mainly a southern church. We split from the North over the Civil War."

"Can Negroes join it?"

I knew what Abe was driving at, but I hoped to avoid it. "Sure, most colored churches are Baptist. The colored church in Clinton uses our old Sunday school material, and the theology teachers at MC hold summer courses for colored preachers."

"Could they go to your church if they wanted to?"

The only answer left was, "No."

I was glad to get off that topic and onto family life. We were surprised at how similar the relationship of family to church was in the Jewish and Baptist communities. Abe had thought all Christian communities were like the Catholic one he knew in New York. Those families were devout, but in his view they got all of their leadership through the priest. I had the impression that Catholic congregations had fewer arguments than we Baptists did, which I thought was because the community's thinking reflected that of the priest.

Abe said, "The Catholics called us 'Christ-killers.'"

"Yeah, we had a revival minister once who was billed as a 're-formed Jew.' He was vicious about the awful things Jews had done.

The board of deacons decided that we didn't need any more preachers like that."

Abe wanted to know whether the Baptists were anti-Semitic. The question took me aback. There weren't any Jews in Clinton. I had known some Jewish boys in Hattiesburg. They went to a different church on a different day, but I don't think there was any resentment. We went to school together and all belonged to the same Scout troop, which was sponsored by an Episcopalian church. We didn't get along well with Catholics because they went to a different school and belonged to the Catholic Scout troop.

I enjoyed my talks with Abe; we both had learned from the same book. My training had been through the Scotch-Irish Celtic culture, and Abe was Russian Jewish, but we had arrived at the same point. Abe also liked the psalm that said, "Yea, though I walk through the valley of the shadow of death." He didn't lean on it quite as heavily as I did. He taught me the Hebrew phrase "Hear, O Israel, thy God is one." It couldn't protect me in the valley of the shadow, but I was comforted to see that we worshipped the same God in different ways. Abe showed me that the Muslims also worship the same God, but seek him through the teachings of Mohammed. I was beginning to see a kingdom of God that was much larger than the one taught at BYPU.

Dale Proctor was an atypical ASTP boy. He was not skinny or pudgy. Before joining the program, Dale had been an end for the University of Nebraska football team. The Cornhuskers lost a fine player and I lost a treasured friend on a hill near Quimperlé. Dale was from Bruno, Nebraska, but the high school was at the county seat, David City. During the week he lived in a room above the bowling alley where he set pins to pay his rent and earn spending money. During football season he played end and was the team's drop-kicker. He was also a track star (shotput, discus, and javelin) and nearly a straight-A student.

The David City High School was more than twice as large as Clinton's, but Dale had earned all the honors that I had yearned for. He had lettered in football for four years and track for three. During his senior year, the football team achieved the first undefeated season in the school's history. Dale sang in the school chorus and was leading man in the senior play. Nobody at Clinton High had even approached such honors. Dale and I discussed politics and race during the hikes. He was particularly bitter about racism. There had been only one black family in David City. Bernie Coleman at halfback and Dale at end had been the consistent stars of the football team. At first there had been some resentment of Bernie, but he and Dale were close friends. Both boys had a great junior year, with football honors being shared about equally among them and one senior player. At the end of the school year, some of the civic leaders went to the Colemans' house with gifts of a car, gas ration stamps, and a road map. It seemed that Bernie was becoming "too socially integrated." The girls had been thinking Bernie was "cute" throughout the year. When Dale and a few friends protested what had been done, they could find no one who would admit to doing it. The party line was that the Colemans had simply decided to move to Chicago, which was their privilege.

Dale wanted me to explain how decent people could act that way. I had no idea. That kind of situation was entirely outside of my experience. The family wouldn't have been forced out of Clinton because Bernie would have been in school with his own race.

Although Dale was planning to be an electrical engineer, he enjoyed European history. It was through his talks that I learned the southern–Scotch-Irish–Celtic relationship. Until then I had thought the Celtics were a basketball team. They came to Jackson every year and played a demonstration game against MC. I can't remember for certain, but I think it was Dale who told me that the King Arthur stories are about Romanized Celts and that Merlin was from France. Dale knew Tennyson's *Merlin and the Gleam*.

Dale was so strong and tough that I wondered why he hadn't joined the marines or paratroopers. "I don't know, Leon. I don't like what they stand for. I'm willing to fight, but not eager. It's more than that. They seem to need the prestige of being tough and brave. I'm satisfied that I can do the job physically. I hope I'm strong enough emotionally. I don't want to kill anyone, but if I'm needed, I'll try." I thought of Bob Souder in the same kind of discussion: "I know how to kill, but will I be willing to kill when I meet the enemy man-to-man? God, I hope not!"

We got a full afternoon of instruction on the use of artillery. We didn't fire them, we didn't even see the guns (which were really rifles), but we learned to direct the fire. We were taught by an artilleryman who knew that we had been misled into thinking infantry was the most important branch of the army. "When you get in trouble and hear artillery coming in, it will sound like music. It will be sweeter than Glenn Miller's band." It made a great joke for us, but he was right. A year later, while I was in the hospital, there was a short news story from my division telling about muddy, tired infantry moving back from the line, past the artillery that had been supporting them. One rifleman stopped, looked at an artilleryman, and said simply, "Thanks."

Our artilleryman taught us the principles of directing artillery fire. "This is usually done by a trained forward observer, but you should know how it is done." He was so right. The principle is simple. You have a map exactly like the one the artillery has. You place a transparent grid sheet over the part of the map covering the area to be shelled. Then you telephone the coordinates to artillery, so that their grid is on the same spot. They fire a practice round to let you orient. You tell them where it hit and proceed to adjust from there. The easiest system is to "bracket": you put one round beyond the point, another short of it, and adjust until the guns are aimed directly on the point. Another system is to "walk" the artillery: you start at one point and move the fire forward in fifty-yard intervals.

We sat on bleachers and watched the instructor walk artillery around a field. "If there were a patrol out there, I could herd them like cattle or pin them down and wipe them out." I was greatly impressed. We enjoyed joking about the demonstration, and talked of directing artillery as if it were directing an orchestra. I told my Civil War story about a preacher who commanded an artillery battery of four brass twelve-pound Napoleon cannon, which he had named Matthew, Mark, Luke, and John. "Fire Matthew, fire Mark, fire Luke, fire John. Gospel, on the way."

After our brief brush with artillery, we ran the close combat course, an individual test. You walk along a trail, alert and watching everything. Suddenly a dummy soldier pops up. You drop him with one or two shots (using blanks). Of course, you have a bayonet on your rifle, and if the dummy is very close, you run him through. It was a great game—an early Rambo. Actually, Alan Ladd was the hero of the time.

In one of his movies he picked up a machine gun, slung an ammunition belt over his shoulder, and charged the dirty Japs with the machine gun blazing. We could hardly lift the machine gun and certainly couldn't fire it that way. In about a minute the barrel would get so hot you couldn't hold it. But Alan Ladd could!

Somewhere in this later training we got the school solution lecture. I don't remember how the instructor led into it, but it was probably in a section on tactics. We would be given a theoretical problem and asked how we would solve it. Then the instructor would explain what we *should* have done. That was called the "school solution." In one of those classes the instructor said: "This is the school solution, but remember that it solves a school problem. Don't expect it to work on a combat problem." It was an off-the-cuff remark, but it drew some questions, so he elaborated a little. Essentially, he said that The Infantry School was illustrating a principle by selecting a specific problem and showing a specific solution. He was disappointed that officer candidates seemed to believe they were being taught specific solutions to actual problems they would meet in combat. We should remember the principle of the solution rather than the specifics. The school solution wouldn't work in combat, but the principle would. That was so obvious that it seemed like a joke to us, but at Camp McCain we would find that our regimental training officers had missed the point. They learned later, after the German officers gave them some advanced training, but the cost was high.

Fort Benning was both boring and exciting. It seemed as challenging as a good boys school. The challenge came from the other trainees more than from the training program, but gradually even that worked. Some time after the tactical field problem (wet, cold, and hungry for five days), we began to develop pride. We were still skinny or pudgy, and still inept, but the bonnie blue braid was less of a joke. The infantry was becoming the Queen of Battle. We were products of The Infantry School, the best soldiers in the world. We had dirt behind our ears, we could lick our weight in wildcats and drink our weight in beer. (Drinking *my* weight in beer wouldn't have been too hard. I was six feet tall and weighed 140 pounds dripping wet.) Benning School for Boys had done a job on us bright, cocky kids. As the cheerleaders and band members, we had learned to back the team and support the school. But this was The Infantry School; this time we were on the team instead of in the band. We were on the team, but we weren't going to have to fight. We would have the best of both worlds, wearing blue braid and crossed rifles while we went to college.

At the end of our training period, we had a big graduation parade. The battalion commander announced that our college assignments would be posted the next morning. I was being sent to the University of Arkansas for engineering training. Then a story began circulating that we weren't going to college. The program was going to be abolished. After a week, the company commander announced that the rumor was true. He had received shipping orders for us to go to an infantry division. We were to be ready to leave in three days. He also stated that these shipping orders were secret and that it was a court-martial offense to mention them to anyone outside of the company. That night I wrote home telling them that the program was abolished. I said I didn't know where we were going, but asked them please not to tell anyone about the new orders, because to say anything at all was a court-martial offense. The telephone lines at the service club were in chaos with boys trying to phone home.

At formation two days later, Captain Lowe said: "I have in my hand copies of telegrams which are legal evidence that fifty men in this company have committed breaches of security. I am not going to press the charges because you are due to leave soon and I will be very glad to get rid of you." He read one telegram to us: "Uncle Oswald has left for Washington to contact some senators. He promised that you are not going to have to become an ordinary soldier."

Captain Lowe said: "Men, I give you the same promise. You will not become ordinary soldiers. You will become infantrymen. You are no longer a bunch of smart-assed kids playing soldier until you can go to college. You have been wasting the time of the finest infantry instructors in the world. They could have been training real men who want to fight for their country. Now you gold bricks are going to soldier. Sergeant Smith, do you have anything to say to these men?" The first sergeant got up and railed at us for awhile, but all he really said was that he had taught us to soldier and when we got into combat, he wanted us to remember to keep our butts down.

We were disgusted with both of them. I was amazed to see such venom coming from the men who had trained us. We hadn't created the ASTP. We joined because it was offered and we wanted to go to college. Blame the army, not us.

After the formation, Sergeant Swords still seemed friendly. Our orders remained secret, but he said that we were going to Camp McCain, Mississippi, to join the Ninety-fourth Infantry Division. He also said the orders emphasized that no requests for transfer would be considered.

# 7 Company of the Line

Camp McCain had been built on pasture land in the flood plain of Bogue Creek (*bogue* itself having been the local Indians' word for "creek"). It didn't look at all like a campus, and there didn't seem to be a tree in the entire camp. Every building was wartime tar-paper architecture: barracks, theater, library, PX, and hospital. The streets were straight and all made right angles. I could no longer wear the emblem of the golden lamp. The divisional emblem was as drab and dull as the camp: a black and gray 9/4. Walt Disney's art group was designing insignia for any outfit that asked. But ours was a 9/4. Other divisions had swashbuckling nicknames: Thunderbirds, Timber Wolves, or Tough Hombres. We were the Pilgrim Division.

Going from The Infantry School to an infantry division left me with a feeling of near-nausea. I wasn't just playing at soldiering now; I was a rifleman. While we were standing retreat one afternoon, a rifle shot cracked in from the Second Platoon barracks. One of the ASTP boys had committed suicide by shooting himself in the head. No one seemed to know why at the time, but after the war his platoon leader, Bob Feitig, told me that the shock of being in a rifle company had simply broken the boy. He wasn't able to eat or do simple things like lacing his leggings. Bob had twice sent him on sick call for psychiatric help, and each time the medical officer had returned him as a malingerer.

That day I faced the reality of what I had gotten into. I remembered laughing at the people who had said that I should volunteer for the navy. Why hadn't I joined V-5 with Bob, or the Signal Corps when they had argued with me at Camp Shelby? Because I'm Infantry, the finest soldier in the world. I wasn't absolutely convinced that I was infantry material, but I was working on it. The Ninety-fourth Division was short of riflemen because it had furnished some for the Eighth Division when the Eighth was preparing to go overseas. Now the Ninety-fourth itself was preparing for overseas shipment, and 1,500 ASTP soldiers were needed to make up for the shortage. After six months of mixed signals about where ASTP was taking us, we finally knew.

I was among twelve ASTP boys assigned to the First Platoon, K Company, 301st Infantry Regiment. This was about one third of the normal forty-man strength. We were outnumbered by old-timers, but there were enough of us to cause problems. Colonel McNulty, the battalion commander, had told us that we would find some resentment because the other men considered us a bunch of kids who had chosen to go to school while they were soldiering. McNulty was exactly right. We could argue that we had come straight from soldiering at The Infantry School, but that only made matters worse. The platoon leaders had been bragging about how much they had learned in OCS at The Infantry School. This made us products of an elitist school. We compounded the problem because in spite of our jokes about Benning School for Boys, we thought it *was* an elite school.

We were scared of these older men. Most of them were twenty-two to twenty-six, with a few grizzled vets of thirty. Then there were the noncoms. When we had complained about Sergeant Cohen around the instructors at Benning, they had told us: "Wait until you get to a line company. The noncoms are really rough there." Now we were in a line company. (*Line company* means a rifle company—the men on the fighting line who meet the enemy one-on-one with only rifles in their hands.) I was in First Squad—twelve men—with Dale and two other ASTP boys.

"The noncoms are really rough in a line company." Well, they at least talked rough. Our squad leader, Ray Graziano, was a truck driver from Brooklyn and he played the part to the hilt. (On the other hand, Ray was never "Sergeant Graziano" to anyone but Lieutenant Westmoreland, whereas Sergeant Cohen would have killed a trainee who called him "Bernie.") Ray had two great loves: singing and boxing.

He and Sergeant DeRosa, another squad leader in the platoon, were part of a quartet that had placed second in the regimental talent contest. They were both good singers and loved to ham it up. Ray's ability as a boxer was somewhat less than his talent as a singer. DeRosa was a fine boxer and had won the division championship for his weight. Ray was a good squad leader. He exuded self-confidence and enjoyed being leader of eleven tough infantrymen—or rather, seven tough infantrymen and four ASTP boys.

Once while he was looking me over before Saturday inspection, Ray said: "Jesus Christ. I'm supposed to fight battles with boys who shave once a week."

"Aw, Ray," I said, "I really don't have to shave that often." We all laughed. Ray loved the show of getting mad at us, and our jokes never really bothered him. He knew that when it was absolutely necessary, we got down to business and soldiered. He also enjoyed being in command of boys who knew all the tactics taught at The Infantry School. He was sure that we knew just as much about platoon tactics as Lieutenant Westmoreland. We were not nearly that good, but we promoted the image because it gave us a lot of leverage in arguing with him.

"Sergeant Ray, not meaning to 'spute your word, but those circles on the map mean that we should be on the hill over there." We were careful to needle him only within the squad, but Ray never did learn much more about map reading. In combat, when he was leading a platoon, Ray once captured the wrong German town. Colonel Hagerty raised hell about it.

I suppose Ray tolerated us because we helped him to understand the orders of our platoon leader, whom we all admired. Jim Westmoreland was the epitome of a good infantry officer, even though barely a year earlier he had graduated from a small liberal arts college in South Carolina with the intention of becoming an architect. (After the war he got a master's degree at Yale and practiced architecture at Spartanburg until his death, in 1987.) He went to infantry OCS because the Westmorelands had always fought as infantry. His cousin W. Childs Westmoreland had gone to West Point and was already in combat under General Patton. Childs was in the artillery at the time, but fought as infantry later. He went on to become commander of the American forces in Vietnam.

Jim was a smooth, soft-spoken gentleman. He respected his riflemen and always gave them a full orientation of what he knew about a mission, whether in training or in combat. I didn't know Jim personally until after the war. To us, he was the platoon leader, and we had no social contact. He never called his noncoms by their first names, and all orders went through them to us. I am sure he did a lot of worrying about how he was going to integrate that bunch of cocky ASTP kids into his dull, discouraged platoon. He never let us know he had any doubts about doing it. He gave us all temporary assignments until he learned more about our abilities. From that time on, we were his riflemen, and our age or background made no difference. It did make a difference, of course, but his attitude helped a lot. There were a lot of flare-ups before we were grudgingly accepted, and even then acceptance did not mean integration. After the war, as we began returning to the company from hospitals all over Europe, we were so integrated that we had trouble remembering who had been ASTP—but it took that long and that many shared hardships.

After the first week, they took us out to the rifle range to see how we could do. I had never fired the BAR (Browning Automatic Rifle) but knew it pretty well. It was the base of a squad's firepower, too heavy to fire from the shoulder (although in an assault you might fire it from the hip). On the range you only had to lie behind it and shoot; the front of the barrel was held up by two legs. I did pretty well on it and was a little afraid I might be assigned to one. The BAR (which we also called the AR) is too heavy for a skinny little boy to carry. Dale and another boy, George Faber, had better scores than mine, so they both got ARs. Dale was transferred to Third Squad; George remained with First and became my closest friend. I was named first scout. Another ASTP boy, Ed Blake, was second scout. As scout, I could keep my M-1, but I had landed one of the two most dangerous jobs in the squad. Stripped of army jargon, the job of first scout is to draw fire. He ranges in front of the patrol, investigating potential ambush sites. If he finds one he dies, but the patrol has a chance to escape. The BAR position is equally dangerous because when the AR man fires, the enemy riflemen all begin trying to eliminate him.

First Platoon's marching songs were what Fort Benning had tried to push on us—dull. "I've Been Working on the Railroad" was the standard, supplemented by "When the War is Over, We Will All Enlist Again" and "I Used to Work in Chicago." The rest of the platoon thought most of our ASTP songs were stupid, but they did like our parody of one of Sousa's marches: "We're a bunch of bastards, scum of the earth." That one went back to high school band, but it fitted well in the infantry. There were some pretty good stock jokes. On one hike Herb Adams, a mountain boy from Kentucky, was listing the many things that had gone wrong: the cook truck had gotten lost, so there was no lunch; the platoon had attacked across a field full of briars; Herb was getting blisters from slogging through the mud—it went on and on and ended with, "An' hit a'rainin'." That phrase became our means of complaining without bothering to detail the problems. It got us through hard times in training and helped during the miserable days of drizzle and fog and rain while we tried to fight Krauts in France.

The upbeat joke belonged to Thomas Richards, first scout in Second Squad. With any delay on hikes, or while we were pinned down during a tactical exercise, he would yell: "Let's go, let's go! Goddamnit, let's go!" The demand was pretty much parallel with "an' hit a'rainin'" in that it complained about the injustice of life, but it breathed humor and defiance as well. Richards helped to release tension for us until a machine gun stopped him in France.

The daily routine in First Platoon was much more relaxed than what we had known at Benning. At five thirty every morning the first sergeant would walk through the barracks and turn on the lights; that was reveille—I can't remember ever hearing a bugle call at McCain. We had fifteen minutes until roll-call formation. A whistle would blow, and we would walk out to the street and stand in line. Our platoon sergeant would ask, "Ray?" Ray would nod his head that we were all there. The first sergeant would call for a report. "First Platoon all present or accounted for." Usually there was nothing else. "Dismissed." We had until seven thirty to dress, wash up, eat breakfast, and mop the floor around our bunks. Nobody cared when you did what. I particularly liked walking slowly to breakfast and eating at my own pace.

Guard duty was a revelation to me. The squad had one four-hour shift during which to guard the battalion area. When we assembled, Ray would look us over and say: "Be sure you know your General

Orders. Prado what's the twelfth one?" Prado: "To walk my post in a military manner and take no crap from Graziano." Westmoreland was our officer of the guard, and he didn't inspect us at all. We just drew our assignments and walked our posts until Second Squad relieved us. (At a reunion after the war I asked Jim Westmoreland about this lax approach to guard duty. He said that it was standard practice: most of the men knew how to walk a guard post, but some couldn't possibly have learned all eleven General Orders.)

Training also was easier. Some of those older men couldn't have kept up with the pace we had known at Benning. We did fewer push-ups, didn't run as much, and went slower on hikes. I was supposed to be alongside Ed Blake but usually switched to be with George Faber. As the day wore on, our company commander, Captain Simmers, would fall back and check on his men. He chewed tobacco only when we were on a hike, and had a contemptuous way of spitting the juice—it amounted to bragging about how tough we were: "*Pe-taugh!* All right, men, lean into it. The day's going to get worse. God, Standifer, you're so tall you can see over the next hill. You goin' to have to carry Prado's pack for him again today? Faber, you carry that AR like it was a carbine, nothing can wear you down." Then he would pick up his pace and move up to somebody else. It was easy for him to move along the column because he was carrying only a light carbine and no pack at all. As things got tougher he would fall back and spit for us again. I glowed when he joked with me and called me a man. I had been a trainee at Benning, but now I was a man.

Looking back, I can see that Captain Simmers was carefully building K Company into a proud, close-knit unit. Before the war he had been an officer in the Pennsylvania highway patrol. It had been strong on military discipline, proper conduct, and sense of community. Our phonetic designation was King Company, and he considered us as just that: the best rifle company in the regiment. He demanded that the platoon leaders know each rifleman personally; if we were ordered to risk our lives, it would be from a man who knew who we were and what we could do. Simmers reinforced his demand by showing that he knew the name, hometown, and personal aspirations of every enlisted man in the company—I remember our platoon sergeant being embarrassed at having to ask each of us what we planned to do after the war.

We were Captain Simmers' family; he required absolute obedience from us but loved each of us deeply.

I enjoyed my new family. King Company was home and I was more relaxed than I had been since leaving Ninth Company. Every platoon had one or two people who played a guitar. Until then, I had looked on the guitar as a hillbilly instrument. I suppose it was; the boys who played it were either cowboys or hillbillies. But it was relaxing at night to lie in my bunk and listen to someone plunk out a tune: "He had a young daughter, he had a young son. / His son went to college, his daughter went wrong." That was aimed at the ASTP, saying that a son going to college was as bad as the daughter becoming a prostitute, but it was family joking. One of the cowboy songs was fairly grisly, but it too came to be part of home:

> When I die, take my saddle from the wall.
> Just put it on my pony, and lead him from his stall.
> Tie my bones to his back, turn our faces to the West.
> We'll ride the prairie that we love the best.

And there were the standard mountain songs:

> Old Uncle Snort, he was sawed off and short,
> Measured 'bout five foot and two.
> But he felt like a gi'nt when you gave him a pint
> Of that good ole mountain dew.

And the bawdy: "I've got a gal, she lives on a hill. / She won't do it, but her sister will."

My first KP duty was at officers' mess. "You drew an easy one. There isn't as much work and the food is better." Yes, but I resented pulling KP for men who never had to take their turn. While they ate, I stood beside the table at parade rest, waiting until they needed something. Three of them were discussing the new ASTP kids in the battalion.

"I know they're sharp and they seem to soldier well," one man said. "But they are such kids." The second agreed: "Yeah, skinny, most of them wear glasses. They know the book, but can they fight?"

Only the third officer spoke up for us: "Mike, you're missing the point. This war isn't a boxing match, they're going to fight with rifles.

Most of them qualified expert and the worst are sharpshooters. Okay, they're sharp, cocky, and conceited, but these kids are winners. They've always been at the top of their class and they aren't willing to lose. When the chips are down, that bunch will fight like tigers."

I suppose I should have felt proud, but I was disgusted. They knew we were going to do the fighting for them, yet they were treating us like trash. I could probably outsoldier any one of them. I was one of the bright kids they were discussing, but they considered me no more than a piece of furniture. "Can they fight?" Hell, yes, we can fight. We're Infantry.

In fairness, I must say that most of the officers were glad to have us and believed we could soldier. The incident I just described is the only one in which I remember resenting the caste system. I was raised in such a system and was taught to "render unto Caesar." Also, I was from The Infantry School. I accepted that a fighting unit required leadership and that I was far too young to participate in it. An officer didn't have to be brilliant to lead men, he only had to be a leader. (I hoped he also had at least a reasonable amount of common sense.) I think that all through combat, I believed I was at least as good a soldier as Jim Westmoreland, but it wasn't a point that bothered me. He was the leader, I was the soldier, and we were good.

About a month after we joined the platoon, we went on a six-day combat problem in the Holly Springs National Forest, a large wooded area in the rolling hills of northern Mississippi. It was a good place for training, except that it wasn't a single, unbroken unit. There were small towns and farms scattered along the gravel roads that ran through it. The combat problem wasn't actually for us as a platoon. It was a training exercise for the platoon leader. We were just the unit he was to use as a learning tool. Our assignment was to act like a combat patrol following a small road and clearing out any enemy resistance. Following a road doesn't mean walking on it. One flank scout walked within sight of the road, but the rest of us were in the woods or walking carefully across the open fields.

I remember those six days as a wonderful time to be young and a soldier. It was early spring and the dogwood was in bloom. The weather was beautiful, not too hot by day, not too cold by night. It was my first time to perform as scout. I was proud of having been selected, but nervous. The boy that I replaced as scout had filled the role much better than I could. He was stocky, with a black mustache and a cynical, confident look. His confidence was genuine—but that was because he wasn't very bright. Thomas Richards, in Second Squad, was an excellent scout, probably the best in the company. A country boy from South Carolina, he wasn't ASTP material, but a shrewd scout. "Take your time, Standifer, don't let anybody push you. Study the land slowly, decide where you would set up a position, and assume the enemy would do the same."

The problem was flavored by continual suspense. At any minute, rifle or machine-gun fire might explode around us. Hit the ground, roll, and try to locate a good firing position. After a minute, Ray would begin calling. It was like a covey of quail regrouping after being flushed: "Standifer?" *Ho.* "Blake?" *Ho.* And so on. He was locating the approximate firing positions and calling roll to see who was theo-retically wounded or killed—one little joke line was, "Sergeant, count your men." Actually, Westmoreland would say, "First Squad, report." Some postwar critiques of American infantry said that our troops were too quiet, in contrast with the Germans, who talked incessantly in combat. But First Platoon chattered freely. We were quiet until fired on, then we yelled at each other and at the enemy. "Ya missed me, you stupid krauthead." There was a bit of bravado in it, but Westmoreland used the Fort Benning philosophy: the terror of being fired on is com-pounded if you don't know where your support is, who is alive, and who is too scared to fight. Yelling breaks the tension and doesn't reveal very much about your position. "Let's go, let's go! Goddamnit, let's go!"

The most serious criticism the umpires had of First Platoon was that we were reluctant to fire our rifles. They pretended to believe that this indicated a lack of aggressive spirit. We ignored their comments because the truth was so obvious. Firing the rifle left a residue of cor-rosive nitrate salts in the barrel. For the next three nights you would have to swab it out repeatedly with a soapy water and oil emulsion called "bore cleaner"—or, inevitably, "boring cleaner." As a final treatment, you would swab until the cloth patches came out dry and clean, then oil the barrel. If you hadn't fired, the nightly routine was to simply run an oily patch through the bore. Naturally, boys who had already fired their rifles were much more "aggressive" than those of us who had clean rifles and wanted to keep them that way. I didn't fire a shot during the entire problem.

Scouts of the three squads rotated as point or flank scouts. Each morning Westmoreland would assemble the platoon and outline the plan for that day. As in everything else, the army had a distinct system by which things were done. The leader would describe our mission, tell us what we should expect to meet, outline any alternate plans, and indicate where we should end up. Then he would lay out each squad's position in the patrol and where the scouts were to be for that day. Finally he would say: "Any questions? Check your gear. Lock and load. Scouts out." *Lock and load* meant to put the safety on for your rifle and then load it. *Scouts out* told the first and second scouts to start down the trail.

I don't know how to describe the excitement that second command put in me. Westmoreland was not a man of high drama, he gave the command calmly and professionally, but to me it said: "From now on we are in danger. This is the beginning of our mission." At Holly Springs, it wasn't actually a mission, and we were loading with blank ammunition. But we were preparing for a real mission, and I enjoyed the excitement. I thrilled at being point scout in front of the entire platoon. It was Westmoreland's show, but I worked like his bird dog. I kept visual contact to see general directions, but basically I worked the area on my own, looking for ambush sites. I would find a high point that looked as if it might have good places for machine guns. Then I would stop, drop to one knee, and look for motion or silhouettes against the sky. Ed would join me and discuss what we should do. Occasionally Westmoreland would come up, but usually he let us decide.

The standard procedure was to "advance boldly and aggressively" directly at the suspected enemy position. Under that concept, the real purpose of a scout was to draw fire. The scout got killed, but the patrol escaped. Sometimes you didn't have to do it that way. If you could slip to the side or toward the rear of the site, you might discover what was there without being shot at. I preferred that approach. Getting killed in a combat problem didn't mean anything because you came back to life after the fight was over, but we were practicing for times when you couldn't be brought back to life.

Every evening Westmoreland would hold a short critique of the day's work. "We did a good job today. The judges say we lost about half the platoon, but the enemy had an excellent position. Most of the losses were just wounded. Statistically, we had only two men killed—probably from First Squad, since they were at the point."

Ray asked, "Who did I lose?"

"Well, Standifer, almost certainly. He walked right into the machine gun. Faber had an excellent fire position for the BAR. When he opened up he would have drawn most of the fire."

"Both ASTP."

"And they were doing an excellent job. There was no way for Standifer to flank that position. He saw where the gun should be placed and took it head-on. Faber saw what was going on. He had selected a good fire position and stayed at it until Standifer drew fire."

That night in the tent, George and I went over the problem. George was from Mount Sterling, Ohio, and had been an engineering student at Ohio State. He was as big and strong as Dale, around six feet tall, with rusty brown hair and a heavy beard—shaved every day. He had played high school football but loved basketball—had played guard when the team won the state championship. At first Ray had tried to box with him a little, but found that George was extremely fast, had a right hook that felt like a mule kicking, and hated boxing.

George and I were an unlikely pair: the stocky, laughing, gregarious boy with his tall, skinny, introspective buddy. Our personalities differed, but I can't remember that we ever clashed. George was also the best poker player in the company. I knew nothing about the awful game, and he liked it that way. When he would get ahead in a game, I would hold his winnings and refuse to give the money back for him to play poker. It took me a while to realize that this was a little scam he used in order to circumvent the old poker proscription of quitting while you are ahead. George was my brother in K Company. He would argue over philosophy or tell me who was stealing sugar from the mess hall and giving it to a girl in town. I still don't know why George chose a shy, blue-nosed Baptist as his close friend. Surely he could have done better.

"Leon, we soldiered today, did everything right, and both got killed."

I agreed with him and was just as worried. "Well, the scout and AR man are going to draw the most fire, but we could have just been wounded. I don't think I handled my part well. Westmoreland knew it, but he wouldn't say so in front of Ray. I was pretty sure of the gun when I hit the opening. It was a classic ambush site, and the blackberry bush was the best gun location. It had three young sweetgum branches stuck in it. Hardly anything will grow in a blackberry clump. Somebody had cut the branches and put them there to hide the gun. I should have called Westmoreland and tried to flank it. You knew about the gun too, because you stopped at that high point."

George shook his head. "No, I just saw that you had slowed down and were being careful. I was at a good position and held it."

I remembered the tense emotion of being almost certain that a machine gun would soon blast away at me. "They sure waited a long time to open up. I must have been about fifteen yards away. It was so close I could feel the muzzle blast of the blanks. With live ammunition I wouldn't have stood a chance."

"I think I would have gotten the gunner when I fired. I was aiming right at him. But Westmoreland was right: the other gunner and all the rifles would have taken me."

I asked the question we were both thinking: "George, is that what's going to happen to us in combat?"

"I don't think so. This was a bad situation. But we're here to fight. We've got to win, and it's going to cost lives."

"I don't want one of them to be mine. George, I hope I'm ready."

"Don't worry, we're both man enough to do it. Let's quit talking about such things."

That night I was brave and proud. I don't think we discussed death again until the night before a real attack that was bound to draw blood. Benning had taught us that the ratio of wounds to fatalities was about nine to one. For a nineteen-year-old, that's good enough. I felt better discussing this with George; he was my anchor. I knew he would always be there, ready to do his share. In October, when I first walked through the valley of the shadow, I knew that George had the machine gun in his sights.

A couple of days later on the Holly Springs problem, I was flank scout, following along the edge of the road. George was the contact between me and the rest of the patrol. Richards and Jack Button, a tall farm boy from southern Michigan, were point scouts, leading the patrol. Richards stopped us at the edge of a field, which left me in the backyard of a small farmhouse. A little colored boy came up and said, "My daddy's a soldier. He's a buffalo soldier."

"Where is he?"

"I don't know, he's way off somewhere. When he gets through whuppin' the Germans, he'll come home and help us farm."

I grinned. "Pretty soon I'll be helping him."

The boy ducked in the house. "Mama, man out here say he gonna help Daddy whup the Germans." He came back out. "Mama say, would you like some buttermilk?"

"Yes, ma'am, I would. Could my friend have some too?" George and I sat on the back steps, watching Richards and Button work the field while we drank buttermilk and talked with the boy's mother. She asked if we knew there was a machine gun at the far end of the field.

"I think our scouts do. The man who plans these tests isn't very good. His guns are pretty obvious." Button was walking slowly toward the gun while Richards slipped into the woods and worked around behind it. The umpires ruled that we had won, and the patrol moved on.

At the next break, George came over to sit by me.

"George, Richards handled that gun the way I should have. I hope I can learn to soldier as well as he does."

George asked what a buffalo soldier was.

"That's the Ninety-second Division. It's a combat unit open to colored soldiers. The father of a friend of mine in Clinton is in it. They have white officers and colored riflemen." Later, I learned that there were many all-black combat units, but the Ninety-second was the only one I had heard of at the time.

George still couldn't understand why the boy's mother had selected us. "Soldiers come through here every day. Why did that woman decide to give you buttermilk?"

"I was home folks and talked with her son."

"But you're white."

"I was still home folks, and she knew I wasn't the Klan type."

The road we were following went through Potts Camp—a crossroad grocery store, post office, and a few houses. We were to move in and capture this hamlet at daybreak. We gathered at the edge of the woods, and the platoon covered me while I slipped up to the closest building, a barn. I had a ditch and brush cover until I was about twenty yards from the barn. Then I had to climb through the fence and cross the open lot. There was no cover at all. The only way was to just get up and run. I slipped through the fence, lay on the ground looking around me, braced my feet, and came up running as hard as I could. I dived into the barn doorway and lay there covering the interior with my rifle. It was pointed directly at a woman sitting on a stool milking a cow. "Good morning, sonny. Is your group capturing us today?"

"Yes ma'am."

The pickup point at the end of this problem was a little grocery store in a fork of the road. About a quarter-mile before we got there, Westmoreland took us all out onto the road. "The problem is over. Sling arms and form a column of twos. At route step, move out!" He wanted us to go in looking like soldiers, but we were in no shape for formal marching. We had worn the same clothes for six days and had bathed out of helmets. We were covered with chigger bites. The older men had stubble beards. But we straightened up and moved out. As we came to the store, the trucks were waiting. A group of maybe ten civilians was sitting on the porch watching us. Westmoreland backed down the column and said, "Infantry, look sharp!" That wasn't a standard command, and the platoon hadn't heard it before. It was straight out of The Infantry School, and we graduates knew what he wanted.

George sounded off with, "I was drinking beer in a cabaret, and was I having fun." At first only Dale, Ed, and I joined him. Then Graziano and DeRosa boomed out the chorus: "Hey, lay that pistol down, Babe, lay that pistol down." The whole platoon was singing when we passed the grocery store reviewing stand.

"Platoon, halt. Sergeant Monti, congratulate the platoon on a job well done and dismiss them." The reviewing stand clapped, and we yelled. We were First Platoon of King Company and we could whip the world. George, Ed, and I were a lot more confident than before those six days. We had shown the old men that we were Infantry with dirt behind our ears. We had shown ourselves that we could soldier. It had been hard to develop confidence in basic training because the instructors were always pressing us to do better.

After Holly Springs, I began trying to know the rest of the platoon better. Ed and I had clashed badly at first. In retrospect, I wonder how we ever became close friends. He was a brilliant boy who had been a physics major at MIT. He had a strong Boston accent and the attitude that any other way of speaking was barbaric. My Mis'Sippi whine and lanky walking gait didn't go over well with him. He was galled about being second scout behind me, although he knew it was a good choice: with Ed's thick glasses he could see pretty well up to about a hundred yards, which isn't a great help on patrols. He was tall and skinny like me but seemed better coordinated, or perhaps was more careful about his movements. At any rate, he didn't lope along like a plowboy.

Ed and I argued continually about scouting procedures. Besides having better eyesight, I understood the open country better. I could detect slight differences of pattern that might indicate trouble, although sometimes they were so subtle that I couldn't explain what was wrong.

"Ed, something over there doesn't look right."

"What doesn't?"

"I don't know."

"Christ, Leon, that's no answer."

He came to trust my hunches even if I didn't understand them. He saved his bitter criticism for my inconsistency. I could start the day being very thorough and careful, then begin moving faster, ignoring danger points. Ed would signal me to stop and walk up to consult.

"Leon, you are getting sloppy."

"Naw, there isn't anything out there. This isn't ambush country."

"It is just like the fields we were in two hours ago. You did a good job then."

I got into serious trouble if I tried to argue that this was just practice anyhow. Ed was right. We were practicing methods that could mean the difference between life and death—for us and for the patrol. I gradually improved but never got to be as careful as Ed. His stubborn harassment probably saved my life, and his too, in combat. Occasionally, Ray would come up and raise hell about our being too slow, but Westmoreland usually supported us.

As Ed and I became closer, I saw how deeply he hated the army. His personality was suited to math and physics: everything should be honest, orderly, and predictable. Ed was a strong, capable soldier, but he hated the army for incompetence, fraud, and—particularly—the caste system. He hated war and the infantry. His disgust wasn't very obvious because Ed didn't talk much even to friends. He enjoyed watching people and noting their idiosyncrasies, then he might discuss them with me, George, or another buddy of ours, Hubert Cagle.

Ed had strange ways of teasing me about religion or some aspects of culture. I don't think he was malicious, but he liked to see me trying to get out of an awkward position. "Leon, why is a person still considered to be colored when he is seven-eighths or even fifteen-sixteenths white?"

"You can't be a little of both, because our laws are based on a person's being either colored or white."

"What about Indians?"

"That's different. Most old families have a little Choctaw blood back in their past." I knew he was playing with me, but I still couldn't find a way out. Ed's sister was a social worker, and his point was that a person who was one-eighth black had to live in the black community with his mother, which meant that we were talking about culture rather than genetics. He also pointed out that culturally, I was at least one-quarter black. I remember disagreeing with him strongly, knowing that he was right. Throughout my time in the army I was comfortable with southern black soldiers, but not with those from the North.

Ed was one of the many tragedies of K Company. I think he would have become an excellent physicist, but my basis for comparison isn't good. King Company was not a postdoctoral research facility. Gore Vidal and Henry Kissinger were in ASTP, but they didn't have to fight at Nennig after the program collapsed. Ed didn't receive the Purple Heart for his wounds, but he was very much a casualty. His brilliant mind simply broke under the stress of giving more than he had. After being discharged, he slowly recovered and I assume he returned to MIT. He now owns a consulting firm for electrical engineering. The scars remain and he prefers not to remember the war. For this reason, Ed is the only one of my close friends for whom I am using a pseudonym.

Hubert Cagle was the third of my close friends in the squad. He wasn't from ASTP but was with us in spirit. Cagle particularly enjoyed my frogs-and-snails-and-puppydog-tails joke. He had a strip-tease bump-and-grind that became something of a cult act for us. It came from a long-forgotten joke about a carnival barker; I can't remember the joke and may never have known it. Cagle used the bump-

and-grind to express the entire range of emotions from joy to terror. He was the platoon's sniper because he was by far the best marksman we had. The disadvantage in giving him this job was that the sniper rifle was a World War I '03 with a Mauser action. The M-1 wasn't accurate enough for a sniper to use. So Cagle, our best M-1 rifleman, went to war carrying a single-shot rifle and a sniper's scope.

One night as Ed and I were walking back from the mess hall, we saw a soldier we called H. R. carrying a half loaf of bread to the barracks. All my life I had heard of no 'count drunks, but I hadn't known one until I joined K company. H. R. was a classic drunk. He spent all his money on beer or wine. He seemed always to have an evil leer on his face. After I spent time with him at Holly Springs, I realized that the leer was his attempt at a smile. He had a vacant stare, black curly hair, and an overall greasy appearance. I remembered the Greek and Syrian fruit stands in Hattiesburg. Nobody trusted those Greeks and Syrians. Maybe that was why I hadn't liked H. R. at first. Now I was beginning to understand him. His mind was always in a haze, but he wanted to be a good friend. H. R. had a full name, and given time, could print it out in large letters that took up three lines on the monthly payroll sheet. Captain Simmers had decided that H. R. was his payroll name.

Ed said, "Leon, I think I know what he's going to do with that bread. Let's go and watch." H. R. dug into his foot locker and brought out a bottle of liquid shoe polish. He cut off a chunk of bread, dug a hole in it, and put the bread in some waxed paper folded like a funnel. Then he poured the shoe polish in the hole and caught the liquid that dripped out. I asked H. R. what he was doing.

"Well, if I pour this polish through the bread, it purifies it and makes good whiskey."

Ed looked at the bottle and said, "H. R., this isn't the kind of alcohol you drink."

"Well, it sure tastes fine when you mix it with wine."

I thought we ought to explain to him what methanol was and what it would do to him. Ed said H. R.'s system was probably so used to strange drinks that it didn't make much difference. H. R. also had problems with his rifle. He could dismantle and clean it beautifully, but one of us would have to reassemble it for him. H. R. wasn't bright;

in fact, H. R. was dumb. He was also a warm, brave, and loyal soldier. If H. R. knew what to do, it would be done. If I were wounded and under machine-gun fire, H. R. would be crawling out to me. "When duty calls or danger, be never wanting there." He wouldn't know how to help, but H. R. would be there.

Although McCain was only a hundred miles or so from Clinton, I was only allowed one weekend pass a month. Sunday mornings in camp were pleasant even though I had given up on church services. The regimental chaplain was as dull as the one at Benning had been. Once, I persuaded George that the way to meet nice girls in town (Grenada) was by going to church. Wearing clean, pressed uniforms, we expected a warm Christian welcome and an invitation to Sunday dinner. We went to the minister's study before the service. I introduced myself and remembered when he had preached the Sunday night service in Clinton. And I told him Brother Joe Canzoneri's son was my best friend.

No sooner had I established my credentials than he slipped into his ministerial tone. This seems to have become a lost art. The tone is much like that of a funeral director—one of being in a much more serious and important position than those of ordinary people. In Clinton, when we had teased ministerial students about this attitude, they justified it by pointing to the simple fact that salvation was the most serious aspect of life.

Now the minister droned: "Yes, I remember when Bob came up here with him for a revival. By the way, I was saddened when Dr. Patterson was called to his reward. He was a fine servant of the Lord."

We went into the sanctuary with him and sat close to the front so that more people could see us when we stood to be welcomed as guests. The minister welcomed two local boys who were home on leave, and said that he was always glad to see servicemen worshiping with the church family. After he preached, we shook his hand and went back to camp. I had known that the cold reception was possible but thought we could avoid it by meeting with the minister beforehand. Grenada, with a population of maybe five or ten thousand, was being swamped by eighteen thousand infantrymen in search of various forms of entertainment. I knew of tales from Hattiesburg, where you might go out to get the Sunday morning paper and find two Camp Shelby soldiers sleeping on your lawn, right beside where they had vomited. It was easy for the local people to believe that all soldiers of the Ninety-fourth Division were animals, but that their own sons were serving at another camp with a much better class of people. There was nothing the minister or the church could have done about the situation. The divisional public relations officer could have improved relations with informational programs and better discipline on the troops—but he didn't.

Sunday breakfast in camp was from seven to eight o'clock if you wanted to get up. George never did, but I liked the quiet, slow meal with seconds served on anything you wanted. I would bring a cup of coffee for George to drink in bed, then I would walk over to hear the division band practicing. It was as warm and refreshing as a good sermon, and I often found myself singing along with the music:

> In the beauty of the lilies, Christ was born across the sea,
> With a glory in His bosom that transfigures you and me.
> As He died to make men holy, let us die to make men free.
> While God is marching on.

I was content and satisfied. If we had to be at war, this was the place for me: first scout in a line company.

Putting ASTP in the infantry was only part of the army campaign for infantry pride. They announced a series of tests to select Expert Infantrymen. Those who passed were to get a silver badge, a five-dollar-a-month pay increase, and a promotion to Pfc. We spent an entire week preparing for the tests. A review team from Washington was sent to test the division, a full day being allowed for each company.

First Platoon clustered around the line from which we would start, one man at a time, to run through one of the tests. The ASTP group began a football cheer: "Faber, Faber, he's our man. If he can't do it, Proctor can. Proctor, Proctor, he's our man. . . ." We kept cheering men until we got to Ray: "Graziano, Graziano, he's our man. If he can do it, *anybody* can!"

The tests themselves were disappointing. They were simply a rehash of basic training. The ASTP group breezed through it, except for Dale. He forgot to salute after demonstrating how to report in from a patrol. I remembered the emphasis on that little slip later, in October in France, when I reported to Captain Simmers after a patrol. I collapsed under an apple tree and waited for him to come over.

"You saw some Krauts at Locmaria?"

I quit shaking for a minute. "Yes, sir, must have been about a squad, but they had two [machine] guns. Sloppy as ever, had no security guards out. I think they had been foraging for food but were headed home."

No salute. I didn't even stand up. Simmers would have wondered what was wrong if I had.

Dale and some of the old men took the test again the next week. He and a good many of the others passed. The medals were impressive: a simple blue rectangle with a silver flintlock rifle. I forgot that the tests were meaningless: I was proud of my Expert Infantry Badge. Later, many of us would receive the silver-wreathed Combat Infantry Badge, which was to be placed above all other decorations on the wearer's chest.

Thinking back, I can see that the riflemen got no further training at Camp McCain. The army considered a rifleman trained when he completed basic. The replacement training centers gave recruits basic training and shipped them overseas into combat. You learned everything else on the job, as quickly as possible. But the division also had to be trained as a unit. Platoon leaders had to learn to move squads around, battalion and regimental staffs had to practice moving companies, and officers at the divisional level had to learn about moving regiments. Quartermasters had to practice getting food up to combat units, and cooks had to learn to cook in the field—and we had to eat the stuff. One morning on a problem, breakfast consisted of coffee and turnip greens: the morning supplies hadn't come up, so we had only leftovers from the night before. All the logistics of running a division had to be learned with trained riflemen. After a division had been in combat for a while, the logistical people had a lot of experience. Only a few riflemen ever got much combat experience, because they tended to get wounded.

Eventually, someone decided the division was experienced enough for shipment overseas. Preparation for the move meant new uniforms and equipment. Relative to an absolute, the division did need reequipping. Relative to what we had known at Fort Benning, we were in great shape. Despite being the cream, we had trained in austerity. For the first month we each had owned only one set of fatigues (the baggy, green cotton clothes we always wore in training). We could wash them every Sunday, and hang them out to dry if it wasn't raining. If it rained, we had to decide whether to wear dry, dirty clothes on Monday, or wet, clean ones. Dry usually won out over wet.

Now we turned in all our old clothing and were issued everything new. A soldier named Amato had been a tailor, and he helped us with alterations. He showed me how to alter my fatigue jacket to fit: we got one that was too big, cut down the waist, and used the leftover cloth to lengthen the sleeves.

And we got new rifles. I had never had a good rifle. After firing on the range at Benning, we had been issued old M-1s with pitted barrels. The significance of their corroded condition was that the army was strong on keeping rifles clean and oiled. When we came in from a problem, wet and dirty, we first cleaned our rifles and oiled them. After they were inspected, we could bathe ourselves. The pitted rifles meant that someone had let them rust and they couldn't be cleaned well. Also, the old pitted barrels very quickly rusted even more if you let them stay wet any length of time. Now we were getting new rifles. If we took care of them, they wouldn't get rusty. Most of them were made by the Springfield Armory, the military armory, but the platoon also received a few that were made by Winchester. The Winchesters were machined much closer than the Springfields and worked more smoothly. Also, they were two-toned: the barrel was blued more lightly than the housing and gas port.

Because the platoon got only six Winchesters, Westmoreland decided to issue them to the scouts. That Winchester became my symbol for being a scout. The walnut stock had a beautiful curled grain. Every night I would polish it lightly with steel wool and rub linseed oil into it. After field problems I scrubbed the stock with hot soapy water, let it dry, and slowly worked in more linseed oil. The rifle was cleaned and oiled every day during combat; in rainy weather I could only wash the mud off and pour fresh oil over it, but there was never any rust. Bill Henry inherited my Winchester after I was wounded. Shrapnel cut the stock completely off at Nennig.

# 8 Go Get 'Em, Infantry

As we were preparing for overseas shipment, each of us got a furlough to say good-bye. Because Clinton was only a few hours from camp, I had gone home for a couple of weekends, but this time was different. This was the good-bye trip. Bob and Atley were still in the navy program at Mississippi College. They were in class all day, but I could visit in the dorm at night.

On the night I went over to visit, Atley was on "watch." He stood at the entrance to Crestman Hall wearing a white pistol belt (no pistol) and leggings—military regulations required that anyone "under arms" also wear leggings. He looked ridiculous with them laced all the way to the top and with his pants stuck in tightly.

"Atley, you look like an ostrich in those leggings. Why don't you fold them down about four inches and blouse your pants?"

Atley blustered a bit: "This is the way leggings are worn. If I folded them shorter my pants would come out."

I remembered that we had been required to wear leggings that way for a few weeks during basic, but Atley had been in the navy for almost nine months. "I never tuck my pants into leggings." I told him. "What do you think condoms are for?" I was only half joking. The navy certainly wasn't issuing condoms at MC, but my division had undergone a strong venereal disease prevention program, under which condoms were freely available to all troops. Because of limited sexual opportunities, 90 percent of the condom usage in rifle companies was as garters for blousing our trousers over the shortened leggings. Our unit commanders knew this, but the heavy condom consumption looked good on monthly reports.

Atley led me to the officer of the day. I stood at attention, saluted, and said, "Private First Class Standifer requesting permission to visit Apprentice Seaman Canzoneri."

He looked at me and said, "Permission granted." I held my salute and continued to glare at him impassively. I had saluted myself into a dilemma. By army regulations I should salute when reporting to a commissioned officer, indoors or out. I knew that naval tradition is not to salute indoors, but it had slipped my mind. I was going to hold my salute until he returned the courtesy. A military salute is not subservience, but a traditional greeting of fellow warriors.

I enjoyed seeing the officer in a bind. I had initiated the salute following my regulations. Returning it was a standard military regulation that took precedence over naval tradition. I was thinking: "He has granted me permission and I have all night. I'll wait the fool out." Atley cleared his throat and squirmed; I glared. The officer pretended to return to paper work, but he knew I was still there and didn't intend to leave. Finally he looked up, glared back, returned my salute, and said, "Dismissed." I did an about-face and marched out.

Atley was mad. "Leon, that stunt may have gotten us both on report."

"Aw, Atley, he can't put you on report; you followed regulations exactly. And I hope he *does* report it as misconduct to my unit commander. Simmers would enjoy writing a reply." I was a little sorry for having upset Atley, but I had enjoyed standing up to a naval officer. I was a line soldier wearing an Expert Infantry Badge. Nobody was going to insult me.

Bob and I went out on campus and sat for a long time, trying to make small talk. It wasn't an awkward visit. There just wasn't much to say. I was going off to fight. I knew I could soldier but was a little troubled. I wasn't worried about having the courage to do the job: BYPU had taught me about courage, and I was embarking on the most important mission I would ever have. At Holly Springs I had realized I wasn't afraid to die. Well, maybe a little, but I was willing to serve and to die. What bothered me most was knowing that I now had the skill to kill quickly and easily, but still feeling deep revulsion at the possibility of having to do so. Bob understood what I was feeling so there was no need to explain. There wasn't much trivia to discuss either. All my trivia was army and all his was navy. Atley was impressed that I had taken my training at The Infantry School. He thought I should be excited about getting into the fight. "Everybody else is stuck in training programs, but you are going where the action is."

I had a few dates with girls I had known in high school. It was an uncomfortable situation. They knew I was worried, and they assumed I was afraid of dying. One girl thought I wanted a little sex before getting killed. I tried to explain that I wasn't afraid of death or of not getting to be a "man."

"Well, what's wrong?"

"I don't know."

The timing for my furlough was bad because our football star, Snerd Goodrich, was in town at the same time. When he had turned seventeen, he persuaded his parents to let him join the marines. "I can't sit here at home while other people are fighting to defend me." He had been in the marines for nearly two years and was a gunnery sergeant at Parris Island, which is where he remained throughout the war. Compared with Snerd (whose nickname, by the way, came from Edgar Bergan's dummy Mortimer Snerd), I wasn't one of Clinton's success stories. I hadn't volunteered, had flunked out of my army program, had been put in the infantry, and was only a Pfc. When I went to my old church for the last time, the sermon was warm and mellow. I became more confident. I was well trained and wasn't afraid of combat. The invitational song was "How Firm a Foundation":

> How firm a foundation, ye saints of the Lord,
> Is laid for your faith in His excellent Word.
>
> . . . . . . . . . . . . . .
>
> When through fiery trials thy pathway shall lie,
> My grace, all sufficient, shall be thy supply;
> The flame shall not hurt thee; I only design
> Thy dross to consume, and thy gold to refine.

I had a good foundation and still had some dross for consuming, but I hoped the Lord would be careful with the flame.

Finally I had said good-bye to everybody but my family. Even that good-bye wasn't very hard. They understood. Mother had a small service flag hanging in the window, with a blue star and the inscription Serving Proudly. If I were killed, she would replace it with a gold star. My sister said, "Leon, don't get killed." I told her I'd come back. "I may get wounded but they can't whip me."

I got back to camp feeling empty and disappointed. George felt the same way. We wondered why none of our old friends really understood the inner conflicts we were experiencing. Part of the disappointment was that nobody could see we were proud of being Infantry and confident that we were good. I had worn my Expert Infantry Badge. People thought it was pretty, but it was about as important to them as an Expert Janitor Badge. I'm exaggerating a bit. It was a popular war. Everybody was proud of me in the same way Atley was: I was going to fight for my country. I was proud of going to fight as a Rifleman, First Scout in a Line Company. But I was afraid of what I might have to do.

Dale came back with the same disappointment, but a friend had given him a beautiful trench knife. It was hard-tempered steel with a blade about ten inches long and a wooden handle carved to fit his hand. I envied Dale's knife to the point of being ashamed. As a BAR man, Dale also was issued a GI trench knife. Scouts didn't get one unless it were needed for a night patrol. (Actually, when that time came, I had to use a German bootknife.) I saw Dale's knife after the war when I went to visit his parents. It was rusted and pitted and had never been used.

Ed had enjoyed being home and telling his friends what a rifle company was really like. He saw the headquarters group as having mutually contradictory attitudes. On the one hand, the rifleman ranked at the absolute bottom for prestige. Any type of transfer from the position of rifleman was a promotion in status and usually in rank. On the other hand, riflemen had the Queen of Battle attitude. In training, the company existed only to serve its riflemen. In combat, the company would survive only if its riflemen were capable, confident, and well supplied. If the line platoons broke, the company would be overrun and captured or killed. It was essential both that the support units have absolute faith in the valor of the line troops and that the troops know their support was reliable. The rifleman was simultaneously the dregs of the company and the glorious knight who would protect his leaders against all threats.

A few days later Ed showed me a book he had been reading. Religion wasn't an important issue with Ed. He wasn't exactly an atheist; he just didn't care. While he was home on leave his sister (the social worker in Boston) had given him a small book called *The Prophet,* written by an Arab and with weird pictures illustrating it. Because we disagreed on religion, Ed was both embarrassed and pleased at showing it to me. I felt much the same way. He was showing me something we both liked, but it was pagan—I really shouldn't have anything to do with it. Yet even though the Prophet was some kind of Muslim holy man, his themes were love, concern, and help. It seemed to me that he had stolen his ideas from the Bible. I particularly liked the section on friendship. The Prophet said that "your friend is your needs answered," adding:

> And let your best be for your friend.
> If he must know the ebb of your tide,
> let him know its flood also.

I felt wonderful. I had more friends now in K Company than I had ever had in my life; and there was soon going to be a lot of ebb and flood for sharing.

Captain Simmers came by to visit the platoon in our barracks. After the formal "Tenshut!" and "At ease, rest," he had us sitting on the floor around him.

"Men, I want you to know that I am extremely proud to be leading you into combat and that I will be proud of your performance. Colonel Hagerty considers King Company to be the best in the regiment. We will be given tough assignments and will take casualties. Many, perhaps most, of us will be wounded. Some will die. We will be afraid, but will not shirk. This is what our country expects of us—to serve as well as our fathers and grandfathers did." He stopped the talk there, looked at us, and walked out.

I suppose he had intended to give the same talk to each platoon but decided it was too emotional. Everyone was quiet after he left. I looked at the group and wondered. It is well we couldn't know. Seven would die, and of the rest only Bill Henry would survive without frozen feet or physical wounds. Westmoreland would endure a total of ten wounds from four incidents. Simmers would live, but brain concussion and severe headaches would prevent him from ever again functioning well enough to hold a full-time job.

The platoon had to leave behind three men who were ineligible for combat duty. We received two ASTP replacements who had been allowed to finish the semester before being sent to us. I felt a little sorry for them because they hadn't been able to train with us, but they seemed to be good boys and I was sure they would soldier. I was less sure about the third replacement. Bill Lehrer had been transferred out of another company for having a fistfight in the mess hall with his platoon sergeant. Captain Simmers was impressed with his spunk and volunteered to take him. More precisely, he volunteered for First Squad to take him. Lehrer trusted no one. He always had a chip on his shoulder. He was proud of having cold-cocked a tech sergeant without going to the stockade. Except for some smart back talk, Ray didn't have much trouble with him. "Lehrer, anytime you decide you can stand up to me, I'll take you to the woods and beat the hell out of you." Lehrer had watched Ray sparring with DeRosa and didn't want to take that kind of risk.

I didn't like or trust Lehrer. One day he demanded, "Standifer, how the hell did a kid like you get to be first scout?"

I bristled but couldn't think of a good reply. "Beats me. Westmoreland decided I was the one to do it."

Lehrer grinned. "After one week of combat I'll have your job."

I was more disgusted than angry. "Anytime you're that good, you can have it." I didn't look on being scout as a job for which I was competing. I did think I was good at it, and I believed that was why I was there. Of course, although it was fun to be the point for the platoon, it was also a quick way to get killed. So if Lehrer was better than me, I wanted him out front. Well, maybe. I didn't quite know why, but I didn't trust him.

I took the question to George. "Hell, no, I don't want Lehrer up there or on my flank. He won't carry his part of the load when things get rough. Lehrer is a loner. He has the guts to do a job if it benefits him, but he will never be a team man." George had hit the key point that worried me. The squad was my family, and I was ready to risk my life for them. I wasn't sure that Lehrer would, or that I was ready to help him. I don't know if the situation would have been different if he had trained with us, but I do know that Lehrer turned out to be useless in combat. He was wounded, during a small skirmish, while arguing with a new replacement over who had shot a German officer. Regardless of who was right, they were both in the wrong. The replacement shouldn't have stopped during combat to take the officer's pistol, and Lehrer was even stupider to run up and claim it was his.

One night H. R. asked me to take a walk with him. He had thought that overseas meant the jungles of New Guinea, where his uncle had been sent, but Dale had told him it was Europe. "How far off is Europe?" H. R. wanted to know. I explained that we would take a train to New York and get on a big ship. H. R. hadn't known that we would go on a ship, but he liked the idea—he had seen a picture of a ship with soldiers on it. That's about all I could explain to him. I knew he didn't have a very good idea of what combat meant, even after two years in the army. In Clinton, Son Green used to walk with me when I went to get the cow from pasture. I would tell him about flowers, rabbits, and turtles. I didn't try to explain complicated things because Son was only five years old. I had the same kind of feeling with H. R.

I was satisfied that First Platoon could soldier. In one of our last training exercises, we had made a forced march of over fifty miles in less than twenty-four hours, part of it in a driving rainstorm. Then we had moved quietly into an assault line under black-dark conditions. At first light we had attacked behind a rolling artillery barrage across three hundred yards of downed trees, had set up a defensive position on Baker Hill, and had held it until midnight—forty-four hours under stress. The last six hours had been rough, but we had taken turns sleeping two hours on and two off. Months of heat, mud, fatigue, chiggers, and hit a'rainin' had built a solemn, almost sacred, promise of team support. On our honor we would do our best for one another. Would Julius Prado, Peewee Budny, and H. R. know what to do? It didn't matter. Their loyalty was solid and we could provide leadership. Would Ray panic when things got bad? Ed was a bundle of nerves— would he be able to carry the load? Lehrer was a problem. He had made no promises to anyone. But the team was also Westmoreland, Dale, Richards, Button, and George. Swift as a panther in triumph, fierce as a bear in defeat.

On the other hand, "Never a horse that couldn't be rode, never a cowboy couldn't be throwed." Maybe, somewhere, somehow, a Kraut platoon could whip us. But what a price they would have to pay!

Late one afternoon we were told to pack our gear and be ready to leave. After dark we loaded on trucks and were taken to a train. All night we rolled through the dark countryside, looking out to see where we were and guessing whether we were headed toward the East or the West Coast. The next morning we were in North Carolina. We were going to Europe. That's what we had expected and what we wanted. We unloaded in East Orange, New Jersey, at Camp Shanks, which was a processing center for the New York port. Each of us got a one-night pass to New York. George and I went to Times Square, wandered around gaping at the tall buildings, and went back to camp. New York just wasn't very exciting when we were about to go overseas.

About noon one day, we were assembled to leave. We had sixty pounds of pack with an overcoat on top of it and rifles, steel helmets, and duffle bags slung over our shoulders. We were wearing wool uniforms in August with the temperature in the mid-nineties. When we got on the train the windows were closed—the powers that be were afraid we might try to throw notes out of the windows. The logic had to do with spies finding out when we were leaving. We sat on the train sweating. At the port we climbed the gangway of a monster ship. We climbed until I was exhausted, then started down, down, down—much farther than we had gone up. We were well below the water line when we reached racks of bunks. I think they were five high. Climb in with your rifle and bag. There was barely enough vertical space between bunks for the bag to fit. I panicked. I was completely wet. Every muscle quivered from the strain of carrying the load in such heat, and I was getting leg cramps. I looked at the raw, steel bulkhead and thought of the tons of water on the other side. I wanted to run and scream, but there was nowhere to go and yelling wouldn't help. I lay in my bunk and shivered, trying to control my fear.

The next morning we got an orientation. We were on the *Queen Elizabeth*. It was so large that it carried the entire division plus a few small units—more than 18,000 men altogether. Feeding all those bodies was going to be a problem. The kitchen would be serving twenty-four hours a day, which would let each person have two meals. We were to eat at ten o'clock each morning and each night. That was the eating schedule, but we would get in line two hours early and file slowly along rows of bunks and gangways. After eating each night, we were allowed on deck for an hour to get some fresh air. The North Atlantic was cold, but the sky was beautiful. One night George and I climbed to the tip of the bow and looked down at the phosphorescence as the ship pushed through the ocean.

Every morning we set our watches back an hour, and in five days we landed in Glasgow. We loaded on trains and rode all day through Scotland and the beautiful English countryside. It was dark when we went through Oxford, then down to Reading, where forty years later I would unload to study at the University of Reading. We turned west and finally unloaded at Chippenham. There we were met by trucks that took us to nearby fields, where we pitched tents.

The next morning we woke in a picturesque English meadow. I had never seen grass and trees so green. We cleaned our rifles, which had been heavily greased for the ocean trip. Then we exercised and took a march to stretch out. A few days later we went to a rifle range to fire German weapons. Their rifle was good, firm, and accurate, but required manual working of the bolt action. We also fired the Schmeisser MP-40—the "burp gun"—a machine pistol that spit bullets out at a rate of 450 to 540 per minute. It made a terrifying sound, but the 32-round clip would last for only about four seconds. It was difficult to fire only a few rounds. In combat we would notice that the Germans usually fired the entire clip in one burst. They carried six clips, which amounted to twenty-four seconds of "actual combat." We learned about the German hand grenade: the "potato masher." It was a wonderful weapon for little boys who couldn't throw the heavy American grenade very far. It was only a little lighter than ours but could be thrown like a tap stick—the long handle provided leverage. (Hunting rabbits with a tap stick is an old southern tradition. Taps are the metal nuts used on railroads for bolting rails down. A tap stick is a stick with several taps on the end.)

British soldiers dressed in German uniforms staged an assault demonstration. The squad was divided into three units: center, left flank, right flank. The squad leader controlled movement with a whistle. When he blew once, twice, or three times, the right, left, or center would get up, run forward, and hit the ground. After watching awhile, you could learn the code, predict which group was to get up, and be ready to shoot at them. But they were very good at running—low and fast.

We were told to watch how Germans hit the ground. If we saw anyone falling like that in combat, he was German—shoot him! We had been taught to hit with our knees first, lean forward, let the rifle butt hit, fall, and roll. Your knees took the heavy impact, and you hoped you didn't hit a rock. A bigger problem was that when the rifle butt hit, your head would jolt upward. That showed like the flash of a white-tailed deer. If you stayed where you fell, you might get shot. The German never ran upright. He was always crouching. He held the rifle in his left hand, dropped his right to the ground, and slid downward. It was hard to tell where he fell because his head didn't pop up. Also, when he got to be sixty years old, his knees weren't all beat up.

Almost every day the platoon made a two-, three-, or four-hour hike, designed to loosen us up. We carried only our rifles and light combat packs. We walked at a fast pace in rural areas but slowed down to strut a bit in the little villages. Kids and housewives lined the street, watching the Yanks come by. Ray would straighten us up, call cadence, and start a song:

> Yankee Doodle came to Europe just to whip the Germans,
> Stopped a while in England, before he took on Hermann.
> Yankee Doodle keep it up, Yankee Doodle Dandy,
> Mind the music and the step, and with the girls be handy.

We went to town almost every night but weren't very handy with the girls—too many GIs, too few girls. But we learned about the pubs and the beer and the songs. I could drink a few beers, but still felt a little guilty. The British army songs had much more wit than the ones from Fort Benning. "I've Got Sixpence" was a round that started with a soldier who had allotted his pay by priorities: "Tuppence to spend, tuppence to lend, and tuppence to send home to my wife, poor wife." As the money got short, he had no pence to send to his wife, then no pence to lend, and so on. Each chorus ended, "Happy is the day when the army gets his pay, and we go rolling, rolling home." And there was "Roll Me Over in the Clover," which was about what it sounds like it was about.

We learned the infantry taunt. A large number of the American troops still in England wore the blue-star shoulder patch of the Army Service Forces: Quartermaster Corps, Transportation Corps, and so on. As we marched past them we would break into our song: "Take down that gold star, Mother, your son's not going to die. / He's a Blue Star Commando in the Service of Supply—Safe Over Seas."

I joined the singing but felt awkward about it. That man hadn't volunteered to drive a truck. He was assigned to it, just as we were assigned to the infantry. We were robbing the truck driver of his dignity and saying that even his mother shouldn't be proud of him.

A few months later I would remember the taunt and see that it had contributed to our problems. It was going to cost Patton the fuel he needed for the drive across France. It was going to give me frozen feet. A lot of kids were going to lose their feet because we were saying that the truck driver wasn't important. In France he would find people who respected him—if he sold them some fuel or warm shoes.

Early one morning we packed our gear and loaded on trucks headed for Southampton. We assembled in a large dockside warehouse. "Stack arms, drop your packs in place, and fall out." A Red Cross clubmobile was there with coffee and doughnuts. There were two girls at each coffee urn—a total of maybe ten or twelve girls for the battalion of about eight hundred men. After the coffee gave out, the girls played records over their public-address system and started dancing with the boys. Playing Glenn Miller's "Little Brown Jug" and the Andrews Sisters' "Boogie Woogie Bugle Boy," the girls showed us some serious jitterbugging. Boy, could they dance! The K Company boys were good, considering they were wearing heavy shoes and leggings. One would dance awhile, another would cut in, and the girls danced continuously. "Ah, go git 'em, Red Cross!" and "Show 'em how, Ray!" I wanted to try but knew I would make a fool of myself.

An announcement came over the loudspeaker: "Company commanders, assemble your men."

"K Company, form on your equipment, load up, and recover your weapons." We stood in formation while I Company prepared to leave. The sound system was turned low now, playing, "The last time I saw Paris, / Her heart was young and gay." Those girls sent troops off every day. They knew how to work the moods. I thought, "Stand fast, Paris, the infantry is coming. You'll be free soon." (Actually, Paris had already been freed.) All the girls except the one playing records had gone over to the exit area. They formed two lines, like cheerleaders waiting for the football team to come out for the big game. This was the big game, the championship game. The prize was the freedom of the world. This time I was playing on the first team.

As I Company started toward the exit, the music changed to marches. After a few songs "Stars and Stripes Forever" came up. I was a kid again, strutting barefoot behind the MC band. Back then I hadn't known the words, but now I did—Smitty had taught them to me— and the old song seemed to have a powerful new impact:

> Let despots remember the day
> When our fathers with mighty endeavor
> Proclaimed as they marched to the fray,
> That by their might and by their right
> It waves forever.

I was covered with chill bumps. Stand fast, Paris!

"K Company, ten-hut! Platoon leaders, move your men out."

Westmoreland said, "First Platoon, sling arms. Move out as a column of squads, route step."

Ray yelled, "First Squad, forward."

DeRosa bellowed, "Second Squad, stand fast."

"March!"

It could have been done with no commands at all, and probably would have been if the Red Cross girls hadn't been watching. Captain Simmers was in front. He had a British officer's swagger stick and was strutting like a rooster. Then came Westmoreland and the platoon headquarters group. Ray led First Squad, and I was next as first scout. Behind me were the finest soldiers in King Company: Ed, George, Herb, Cagle, Herman Wendler, Prado, and Bill Henry. I was proud of them all. We straightened up as we marched past the line of Red Cross girls. They were not quite like backslapping high school cheerleaders because they also had to meet shiploads of returning wounded. They were proud and brave, but deadly serious.

As I marched by the line, one of them said, "Go get 'em, Infantry!" I hadn't cried since I had been in the army, but tears were rolling down my cheeks—no fear and tremendous pride. Ray turned around to check the squad; the Brooklyn truck driver was crying as hard as I was.

The author in May of 1944, soon after being assigned to the Ninety-fourth Infantry Division.

*Photo courtesy of the author*

Part of First Squad, First Platoon, at Camp McCain, Mississippi. *Clockwise, starting at top:* Leon Standifer, Herb Adams, Alton Evans, Bill Henry, Herman Wendler, Hubert Cagle, Ray Graziano, George Faber.

*Photo courtesy of the author*

*Left to right:* Gus Amato, Jack Button, and Roy Brown during training. In France, Brown lost his hand in a grenade accident, and Button was killed in action.

*Photo courtesy of Helen Simmers*

From a group photo of K Company at Camp McCain. Among the company's officers are, *front row, left:* Lieutenant Ruben Schroeder; *second from left:* Captain Richard Simmers (company commander); *right:* Lieutenant James Westmoreland.

Photo by W. R. Thompson and Co.; courtesy of the author

Dale Proctor as a high school senior.
*Photo courtesy of Don Proctor*

The Germans conduct a burial with military honors at Lorient for the dead of the Third Platoon after its ambush and capture near Cap Kerdudal.
*Courtesy of Mrs. David Devonald*

Lieutenant David Devonald, center, reports back with his Third Platoon at Etel after an exchange of POWs.
*Courtesy of Mrs. David Devonald*

German dead, Nennig, Germany, January 29, 1945. The men were killed by rifle fire and grenades as they took cover in and around the house in fighting two days earlier. The photo was taken on the day the author arrived in Nennig, and shows one of the first sights he saw.

*Photo courtesy of National Archives and U.S. Army Signal Corps*

German POWs under guard, Nennig, May 8, 1945. The damage to the town is typical. The sign on the building identifies it as a bicycle repair shop.

*Photo courtesy of National Archives and U.S. Army Signal Corps*

In December, 1944, K Company captured this German coastal bunker at Etel, France. By 1984, when this photo was taken, the bunker had been converted into a summer house for vacationing Parisians. Note the awning.

*Photo by the author*

The stone wall where the author was wounded during the attack on the coastal bunker at Etel. In this 1984 view, a new housing development rises in the background. As cover, the wall had its drawbacks: American machine-gun bullets ricocheting off it apparently caused the author's wounds.

*Photo by the author*

# 9 Lock and Load: Scouts Out

We landed on Utah Beach late on the afternoon of D-plus-94. We climbed down the cargo nets and dropped into a little assault craft that roared off toward the beach. It hit the sand. The front dropped down, and we prepared to storm the beach just as we had seen it done in newsreels. The sailor running the craft said: "Wait. There's no rush, and the tide is going out. Pretty soon you won't have to wade." So we stormed the beach with dry feet. We formed into a column and hiked up the hill past the debris of war and beyond the big fortifications. We were carrying sixty pounds of equipment, with an overcoat rolled over the top of the pack. It wasn't really heavy, but bulky and awkward. You don't march with that much equipment, you walk.

We passed a group of GI engineers who were cleaning up the mess and taking out mines. They started jeering us: "Hey, the war is over. Here comes the army of occupation. Hey, Infantry, you're too late." It started getting to us, and there was nothing to do but take it. Westmoreland fell back along the line and said, "Infantry, look sharp." The imprinting worked just as The Infantry School had planned. I could hear the battalion commander at Benning yelling, "Infantry, pass in review." You can't look sharp while plodding along, and you certainly can't sing—but you can feel like Infantry. We were the Queen of Battle. Everything else in the army, navy, and Air Corps existed to get the infantry up there to win the war. All right, Infantry, let's see what you are made of. Frogs and snails and puppydog tails.

It started raining. An August rain in France is a lot colder than an October rain in Georgia. The cobblestone road was slick with mud. Every few minutes somebody slipped and fell with sixty pounds pushing him down. Every time I fell, I said: "The next time I'm not going to get up. I'm going to roll into the ditch and rest." But I wasn't going to do that no matter how tired I was. First Platoon was going to war and I was going to be there. We slipped and slogged through the rain until about midnight. We stopped in a wet field, unrolled wet shelter-halves, made tents, and went to sleep. The next morning we woke up in a pasture with the wreckage of two British Horsa gliders. Dale thought that Horsa was a strange name for gliders used to drive the Germans from France. The mythological first two leaders of the Germanic (Saxon) invaders of England were Hengist and Horsa. Well, these weren't gliders anymore. They were made of plywood and had become firewood. We used the day drying our gear and getting it ready for combat. The nearby farmhouse had a large whetstone where we sharpened our entrenching tools. Lehrer stayed to sharpen his bayonet despite our comments that he would never use it, and besides, the blued surface was intended to retard rusting. Later we found that bayonets could be used to clear brush and open cans, but they didn't need to be sharp.

The next day we loaded onto trucks and rode to Brittany. It was an exciting, depressing, frustrating trip. We passed through small towns that had been shelled to rubble. St.-Lô had been a large town, and it hardly existed anymore. Wrecked, burned-out vehicles had been shoved off the road—German and American, tanks, buses, trucks, jeeps. We also saw many towns and farming villages that were nearly untouched by war. They looked like quaint pictures from an old *National Geographic* magazine. The streets were lined with cheering French people. They threw us apples, flowers, and bottles of cider. Finally we felt like Infantry again, but we would soon have to prove it. We unloaded near the small town of Rédené, about five miles west of Quimperlé and maybe fifteen miles from Lorient.

"Draw ammunition and K rations for two days. We will be moving into combat positions after dark."

This was it. We were all too excited to think, to be afraid, or to be very cautious, but we would learn about that tomorrow. Ray and DeRosa were handing out ammunition and grenades for the platoon:

> Praise the Lord and pass the ammunition.
> Praise the Lord, we're on a mighty mission.
> Praise the Lord, we're not a'goin' fishin'.

Someone said: "Shut up, Ray. The Krauts will hear you."

Peewee Budny had drawn three bandoleers of ammunition and six hand grenades. The clips from one bandoleer filled his cartridge belt, and he had the other two crisscrossing his chest like a Mexican bandit. He had a grenade in each upper jacket pocket, two in each lower pocket, and was trying to decide where to carry his K rations.

"Peewee, if you ever have to hit the ground, you won't be able to get up."

"Man, I don't want to give out of ammunition."

"You've got enough to kill 240 Krauts, 120 if you miss half of them." We persuaded him to put back a bandoleer and four grenades.

Westmoreland called us together and had two men hold a map of the area to show where we were. "I will fill you in on the details tomorrow. We are the first company in the division to take up a combat position. I Company will follow us on the left flank. As soon as it gets dark, we will move up this road about two miles and take up temporary positions. First Squad will lead off with Standifer and Blake as scouts. There will be no flank scouts. This is a narrow road with hedgerows on each side." Then he had to stop while Standifer went to the bushes. I had been eating cider apples all day and had what Cagle called "the green apple quick-step."

Westmoreland started again. "Okay, lock and load as you move out, but nobody is to fire at anything tonight. We will move past a tank of the Sixth Armored and set up a position along this hedgerow. Don't try to dig in tonight. The ground is hard and rocky. Now what, Standifer?" I had to go again.

Westmoreland laughed. "All right, Second Squad leads off with Richards and Button. Standifer, Staton needs someone to ride shotgun on the jeep."

So I missed being the division's first rifleman in a combat position because of eating green apples. Hoyt Staton, our jeep driver, needed someone with him because he was terrified of driving along the narrow roads—trails, really—with no lights. I wasn't much protection with two hand grenades and a rifle, but I wasn't any trouble either. Somehow, fear of stopping the jeep and walking off into the dark bushes cured my diarrhea.

We slept that night at the headquarters of the tank company we were replacing. I woke up the next morning to the sound of American rifles, German rifles, and the ripping of a burp gun. I grabbed my rifle and joined Captain Simmers, who was listening to the tankers on the radio. "Better get some tanks back up here," someone was saying. "The infantry is going to break."

Simmers said: "Like hell they will. Those are my men. They won't give an inch. Let's go, Hoyt." I jumped in the back of the jeep, excited and scared.

There hadn't been much of a fight. A German patrol had hit an outpost and been thrown back. I Company had been hit harder, or maybe weren't careful enough. Two men had taken up positions behind a haystack. Both were wounded before tracers set fire to the stack. The two screamed for help, but nobody could get to them. When we found First Squad, the whole crew was acting like chickens after the hawk has flown away. Ed, George, and Cagle were standing there giggling and making jokes to hide their fright. Ray was quiet and pale.

Ed said: "We could see the Germans over on the hill. They were too far away for anything but Cagle's sniper rifle. He wouldn't shoot, but he got up on the hedgerow and gave them a bump-and-grind."

That shook Ray out of his terror. "Cagle stood on the hedgerow? Jesus Christ, I'm going to have to fight a war with kids too dumb to be careful."

Cagle said, "Frogs and snails and puppydog tails."

A little later Westmoreland came by to let us know where we were. Patton's Sixth Armored Division had swept across Brittany and driven the Germans into three seaports: Brest, Lorient, and St.-Nazaire. All three had been made into German submarine bases, but their value to us was as ports for men and materiel shipped directly across the Atlantic. There were three American infantry divisions at Brest, with artillery and heavy air support. After they took Brest they were to move down to help us at Lorient and then St.-Nazaire. Until then we were just to hold the line.

The problem was that there were about 25,000 Germans in Lorient and 35,000 in St.-Nazaire. With a successful breakout they might be able to reach a fuel depot, and possibly some of the badly overcrowded POW enclosures. The danger wasn't great because cornered Germans were not organized combat units. About half the troops were infantry, but they were a mixture of units that had retreated here from Normandy and the rest of Brittany. There were some Kriegsmarineinfanterie, basically naval guards, although the Germans were trying to retrain them as combat soldiers. There were paratroops and a few SS troops, but most of the infantry were Wehrmacht (army). These soldiers were *Ländser,* counterparts to the GI foot soldier, dogface, or straight-leg infantry. The Germans in Lorient had a lot of artillery and all the ammunition they could use. Their biggest guns were 340 mm, firing seven-hundred-pound shells. The Germans had a lot of armored vehicles but were low on fuel, and they probably were going to run short of food.

The 25,000 men in Lorient were being surrounded by our regiment—about 2,400 infantrymen with some supporting units. I suppose the worst aspect of the situation was that we were rationed on ammunition of all kinds, from rifle to artillery. The ammunition was going to Brest. Our assignment was to hold.

Westmoreland tried to sound optimistic. "It's not as bad as it seems. We have enough ammunition to defend ourselves. We have no armor, but we can have air support within two hours."

Ed wasn't convinced. "The Germans could wipe us out in two hours—then a heavy air bombardment will make them sorry they killed us."

First Squad didn't have a good defensive position. It was a good location for a tank, but not for infantry. Westmoreland was planning to move us forward the next day, but until then we would set out single man outposts along the hedgerow. The tankers said there wouldn't be any more activity that day. The Germans never attacked in the afternoon. My outpost was beside a gap in the hedgerow, through which I could look beyond a blackberry bush and down toward a small creek. I noticed that the bush had ripe berries, which seemed strange for September. I slipped out and tasted one. They were pretty good—a little bland. I could sit behind the bush and watch if I took off my helmet. Then the bayonet on my rifle belt got in the way so I took the belt off. I sat there watching and eating, mostly eating.

"Burrp!" Bullets from a burp gun cut the branches off the top of the bush, right where my hand had been. I slid to the ground and peered into the brush along the creek. I saw a little movement, but nothing to shoot at.

Westmoreland came roaring along the hedgerow. "Standifer, what's happening?" When I came scurrying back through the gap with my helmet in my hand, he had no problem knowing what had happened. He laughed. "Welcome to the war. Don't let them catch you again." I had received a cheap lesson and we both knew it. It was one I would never forget. Almost never.

That night, on guard, I wondered about the German who had shot over my head rather than killing me. Was he nineteen, and did he know why he fought? He hadn't just plain missed. It was a full four-second burst. I wondered about that for a long time and got nowhere. I had seen him moving down by the creek but couldn't get an aimed shot. I had refused the sucker shot. But if I could have aimed, would I have tried to wound him or shot to kill?

The next day we moved forward and spread out along a hedgerow that was fairly straight and near the rise of a hill. That hedgerow line was our basic position, extending left to connect with I Company. To the right were our second and third squads. The small triangular field to our front was on the crest of a hill overlooking the fork of two narrow roads. It was an excellent defensive position, except that it stuck out in front of our main line. Westmoreland decided that we would use the triangular field as a daytime outpost, pulling back at night. We called the daylight outpost Strongpoint Graziano. Ray liked the name. We didn't tell him that the position stuck out like his nose.

Strongpoint Graziano boasted one .50-caliber machine gun that we had gotten from the tankers. It was placed to cover both of the narrow roads. Because .50-caliber slugs were so much larger than our little .30-caliber (about the diameter of a pencil) rifle rounds, the machine gun seemed almost like artillery. We wouldn't be able to use it much because the tankers had given us only two boxes of ammunition.

Our primary position and living area was a rectangular field of about 50 by 150 feet. I suppose the field had been a pasture enclosed by hedgerows. "Hedgerows" was what we and the British called them; the German word was *knick*. The term I heard the French use most often was *talus,* which carries the geological connotation of a sloping bank or bed of stones: unlike the true hedgerows of Normandy, the typical talus in Brittany had a low stone wall as a core. Earth was mounded over the stone to a height of about four feet, with hawthorn bushes planted on the top. Every spring the farmer would cut the hawthorn branches, tie them in bundles, and build a large stack beside the house to use as firewood for cooking. Because the sloping mound came down at a sixty-degree angle, it made a poor firing position. We dug slots into the wall for guard positions.

George, Cagle, and I pitched our tent over a pit we had dug to a depth of about a foot. This depth represented a compromise that afforded a little protection against shrapnel without digging so deep that the pit would be cold and wet. Just beyond the tent was our pee post. At Benning, we had undergone a demonstration that involved listening to a man urinate at night fifty yards away. I remembered Snerd's verse from 1 Samuel about all who pisseth against the wall, and wondered if it meant that David's soldiers practiced noise discipline.

First Squad had four three-man guard positions, each spaced 30 to 50 yards apart. We had no communication system between positions, but the squad had a German telephone that we connected to the dugout that functioned as platoon headquarters. After our positions were established, Ray let us roam a little. "Leave one man on the machine gun, and stay within running distance."

Running distance was a matter of interpretation. George and I went over to see Dale, who was in his historical glory, quoting Tennyson: "When over the valley floated the gleam." Merlin and Lancelot were Breton Celts. Their ancestors had been driven from Wales and Cornwall by the Anglo-Saxons. The refugees had settled here and called it "Little Britain." The old people still spoke a language like Welsh, and even the local French was full of Celtic slang. Gauguin had lived about twenty miles down the road from our front lines. His earliest paintings are of Breton scenes. Carnac, not far down the coast, had stone menhirs older than Stonehenge. Not that any of this mattered much— nothing interesting was within running distance. There was one small town, Kerdudal, behind the Third Platoon lines. It consisted of three stone houses and a quiet, pretty girl in her early twenties. Carl Nance, an ASTP boy who was a Third Platoon scout, was trying to teach her some English phrases. She couldn't even repeat simple words, but she seemed to enjoy smiling at us all. George, Cagle, and I didn't stay because we didn't stand a chance with her.

We gradually settled into a routine that revolved around nighttime guard duty. Guard duty required standing by the hedgerow for two hours and listening. More accurately, it required staying awake for two hours. You tried to be absolutely alert, straining to hear any sound that was unusual. The procedure was to throw a grenade at any sound you couldn't identify. Firing a rifle at night was useless, and the hedgerow would protect you from the grenade fragments.

There was one tricky point about a grenade. It had a spring-loaded handle held in place by a cotter pin with a ring on the end of it. You pulled the pin while holding the handle against the grenade. When you threw the grenade, the handle flew off, releasing a firing pin. The grenade exploded in five seconds. After pulling the cotter pin, you could hold onto the grenade safely as long as you kept the handle down. But the handle was made in such a way that if you held it tightly, the holes for the pin didn't line up. Suppose you heard something out there in the darkness, pulled the pin, then realized the sound was only a pigeon. That was when the fun began. If you let up on the handle just a little, you could slip the cotter pin back in place. If you let up on the handle too much, it would fly off and the grenade would explode in five seconds. If you didn't drop it when the handle flew off, you could throw the thing on the other side of the hedgerow. The explosion would wake the entire company. Somebody would get excited and start firing parachute flares. You would have to go to the phone and explain what had happened, and everybody would tease you for a week.

The occasional live grenade aside, guard duty was pretty dull. I used it as a chance to think over what had happened during the day. Usually nothing had happened, but I would analyze it in depth anyway. That took about twenty minutes. Reciting all the poems I knew could use up an hour. If I got stuck on one, George or Ed would help me the next day. As a last resort, I worked out math problems in my head. Expanding a binomial took about an hour because I kept forgetting the parts I had already done.

Nights differed in quality. Dark rainy nights were uncomfortable but boring. The really bad nights were those when the moon was bright. Ghosts walked the earth when the moon was full. I could see how far the next guard post was and how weak we were. I would spend the time slowly moving my head from side to side. If my mind drifted, a German would run from behind one tree to the next. I would grip the grenade ring and watch the tree, thinking: "Nobody could hide behind such a thin tree, but maybe he's on the ground. Leon, there's nobody there, you moved your head too fast and made the image move." And a dog would howl, and a Frenchman would get up to draw a bucket of water from the well—only when the moon was full. I drew some comfort in knowing that the moonlight affected everybody, even the German guards standing their posts three kilometers away. Every hour or so we would hear a grenade explode near the German lines. A flare would go up, or someone would fire a burp gun. We had no night patrols out. They were shooting at things that go bump in the night.

Prison life may be more boring than holding an infantry position, but probably not by much. We had a few paperback books that were interesting, and a pocket chess set—but the game loses some of its appeal when the knights are pegs the size of matchsticks. We spent a lot of time talking about home. Mount Sterling and Clinton were so small that George and I could describe the entire towns; Cagle and Ed were limited to telling about their neighborhoods in Knoxville and Boston. We drew elaborate maps in the dirt and giggled over the yarns we told. When I visited Mount Sterling after the war, I knew every street and who lived in most of the houses. Once when I was in Boston for a meeting, I easily found Ed's old home; I drove by but didn't stop.

The apple orchards were beautiful. The only apple trees I had ever seen were crabapples. These were big trees loaded with apples. Most of them were cider apples and too sour to eat, but every field had one tree that bore good eating apples, which the French called "apples of the knife." To find that good tree, you had to taste an apple from every tree. Cider apples at least were good for throwing. We developed a game we called "playing the apples." One person sat on the hedgerow acting as artillery observer, and picked a spot he wanted to hit with the apple. The other player sat behind the hedgerow with a pile of apples and a pointed stick. He would spear an apple and sling it over the hedgerow. The observer would give the range and direction corrections, and the apple slinger would sling another one. It was a useless pursuit designed partly to irritate Graziano.

Our daily serenade to the Germans was more fun. Every morning when there was barely enough light to see, the guards would wake everybody to take position on line. The idea was that a patrol could creep close to our line at night and attack at dawn when we were asleep or only half awake. It was cold in the half light. Slip on a jacket, get your rifle, and stumble up to the firing position. Look through the thick mist, knowing there isn't anybody out there, but afraid there might be. As the mist began to clear, George, Cagle, and I would begin singing little songs to the Germans: "Good morning, breakfast clubbers, good morning to ya. / We got up bright and early just to try to shoot ya." Or: "We must be vigilant, we must be vigilant, American patrol."

Ray would say: "Shut up. The Germans will know where you are."

"But Ray, if they are waiting out there, they already know where we are. If they hear us, they'll know we're awake and won't attack." I'm sorry that Ray didn't understand we were all frightened and needed to break the tension. He would have been a great addition to the harmony on our masterpiece:

> They'll be comin' around the hedgerow when they come.
> They'll be comin' round the hedgerow when they come.
> We will all go out to meet them, and we surely will defeat them.
> We will all go out to meet them when they come.

Finally Ray would say: "Standifer, shut up. That's an order!"

One morning Westmoreland came by to take us on an orientation patrol. He had taken Richards and Button the day before. Ed and I were to be the scouts, with Ray and Westmoreland behind us.

Westmoreland spread out a map. "We go across the railroad to Ste.-Marguerite, follow the ridge north, cross the highway, cross the ridge north of Kervalze, and come into Locmaria from the high ground. There's an old antiaircraft outpost at the edge of town. Graziano and I will cover you from the ridge while you check the barracks. You won't find anything there, but be careful because German patrols use that route. We have an FFI man, Emile, who will go with you to observe. Blake will work with him because he speaks no English. Button had a lot of trouble keeping him from exposing us too much."

Ed, with two years of high school French, was our only means of

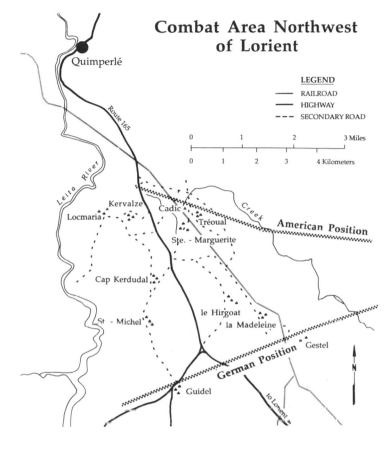

# Combat Area Northwest of Lorient

Quimperlé

**LEGEND**
——— RAILROAD
—— HIGHWAY
– – – SECONDARY ROAD

0     1     2     3 Miles

0    1    2    3    4 Kilometers

Leita River

Route 165

Kervalze    Cadic
Locmaria            Tréoual
                Ste. - Marguerite    Creek    American Position

Cap Kerdudal

                le Hirgoat
St - Michel        la Madeleine
                        German Position    Gestel

Guidel    to Lorient

N

speaking with Emile, the resistance man. I can draw no mental image of Emile but believe he was tall and rather slim. Before the war he had been a fisherman at Lorient. I know this because he showed us a picture of his fishing boat. His brother-in-law was taking care of the boat, but occasionally Emile would slip into Lorient just to look at it. The FFI wore no uniform, used captured German weapons, and assumed code names that could not be traced. If captured, they were always shot as vandals.

Emile thought he should walk alongside me to show the way. "Tell him I know the way," I said to Ed. Actually, Emile thought the three

of us should go in as a group; the compromise was that he would follow me, and Ed would cover both of us.

I was getting disgusted. "Tell him to go exactly where I do and to
stay about ten yards behind me." We crossed the railroad in good
order, but then he walked ahead of me and went right over the crest of
the hill, exposing us to anybody in Kervalze.

"Ed, come up and tell this fool what's wrong."

"He says he knows this area well. We're a long way from Locmaria,
and he isn't afraid of the Boche anyhow."

"Tell him it's not the Boche he should be afraid of. If he exposes us
like that one more time I'm going to ram my rifle butt down his
throat."

Emile and Ed talked for a long time. I asked what was happening.
"Well, I had trouble with the phrase, and then I added what I was
going to do when you were through with him." We had to get Emile's
attention one more time before we got to Locmaria, but otherwise the
patrol went pretty well. I wasn't as careful as I should have been.
Maybe I was rusty, but those green rolling hills didn't look dangerous.

A long hill sloped down to Locmaria, a Celtic name meaning something like "holy lake of Mary," although there wasn't so much as a
pond there when we saw it. The road/trail was narrow and muddy,
flanked by hedgerows. Ed, Emile, and I started down it, stopping just
at the point where the firing should start if an ambush were set up. Ed
had developed this system during the Holly Springs exercise. His idea
was that if we dawdled long enough, the enemy would get nervous
and make a mistake. It had worked once at Holly Springs, but usually
Westmoreland himself would get nervous and make us start moving.

Now it was Ed who seemed worried. "Leon, we can't stay on this
road. A machine gun in that first house would tear us up."

"But, Ed, there's nobody there."

"Don't bet our lives on it. You take the open field on the right, but
stay away from the path along the hedgerow. That's the best place for
booby traps. I'll be in the orchard on the left. Emile can follow the
road. Maybe they'll shoot him."

I climbed the hedgerow and saw why Ed had given me the open
field. It was full of knee-high gorse, a thick spiny weed. I blundered
along in it, stepping high and hoping I wouldn't stumble, keeping my
eyes on the closed attic window of the first house.

I climbed over the hedgerow and motioned to Ed that I was going to check the barracks. It was fitted tightly between two houses and had a straw roof that, from the air, made it part of the town. The anti-aircraft gun site was a cement slab in the street; it had been camouflaged to look like a well, but the gun and shelter were gone. Ed covered me while I followed Infantry School procedures: push the door open slowly, then jump in ready to fire. I came face to face with my first German: a kid about my age, with a neat, clean uniform and his hands over his head. "Ed, I caught a Kraut. We're coming out—he's first."

Emile raised his rifle and pointed it at the German's head. Ed knocked it down and they had a little discussion. "Roughly translated, he wants to shoot the dirty Boche swine. I don't know. The noise would attract attention. My thinking is that we could cut his throat quietly inside the barracks. It would be hard to take him back to our lines."

I knew Ed was right, but the German, who understood French, was terrified. I thought of the Good Samaritan: "But he, willing to justify himself, said unto Jesus, and who is my neighbour?"

"Ed, our bayonets aren't sharp enough to cut hot butter. We're taking him back. If Westmoreland wants to kill him, that's his decision. You cover him and Emile, while I search him." He had a beautiful polished cartridge belt with a *Gott Mit Uns* buckle. "You take this Ed, the next is mine." I ran my hands down the German's sides and legs. He was shaking like a leaf. I reached inside his jacket and pulled out his wallet with the soldier card: name, rank, and serial number. He had a picture of a girl and another that was probably of his parents. He had some French occupation money. The motto on it was pitiful: *Etat et Travail*—"State and Work"—instead of *Liberté, Egalité, Fraternité*.

Ed watched Emile and the Kraut while I quickly checked out the rest of the area. Then we went back up the hill to Westmoreland. "You said we wouldn't find anything. What do we do with him?" Westmoreland agreed that we should take him back, so we returned from the orientation patrol with a prisoner.

That night on guard, I thought back over the patrol. It had felt good to be the point scout again, but I hadn't done well at all. The rolling hills had been so beautiful that I had forgotten to be careful. Fear was my best insurance. I was most worried about my attitude toward the prisoner. It didn't matter that my decision to bring him back had been right. The problem lay with my reasons. "Don't ever think of the enemy as human. If you hesitate in combat, you may become the one who dies for his country." I had no argument with the logic. It was just so hard to do. What happens if you make a quick decision and it's wrong? You can't tell the man you're sorry you killed him. Leon, are you able to fight? I'm a good scout and one of the best marksmen in the company. But can you fight? I had no problems in the practice assaults under machine-gun and artillery fire. I'm not afraid to die. Can you kill a man? That's what they sent me here to do. I hope I can.

It became common for a patrol to bring in one or two prisoners. A lot of Germans would desert while on patrol and wait for a chance to surrender. Occasionally, we found a man who had been wounded or killed by artillery and left for us to pick up. We quit using Emile with the scouts and kept him with the body of the patrol. He was a guerilla fighter and had never learned to soldier. He told wonderful stories of how he used to blow up trucks and steal supplies. Well, maybe. He was good at telling stories. He was also sloppy, careless, and devoid of foresight. But he was a real clown, and we became fairly good friends. He called me "Babee," both because of my looks and because I couldn't drink the vile-tasting Calvados that he kept "discovering." When we were in reserve, he would come by and take me into town.

During our first week on line, a fourteen-year-old French boy came up to practice his English with us. His name was Francis Peramont— Francis, not François. He had taken only two years of English, but he learned fast and enjoyed teaching us his language. Ed was adequate with basic French, but he had trouble understanding this Breton dialect with Celtic slang thrown in. Francis lived in front of our lines. That area was supposed to be evacuated, but he and his mother had no other place to go. His father had worked for the railroad before being killed in an accident. As part of the pension system, the widow and son lived in a company house where the Ste.-Marguerite road crossed the tracks. Their job was to lower the barricades when a train was coming. That wasn't a big job at the time. About three kilometers down the line, the Germans had the railroad covered with machine guns and artillery. School wasn't being held that fall, so every morning Francis got on his bicycle and rode through the American lines. Occasionally he went the other way, but the German soldiers weren't as friendly as the Americans and didn't have any food to offer him.

Ray didn't like having Francis around; he said the kid might be a spy. What was there to learn? The Germans knew where we were and we knew where they were. Most of our discussions with Francis were about French and Breton words. He learned a lot of English from us, but nothing that would help him in school. Once he went home and looked up *son of a bitch* to see why it was such a popular phrase. It didn't make any sense, but the Americans liked it. The next year he used it in a written assignment in school. It didn't go over well there. He learned other phrases that were not English or American. At McCain, because Westmoreland didn't look kindly on the use of vulgarity, Ray and DeRosa had taught us some Old Country words. (I don't mean that the old Anglo-Saxon words were forbidden, just that it was obvious that Westmoreland didn't like them.) The most popular "Italian" terminology we learned was "falan goule." We thought we knew what it meant, but it turned out later that Ray's Italian wasn't very good. No matter; it was fun to cuss in a foreign language.

Because nothing was happening, Ray finally let us go in front of the lines to the little towns of Tréoual and Cadic. They were really just farm clusters of one or two families. The farms were muddy and smelly—and old. One building had the date 1528 carved over the entrance. It was being used as a barn. Those houses were built to last, made of thick granite stones and covered with thatch roofs that were replaced every eight or ten years. Both Tréoual and Cadic were deserted. The people had moved out about a month earlier, and the Germans had taken all of the livestock except a few wild chickens.

One afternoon while Dale was on an outpost, he saw a German patrol slipping toward our lines. He called back to company headquarters, which alerted everyone. Then headquarters connected him with the artillery. Dale didn't have any kind of reference map, but he thought he could stop the patrol with artillery before it reached our lines. He played the artillery the way we had been playing apples. He told them approximately where he was, and they dropped a reference round. Keeping that point in mind, he walked the artillery across the patrol. When several Germans were wounded, the others spread out and continued the attack. Dale dropped a few artillery rounds on the edges, pushing them back together. As the attack faltered, he interrupted his directions to tell headquarters that someone was wounded and they should send a medic up. He kept playing the artillery until the patrol retreated. Then he said: "Get a medic up as soon as you can. I'm dying."

We knew only that Dale was badly wounded and was in the hospital. The next morning word was passed along the line that he had died. I remember the helpless, bewildered emotion. When someone died at home, we visited the family and helped with the wake. Here, we were Dale's family, but there wasn't any ritual we could use to help with the grief. We couldn't have a memorial service or even see the body. I sat under a tree and cried. I had known that some of us would be wounded, and a few killed—but not Dale. I composed a funeral service that would never be. I couldn't use a Scripture because Dale was not religious. I thought of Merlin: *I am Proctor and I am dying. I am Proctor who followed the gleam.* But Dale wasn't dying. He would live as long as we would remember his strength, depth, love, and wit. In my mind I could sit beside him and say the things I should have told him earlier. I loved him as deeply as a brother. I was thankful for what he had meant to me. His depth and insight had helped me to grow. I was a better person for having known him.

We heard that Simmers was recommending Dale for a Distinguished Service Cross, second only to a Congressional Medal of Honor. I was pleased, but at the same time troubled by the implication. "Above and beyond the call of duty" seems to suggest something more than would be expected of a good soldier. But Dale had done exactly what we would have expected of him. None of us would have considered any possibility that Dale Proctor might break and run. "On my honor I will do my best." Dale was family; he had kept his promise. If you extend those concepts, there is no such thing as individual courage, and medals don't mean very much.

After Dale's death we became more careful about security procedures. We stripped down and cleaned our rifles every morning, working in relays of only two or three men. George and I were talking while we cleaned and oiled our dismantled rifles, which were spread out on a blanket. "George, the bayonet instructor at Benning said that combat is boring most of the time. You sit around trying to get warm or dry, and suddenly the whole thing explodes on you. He was right, and I'm scared. We aren't really fighting, but Dale got killed, and now things are dull again."

"This place is a mess, Leon. The Krauts can slip up on us because we aren't strong enough to have a defensive line. We ought to have a screen of patrols out in front. These guard positions are useless."

"Do you suppose the man who planned the Holly Springs exercise is in charge of our defense?"

A standing order for daytime guards was to fire their rifles only in an emergency. Just seeing a German patrol did not qualify. In that case, you should alert the squad so they could take up firing positions. Someone would contact company headquarters by telephone, and there might be time for artillery to prepare. If a German popped up fifteen yards away pointing a burp gun at you, then you fired. You were going to die because he would not be alone, but the shot would warn the squad.

Ka-*pow!* An M-1 had fired from the guard post across the road to our left. Lehrer, Peewee, and Prado were there. Pooling their intelligence, those three were as smart as a jackass. I finished slipping the trigger housing of my rifle into place and was ready to go. George's BAR was more complicated, but he was always cool under pressure. He would be ready in about two minutes. I started planning where we would set up to fire. The .50-caliber machine gun was quiet, which meant the road was safe. The Krauts must have their position in that stone house at Trévual. It was about seventy-five yards in front of Lehrer's group. But the M-1 had fired once, and no German weapon had fired at all. How had they killed our three men? If they weren't dead, why weren't they yelling? Were they captured? There was absolute silence except for the sound of Ray running toward us. He saw me squatting beside George and yelled, "Standifer, get your butt in gear!" I ignored him because I was already in gear. The BAR, our main firebase, was disabled, and my job was to stay as backup. George finally finished the assembly, and we went to our firing position.

Then we heard Ray. "Jesus Christ, Lehrer, you shot a cat?"

We crossed over to the position and there it was—a gutshot cat struggling to walk about fifteen yards away. Even at that distance Lehrer had barely managed to hit. "Get your ass down there and kill him. Hell, no, you won't fire again! Go down and use a stone."

Westmoreland came up and looked at the mess. "Sergeant Graziano, if that man pulls one more stupid stunt he will be transferred to quartermaster, unloading ammunition trucks." He walked away without another word. We had failed miserably in responding to an attack. Lehrer was stupid to have fired, but he had been scared and something had moved quickly. Ray had panicked and run into the fight without calling roll and with no plan of action. George and I had been in the nearest firing position, but we hadn't yelled to learn what was happening or to let people know where the BAR would be. We had learned one more lesson cheap.

After two weeks on line we were getting punchy. We hadn't fought at all, but the stress was showing. We had abandoned the two-hour guard shifts because we couldn't stay awake that long. Now it was one hour on and two off. That wore us down faster, but it was the only way to stay awake. We slept some during the day, but just as I was dozing off, artillery would start whizzing overhead. I hadn't quite learned to distinguish between incoming and outgoing. A little later a BAR would go *bop-bop-bop,* answered by the *rippp* of a burp gun, then a little rifle fire—all about a mile away. It shouldn't affect us. The flies were awful. If I did get to sleep, one would crawl up my nose.

Word came down for us to pack up. King Company was being pulled back for rest. We didn't know when our replacement squad would arrive because the procedure was staggered, with a new squad coming up about every hour. By nine o'clock First Squad was packed and ready to go. Cagle, on the machine gun, was our only guard, and he was talking with the rest of us who were sitting on our packs. Ed looked down the road behind us and saw the first scout of an L Company squad creeping along slowly, giving occasional signals back to the second scout and on to the squad leader.

George recognized the scout as a buddy from Benning. He yelled: "Hey Mike, come on up. We've already whipped the Krauts!"

The squad was a little sheepish about having come up so carefully, but they had been right. We already knew most of the L Company squad from Camp McCain. After the ritual greetings, we showed them the positions and told them approximately what was in front. Somebody asked where our second squad was. "It's over beyond those trees. We don't have visual contact, but they always have somebody on the telephone."

They were a little shocked. "This isn't really a line, is it?"

"No, it's just a series of weak outposts. A strong German combat patrol could tear you up. Good luck."

We lined up in an extended column and started walking to the pickup point at Rédené. We were exhausted, grimy, and sleepy, but we had made it through two weeks of combat. Tonight we would have a hot meal and sleep all night. When we got to the pickup point, Second Platoon was already there. The rest of First Platoon hadn't yet been relieved. A small group of French men and women were sitting around watching. Ray straightened the column up, had us sling arms, and started: "I was drinking beer in the cabaret and was I having fun, / 'Til one night she caught me tight, and now I'm on the run." We came in with: "Pistol packin' mama, lay that pistol down." It didn't go over nearly as well in Rédené as it had at Holly Springs, but we enjoyed it. We were Infantry and we were winning the war.

# 10 We Happy Few, We Band of Brothers

The reserve area was a long, open meadow with a haystack at one end. We pitched our tents and filled them with hay. Tonight we would sleep well. George and I went over to see the boys in Third Platoon. It reminded me of a family reunion. One squad told of the night that somebody had seen movement and pulled the pin on a grenade—and a woods pigeon started flapping around in a tree overhead; he almost dropped the grenade.

Roy Brown did drop his grenade. It rolled into a tent where his buddies were asleep. He dived in after it, grabbed it, and was throwing it out when the thing exploded in his hand. The entire hand and wrist disappeared. He also had two shrapnel wounds, but no one else was hurt. Roy was being recommended for a Soldier's Medal.

Another squad had a strange story of the morning that two Germans walked right up to their position, trying to surrender. That caused a lot of excitement. The guard swore he had been watching them all along and didn't want to scare them off by saying anything.

Dyer, one of the Third Platoon scouts, called me to one side and asked about the orientation patrol I had made. He was a quiet boy from Tennessee, a good scout with much more experience than I had, but he was bothered about how poorly he had done on his first patrol.

I said, "Hell, Dyer, they didn't expect us to be good on the first try. I felt like a fool out there. Nothing went right."

That didn't help him any. "We are lucky the Krauts didn't see us."

"Don't be so shaky. We are better than anything the Krauts have. You heard what happened to that Kriegsmarine patrol that I Company found. It was pure slaughter." I didn't really feel that confident, but he was so scared I didn't want to tell the truth.

When we got back to the First Platoon area, we learned that Third Squad had been assigned guard duty, so we were going to be able to sleep all night. We could sleep with our shoes off, but should be dressed and have our rifles ready. No fires at night. We weren't far enough back for that. The kitchen was preparing a hot supper, our first real meal in two weeks. The smell of frying pork chops and of coffee in the GI cans was spreading over the area. George and I took our food over to the hedgerow and ate as casually as if we were at a fine restaurant. We were back home after two weeks of war.

Sergeant Monti came by. "Has anybody seen H. R.? He bought a bottle of something from a Frenchman and disappeared." We asked the boys in Third Squad how H. R. had held up on line. Considering that H. R. was badly alcoholic, things had gone pretty well. They had rationed him to one cup of hard cider a day and repeatedly warned him about what could happen to the entire squad if he got drunk. Both wine and Calvados were easily available. There was a little bar not far behind our lines, but H. R. didn't drink any more than his ration of cider. He was terrified of seeing Germans and was getting the shakes, but he did stay sober. Well, he was off line now. Maybe he would find his way back. We couldn't go out looking for him in the dark.

George and I sat in front of the tent, watching the stars and making small talk. We didn't want any profound thoughts; just being safe and well was enough. The next morning, force of habit woke me at first light. George was snoring; he hadn't snored much on line, and it didn't matter now. I could hear the kitchen crew rattling around. The roar of oil burners meant that coffee would soon be ready. I rolled out, pulled on my shoes, and walked over to watch. Fergie, the cook's helper, poured me a cup and started asking what it was like on line. I eased out of that one and went over to sit on the hedgerow. I watched the mist drift away, with no worries about an attack. The good things of life were so simple: dry shoes, coffee, and a beautiful red sun rising. I re-filled my cup and got one for George. "George, wake up. Coffee's ready and there's a beautiful sunrise." He raised his head, looked at me, and went back to sleep. So much for the finer things of life.

About nine o'clock an old Frenchman came up carrying H. R.'s rifle. H. R. was tied up in the man's barn. Apparently the bottle had worked very well on H. R.; it also had brought out his fear of Germans. He had broken into the Frenchman's house, pointing his rifle at the man and his wife and calling them Krauts. He took them to the barn, although even H. R. didn't know why. The man knocked H. R. down, tied him up, and took his rifle. I'm sure the French were impressed with our fighting force.

Simmers came by to visit and tease me about the patrol. "I understand you didn't think much of your FFI scout."

I laughed. "Cap'n, if I get shot I want it to be my fault."

It was good of Simmers to stop by, but I wondered why he didn't visit us on line. Later, some officers from battalion headquarters showed up to "talk with the troops." We answered their questions and smiled at their air of self-importance. This was as close to the front as they were going to be, whereas we thought being in reserve was like a vacation. We should have been drilling, taking physical exercises, and particularly keeping ourselves ready to move back on line quickly; but we weren't.

Being in reserve only meant sleeping, eating, and wandering around—and listening to the company radio. Every afternoon Glenn Miller came on live from England, playing all the popular songs. When we heard his theme song, we all drifted back home. Most of the boys remembered high school dances. I remembered warm summer nights on the porch. Then the Crew Chiefs would sing something like "The Victory Polka":

> There's gonna be a hallelujah day
> When the boys can all come home to stay.
> We'll be marching down Fifth Avenue,
> The United Nations in review.

At night we could pick up a German propaganda program. It featured a girl who called herself Midge. She had a strong American accent—George said it sounded a little like Ohio. After the war we found that he was right. The girl was Mildred Gillars, who had attended Ohio Wesleyan College just outside of Columbus. She was popularly known as Axis Sally. Some of the propaganda was heavy-handed. She kept talking about draft dodgers sleeping with our wives back home. Ed and Herb were both married. Ed's wife was living with his mother. Herb was from a small mountain town in Kentucky—anyone messing with his wife would be dead within twenty-four hours. George had a girlfriend at home, but he wasn't worried either.

Midge also delivered a hidden propaganda that was soft, subtle, and effective: "We hear that the Ninetieth Division has been refitted and is ready to try again. You 'Tough Hombres' made a good showing last time. Too bad you were fighting a panzer division with three years of combat experience." Or: "Fighting flared up again in the Brittany area. The Ninety-fourth Pilgrim Division ran into some German marines. I'll bet they hope that doesn't happen again." The theme of her reports was: "You already know the details of these defeats. I'm just making small talk about them." We listened because she had a wide range of good recorded music. She liked to play "Little Brown Jug" and "Sweet Georgia Brown"—which she dedicated to "the boys from Benning." Her staples also included "Long Ago and Far Away," "I'll Be Seeing You," "As Time Goes By," and "Don't Get Around Much Anymore." It was strange to hear the enemy as a girl who enjoyed talking to us. We thought she was a failure at propaganda, which is just what she intended. We went to sleep homesick and wondering what had happened to the Ninetieth Division. We knew what had happened to the Kriegsmarineinfanterie: I Company had cleaned their plows, made them say "calf rope."

After a week in battalion reserve, we went back on line. Our platoon was held as company reserve and used for patrols. They were better than that first little orientation patrol. They consisted of one or occasionally two squads, with Westmoreland in charge. I was excited because this was my kind of war. I was the best scout in the world. I was Westmoreland's best bird dog.

The first few patrols were intended mainly to loosen us up and help us get a feel for the land. Then Westmoreland took us on a long patrol almost to Gestel, which was probably about two miles away. "We will cross the railroad and follow the edge of the ridge between Ste.-Marguerite, pass Cap Kerdudal, and cross the highway to le Hirgoat. Be careful there, Standifer, you'll be exposed in a long open valley. We will cover you from around this bridge. Then we will cut over and locate a German outpost in this area. We will return by crossing the railroad and following the edge of that ridge. We are on a reconnaissance mission. We will fight only if fired upon. Artillery has been alerted, and I have their overlay for the area. Don't shoot a Kraut just because you see him. Questions? Lock and load. Scouts out."

I led off in front of the patrol—point scout in front of the whole army. The next people in front of me were Krauts. I was careful but relaxed. The rifle felt good in my hands. My rifle belt was heavy and biting into my hips. I wasn't accustomed to having it full of ammunition. Maybe I should start wearing the harness of a combat pack. I cocked the helmet to the side of my head so I could hear better. Ed was about twenty-five yards behind me and off to the side. His primary job was to keep contact between me and the patrol. Just past Cap Kerdudal, a creek ran under the road. The patrol formed a line along some brush beside the road. Ed and I began the trip up the valley. It wasn't quite a valley, just a long draw feeding into the creek. I walked very carefully, stopping when something looked strange. Everything looked strange; I had learned that the beautiful rolling hills could explode into chaos. I was going up the draw like a scout in a war movie—one of those exciting scenes in which there is background music until you see that the enemy is ready to attack. Then there is deadly silence.

I realized that the countryside was absolutely quiet. I strained to hear any sound. A bird was singing.

I stopped and looked back at Ed, who just shrugged his shoulders. Either he didn't see anything wrong or it was too late for us to confer. If this was a trap, I had already gone too far into it. The patrol was still safe, but Ed and I were in a bad place. There was a shed on the ridge at the head of the draw, a perfect machine-gun position. A board had been pulled off to make a hole to fire through. The gunner was watching me, waiting. Without looking back, I knew what the squad was doing. George was cool, calm, his BAR aiming directly at the shed. His finger was resting lightly on the trigger. If I were shot, the German gunner would die within two seconds. Westmoreland was twitching his chin and breathing hard. Ray was cursing me for being too slow. Prado and Peewee were relaxed and bored.

"I need a couple guys what don't owe me no money fer a little routine patrol."

My mind was running through options. If I turned around to walk back, the gunner would fire. Flanking was impossible. "Yea, though I walk through the valley of the shadow of death, I will fear no evil." My muscles were tense, my hands were sweaty—the rifle felt slippery. I slid the safety lock off and walked straight at the gun, boldly and aggressively but very carefully.

At thirty yards I stopped and dropped to my knee. The gunner would open up somewhere between here and ten yards. I couldn't see a thing. Where would the enemy riflemen be? There was no cover close to the shed. Rifles would be along that hedgerow.

I thought, Leon, you're stalling. The squad is watching. I came up to a crouch, rifle ready to fire from the hip. Cut every thought out of your mind. Depend on instinct. Fire at any sound or motion, anywhere.

Twenty yards. At this range he couldn't miss. I might get one round off. I stopped ten yards from the shed. I could see nothing through the hole. Maybe there wasn't a gun. I reached the shed and opened the door. Just a few tools. I poked through some brush and signaled the patrol. Nothing had happened, but to survive as a scout, you have to stay scared.

We took a break, which gave me a chance to shake a bit. Then I skirted the edge of Hirgoat (four scattered houses) and entered a group of hedgerowed fields. The patrol formed along the first hedgerow. I climbed over it and started toward the next, about thirty yards away. It had brush growing along the top. Any point could hide a machine gun, but the middle was the best bet, with riflemen on each side. I walked that field as I had done the valley and reached the hedgerow without a shot. I climbed up at a clear spot and saw there was nobody on the other side. Then I looked to the next hedgerow. It had a break in it, and I saw movement beyond. Easy, Leon, you're perched up here like a turkey in a tree. Slide down slowly, signal Ed to bring up Ray and Westmoreland.

While I waited for them, I tried to put my information together. I could see one machine gun. A man with the insignia of a squad leader was slicing bread for everyone. It was probably a squad of about ten men. I couldn't see any movement of guards, but I knew roughly where they would be. I didn't think I had been seen because they were all so calm. I reported this to Westmoreland; he sent me over behind a hedgerow that led to a position where I could spot their guards. Ray set the squad up in firing positions and they waited.

I slipped down along the row, peeked over, and saw no guards at all. I saw eight men sitting together drinking cider and eating bread. I went back and reported to Ray: "We could almost wipe them out with one burst of the BAR. They're bunched up like a covey of quail."

Westmoreland said no. "Wait to see which way they're going. We're here to look for the outpost." While we waited, I realized that the Germans could just as easily have taken their break a few minutes earlier and been sitting at the end of that draw while I walked up it.

I was back at my hidden observation point when the German patrol got up and started moving on toward their lines. I hadn't seen any security guards because they hadn't posted any. I climbed the hedgerow and went up to where they had been resting. I picked up a magazine one of them had left, and signaled Ray. We all watched the Germans walk along the crest of the ridge as if they were on a nature hike. About two hundred yards away they cut into a hedgerow gap and stopped again. Westmoreland looked through his binoculars and said, "Well, we found the outpost." There was a machine gun, flanked by rifle positions on either side. The gunner and all the riflemen left their positions to visit with the returning patrol. Westmoreland watched for a while, took a few notes, and said, "Let's go home." We went back a shorter way with more room for cover, but I was very careful. I had seen how easily I could have walked into the patrol's machine gun, even though I was doing everything right. They had been wrong, but I would have been the one who died.

When we came to the road, I followed the edge of it down to the railroad crossing. Mrs. Peramont watched us go by from the front of her house. She was a mildly interested spectator watching some boys walk by. A combat patrol meant nothing to her. As I started up the road to Strongpoint Graziano, I looked back at Westmoreland. Letting the patrol walk in a line up that sunken road was chancy, but we were only about a hundred yards from home. Westmoreland waved me on to risk it, and after the curve I was looking directly into our .50-caliber machine gun. The gunner waved at me and called to the rest of his squad. The patrol was over. I tried to imitate the casual way Snerd used to leave the field after a football game. My helmet was cocked to one side, a pants leg was hanging out of my legging, and I held the rifle in the crook of my arm as if I were coming in from a hunting trip.

> Swift as the panther in triumph, fierce as the bear in defeat,
> Sired of a bulldog parent, steeled in the furnace heat.
> Send me the best of your breeding, lend me your chosen ones;
> Them will I take to my bosom, them will I call my sons.

The L Company squad crowded around us while Westmoreland went to phone in a report. This was the first combat patrol they had seen. I was glad to tell them about life out where the real fighting was: "It's not bad out there. The Krauts are stupid soldiers. We slipped right up on one of their patrols. Could have wiped them out, but Westmoreland wouldn't let us. We'll clean house if they ever let us fight." I was surprised at how good I felt—a little tired but no longer scared. These front-line kids didn't understand how exciting a patrol was.

After he reported in, Westmoreland led us back to the company headquarters group where we were staying as the reserve platoon. The headquarters boys were just as excited about the patrol as the L Company squad had been, but suddenly I was getting tired. George had walked over into the orchard and was sitting alone under a tree. He didn't want any company, so I selected my own tree. I was relaxed but emotionally exhausted. I had looked fear squarely in the face and walked away. The squad had watched me while I carried the ball—not for a touchdown, but I had carried it. I had experienced the ultimate in courage. Greater love hath no man than this. Ed was still excited, still telling people about the Krauts we saw, but soon he would hit the slump George and I were experiencing.

After a while, I reached in my pocket and took out my little New Testament with Psalms. I wasn't looking for assurance that my life would be spared. People get killed in combat. I didn't expect God to favor me above other Christians. My life would be spared only if I were very cautious and a little lucky. What I needed from the Bible was an anchor to home. I wanted to hear the great booming voices of the Sunday night orators. I wanted to be reminded that "the heavens declare the glory of God; and the firmament sheweth his handiwork," and that "the earth is the Lord's and the fulness thereof." Then my mind drifted to Ecclesiastes. I needed the reassurance that "to every thing there is a season, and a time to every purpose under the heaven: a time to be born, and a time to die . . . a time to kill, and a time to heal . . . a time to love, and a time to hate; a time of war, and a time of peace."

Richards had made a patrol similar to mine—he had returned by a different route—a few days earlier. We spent a lot of time encouraging each other. Or rather, he encouraged me.

"Richards, I'm scared to death out there. Every minute, every step, I expect to be hit. You look so confident and in control."

"It's all bluff, Leon. Only a fool can be calm out there, and he won't last long. Being scared is your best insurance—and don't let anybody rush you."

I started some sort of complaint about why the scout always had to take the risks.

"Richards said: "Back home they have an expression that 'you hoe your own row.' It may seem like the weediest one in the field, but it might change into being an easy one. Even if it doesn't, that's the row given to you."

I liked the thought. A good preacher could have made a great sermon out of it. Do your job to the best of your ability and don't trouble yourself about what other people are doing. The Infantry School had the same idea in its maxim, "Don't fight the problem." Take the assignment given you and get it done.

George and I tried to read the German magazine I had found. We enjoyed the cartoons. "George, that's a *Collier's* cartoon. I remember seeing it last year."

"It sure is. Look at the newspaper that man is reading. It says *Evening News*."

I wondered how an American cartoon found its way into a German magazine during wartime. There was an ad for Dr. Scholl's foot pads. The note below it said that this was entirely a German firm, which no longer had any connection with the American manufacturer. In my letter home, I told about the *Collier's* cartoon, but not about the patrol. It had scared me too much. The fear had evaporated quickly when the patrol ended, but I still remembered it too clearly to want to write about it.

One night we heard German weapons open up about three or four

*"Wot do ya mean, 'It's nice to git back to th' rear echelon'? Ya been out huntin' souvenirs agin?"*

hundred yards in front of our line. Then some American rifles and a BAR began firing. K Company didn't have a patrol out, and any other Americans should have notified us before going in front of our line. The next day the entire regiment was questioned. There had been no Americans out. The next night it happened again at the same spot. From the sounds, we knew they were fighting over near Kervalze, but we didn't know why. The next day Battalion G-2 (operations) called

Westmoreland in to talk about a patrol. He came back very quiet and mad. Right after dark, the entire platoon was to go to the hedgerowed field where the fighting had been. We were to set up within the field and ambush the German patrol when it came up.

I couldn't understand Westmoreland's mood. We had orders to go out there, so we would. Then Captain Simmers came up and talked to us. "If you fight, stick with it and drive them off. The Germans won't continue a fight for long because they are too close to our lines. Bring back all your dead and wounded. You may have to get a wagon from that farmhouse."

What did he mean by that? Fight them off, and bring back your dead. We were King Company. We fought to win. Why shouldn't we win and have German prisoners carrying the wounded? That wasn't the kind of pep talk the coach was supposed to give before the big game.

There was some small talk, then Westmoreland said: "Any questions? Lock and load. Scouts out." That phrase wasn't as much fun as it had been in Holly Springs. I had done enough daylight patrols by now to get a sick feeling when the lieutenant said, "Scouts out." This was our first night patrol. After we started I settled down—scared, but only cautious-scared. At Benning, the ASTP boys had loved night fighting and we were very good at it. The other First Platoon men hadn't had much night training. But we all considered our platoon to be good at everything.

The grease paint on my face was making me sweaty. "Sergeant Cohen, there aren't any Japs out there." No, but the *Ländser* are going to be coming, and they are good. Not as good as the Benning School for Boys, though. We can lick our weight in wildcats.

The trail went under an oak tree. I had goofed. I should have skirted it. The noise of cracking acorns sounded as if it could be heard a mile away. A dog started barking. But the field was still a couple of hundred yards ahead, and after the oak tree we went quietly. When we reached the ambush site, I slipped through the hedgerow and went to my position, watching the rest of the platoon ghost by as quietly as clouds passing over the moon. We were good. The Germans were in for a shock. Tonight I was going to kill for the first time. I remembered Bob Souder. "Will I be able to kill? God, I hope not." I could kill. I had prepared myself long ago. I was also prepared to die. I sat there with my rifle between my legs. When we heard the Germans coming, we were to get into position but not fire until Westmoreland did. He had a carbine, which had a tinnier sound than our rifles.

We waited. Not a sound anywhere. The nights were strange in Brittany. At home you would hear crickets and frogs. I wondered why regiment was so sure the patrol was coming. Slowly I saw what had disgusted Westmoreland and shaken Simmers. The only reason for staging a mock battle is to draw a patrol out and destroy it. How? Well, artillery is the best bet. Select a spot on which you had registered in your big guns a few weeks earlier. Send a few infantry out to capture the wounded survivors, but play your music with artillery. We weren't going to shock the Germans. We were going to die.

A shot rang out. That scared me. How did a patrol slip up without my hearing a thing? Then I realized it wasn't a German rifle or Westmoreland's carbine. It was an American M-1. Had they started another mock battle?

Westmoreland came running down the line hissing, "Get the hell out of here."

Forty American infantrymen ran four hundred yards back to our lines.

For the next few weeks, we listened to countless variations on the big joke about the night First Platoon broke and ran. But we saw a much deeper truth. Our patrols were being planned by the men who had organized those imaginative field problems in Holly Springs. This time it really mattered if you were killed. The German trap hadn't been brilliant, but it had shown some thought. I don't know why the Germans wanted to wipe out an American platoon. Maybe they only wanted a few prisoners. Nobody had been captured since the division took over. The French underground later reported that German artillery was ready to shell us as soon as their infantry was in position. The plan was blown because one of our men forgot to lock his rifle and fell asleep with his finger on the trigger. Westmoreland was looking for a good reason to abort, and the rifle fire was it.

We kept patrolling almost every day. Regiment had finally decided to defend the line with a protective screen. We saw a few German patrols, but they weren't heading in our direction. I was appalled at the loose, careless way their patrols operated. Sergeant Cohen would have made them scrub the barracks every night for a week.

Ed and I were improving in our communications and ways of operating. He was teaching me to be more cautious. On one of the patrols we were to pass through Cap Kerdudal from the far side. *Ker* is a Celtic word meaning "house or home of"; thus Cap Kerdudal was where the *dudals*—"strangers"—lived, located on a large hill, or *cap* (in Brittany *cap* often is used in a broader sense than our topographical term *cape*.) The road followed a gentle slope in a rectangular field that had been cultivated in the spring but was bare at the time. At the edge of the field, I looked up toward the town, about a hundred yards away. I saw two stone houses with excellent hiding places for machine guns. Thick, bushy hedgerows extended along either side of the field. I saw nothing suspicious, but it was no spot to be caught in. I looked back. Ed was signaling me to come out.

"Leon, we've got to do something, this is a bad place."

"I know, but we have to go through the town, and I can't see anything wrong. I don't think we have any Krauts."

"Look at that hill behind us. A few machine guns there, plus some in town, would turn this into a slaughter area."

As usual, Ed was right. The squad was in an exposed spot between two hills. If anyone were planning an ambush, they had us in a dangerous position.

Westmoreland came up and listened while we said that we saw nothing suspicious but didn't like it. "Okay, what do you want?"

I hadn't thought that far, but Ed had. He wanted the patrol to wait along the sunken road where they would have a little protection. He and I would clear the hill behind us, then go up to the town. He wanted to climb the hedgerow on the right and me to climb the one on the left; from there we would work our way up to town. If there were any Krauts in the area, they would certainly be lined up behind those hedgerows, taking advantage of the obvious ambush site. Ed had an apple orchard on his side. I had a small field flanked by an old road. The field was so obviously clear that I crossed it at a trot; if Ed had been with me, he would have insisted that I walk cautiously, watching for booby traps. I was in the town and had checked out both houses before he got there. That was the only bit of excitement on the patrol. We would remember it a few weeks later and realize how easy to work for Westmoreland was.

Not long after the Cap Kerdudal patrol, we replaced a squad from I

Company at Strongpoint Graziano. They had used about half of our .50-caliber ammunition. One day the man on the gun had seen a German climb the hedgerow and head down the road to Cadic without looking back. Then another and another, until there were six Germans lined up on the narrow road, with a hedgerow on each side. The gunner saw no reason to shoot—the Germans were headed back toward their lines. Then the seventh soldier climbed over. He looked back, saw the gun, and raised his rifle to shoot. That's when the American fired. The I Company squad told us: "Don't fire the .50 unless you have to. It makes an awful mess."

They also told us the Germans were stealing our chickens at Tréoual. The town had been evacuated, and the chickens were ours because we had decided they were. But on two recent mornings, German patrols had caught chickens just before dawn and spirited them away. The Krauts probably went back and reported to their officers that the Amis were too alert for an attack, so they hadn't made one.

We agreed with I Company that we ought to eat the chickens to keep them out of German hands. One day about noon, Ed and I decided to go over and try for one. We had been nabbing them pretty regularly, and they were beginning to turn wild and hard to catch. I wasn't exactly trying to catch the rooster I spotted that day. I was chasing him with a stick, meaning to throw it at him. You can't throw a stick accurately with a rifle slung over your shoulder and a steel helmet bouncing on your head, so Ed stood at the edge of the town guarding my rifle and helmet while I chased the rooster around a farm building. As I rounded a corner in hot pursuit, the rooster squawked and ran back between my legs. Then I saw why. A German soldier wanted the bird too, and he hadn't been dumb enough to leave his rifle lying on the ground. I turned and ran back to Ed. He hadn't seen the German, but I had no trouble convincing him that we didn't really want a chicken. When we got back to the line, we said the chickens were too wild to catch.

I wondered if we should tell Ray about the German.

"Not on your life," said Ed.

# 11  But Can They Fight?

I was beginning to have trouble with my letters home. Censorship allowed us to say only that we were in combat somewhere in France, but Ed had worked out a code with his wife, Betty, so that in each letter his complimentary closing spelled part of a word. The first letter closed with "Love," the next with "Only," and so on until Betty could write to my mother and Mrs. Faber saying that we were outside of Lorient and near Quimperlé. Mother knew that the fighting wasn't very intense in our sectors, and I kept telling her we weren't in much danger, but then she heard from Mrs. Proctor that Dale had been killed.

A boy from Jackson was in division headquarters, working as an optical technician. Mother knew his parents, and she began comparing my letters with those he was sending home. I tried to set her straight:

> Mother, why don't you believe what I tell you? Carl is lying. Division headquarters is so far back it's out of artillery range. They haven't ever been attacked by German patrols. They do stand guard at night, but it's like we did at Camp McCain. They aren't allowed to have ammunition in their rifles. Occasionally, Frenchmen try to break in and steal rations, but the guard turns on floodlights and arrests them. They sleep on cots and watch movies once a week. I don't know why he tells about machine-gun fire keeping him awake at night. We hear machine-gun and rifle fire occasionally during the day, but being on the line is really pretty boring.

It was hard for her to understand that combat is dull. One friend had been killed, but nobody else had even been wounded, and we weren't doing much fighting.

One result of boredom was that we developed daily rituals. Sunrise serenade of the Krauts was followed by breakfast—C rations and powdered coffee heated over a small twig fire. Then we cleaned rifles, washed up, and shaved. All of the other platoons were allowed to grow beards, but Westmoreland thought it looked sloppy. A one-day stubble was acceptable, and we could grow sideburns or a mustache. Except for Leon: I could grow only a ball of fine fuzz on each side. Every day the squad got a five-gallon can of iodine-treated water for drinking, washing, and shaving. There was a strong rule against using local well water. The French used it to wash with, but nobody drank the stuff.

On sunny days George, Ed, and I would top off the morning with a trip to the creek. Because it was within running distance, we didn't need permission to go, but we usually let someone know where we were. In fact we usually made a show of it:

> Yes, we'll gather at the river,
> The beautiful, the beautiful river;
> Gather with the saints at the river
> That flows by the throne of God.

When we felt good, George and I enjoyed hamming it up with revival songs. Ed thought they were ridiculous, especially the blood-cult ones: "There is a fountain filled with blood,/Drawn from Emmanuel's veins." He usually joined in, though; it was bad theology but great fun.

The creek was rather pretty, clear water flowing over rocks with patches of almost sandy beach, but we knew that it drained from the muddy farmlots. It wasn't a face-washing place. We would strip off our clothes, soap down well, and squeal while we rinsed with the cold water. Once, I asked George what he would do if the Germans were to attack while we were standing there naked.

"Dress. I'm not going to kill Krauts barefoot and bare-assed."

We giggled over the idea and decided we would need shoes (not necessarily laced), pants, long-sleeved undershirts to hide our white skin, cartridge belts, and rifles. Dressing would take a while, but the rest of the squad could hold the line until we three came heroically to their rescue. Nothing like that happened. We washed, dressed, stretched in the sun, threw rocks, and joked until we had been gone for about an hour.

Once when we came back, Ray was yelling. "Standifer, where the hell were you?" Third Platoon had come by wanting two scouts for patrol. Westmoreland had sent Richards and Button instead. Battalion G-2 had gotten word of a group of Germans who wanted to surrender but needed to be confronted by a strong combat patrol. It was arranged that we would have a forty-man patrol approaching Cap Kerdudal at noon, and the Germans would surrender to them.

Ed said, "They sure picked a fine place to surrender." We still remembered the scary road leading up to town, the thick hedgerows on either side, and the hill behind us. To be honest, at the time I didn't suspect a thing. As with the night-patrol ambush fiasco, I made the mistake of assuming that the people planning the patrols were competent. Third Platoon was assigned to patrol, just as we had been earlier, so it was natural that they should have been sent. Their platoon leader didn't know the area, which is why he picked up some First Platoon scouts. I didn't wonder whether he would let Richards and Button work the ground properly. That was what scouts were for. Besides, this was such a simple patrol that it had no backup at all. I Company, in reserve, had been trucked to Quimperlé, where they were showering in the local high school.

Richards was point scout, going slowly, carefully, and scared toward a bush where, if anyone had planned an ambush, there should have been a machine gun. Someone had, and there was. When Richards got close enough to see the gun, they opened up point-blank. He had no chance at all. Button ran for the hedgerow on the roadside but didn't make it. Dyer, the scout who had talked with me about the job's dangers, was cut off in his rear guard position; he didn't make it either. The rest of the patrol took cover in the sunken road, which was a fairly good position except that the enemy had high ground on both sides. The patrol was well out in front of our line, but we heard faint rifle fire, then artillery. We hoped it hadn't happened in that ambush site but knew it had. The sweet little children had finally been caught and were going to have to fight. "Let's see what you are made of."

Luckily, our artillery knew the patrol was out, and the platoon leader, Lieutenant Devonald, was carrying the overlay map on which to plot concentrations. He took a bullet to the head, which paralyzed the left side of his body, but he could still read a map and call artillery. At Benning they had said that artillery could sound as sweet as music. Devonald made a great orchestra leader. As the shells whistled over us, I remembered my Civil War joke: Gospel, on the way! We stood there and cried. It wasn't joy or fear—possibly relief. We knew we couldn't help and the artillery could. Battalion radioed for I Company to get dressed and hustle back from Quimperlé, but that would take an hour. Simmers put together a small relief patrol with a few men from company headquarters, led by Westmoreland and the company executive officer, Lieutenant Schroeder. They came by us on the run, went past Ste.-Marguerite, took the highway—and ran into German machine guns dug in on high ground. They couldn't get through. Third Platoon was in trouble.

But, boy, did they fight! One of the survivors of the ambush later said, "I saw acts of bravery that day which it seemed could only happen in motion pictures: men charging machine guns and wounded men firing their weapons with one hand."

After fighting for five hours, Third Platoon began running out of ammunition. The old battery radio had been calling artillery for too long and was getting weak. I Company was still trying to get through, but the German position was too strong. Of the thirty-nine Americans who surrendered, thirty were wounded. Five of the platoon were dead.

Back on line we heard the artillery stop. Then the rifle fire stopped. Cagle said, "Maybe the Germans surrendered." It was just a hope. Word came down that Third Platoon had given up. I felt sick in the pit of my stomach. Someone had beaten us. How? We were King Company—the home team. On every tactical problem back in the States, we had come out as the winner. We knew what had happened here. We had heard the German guns, particularly the machine guns. It was a big ambush in a classic location. Well, almost classic: the Germans couldn't have had much protection from artillery. What happens to men who surrender after they have been calling artillery down on their captors for five hours?

It was getting dark. Word came through for us to be on full alert all night. Maybe some of Third Platoon had escaped and would come in tonight. We thought about that and realized German patrols might be looking for them.

"Ray, ask Monti if we can patrol our sector."

"No, orders are for full alert on line."

"Let us put an outpost at Ste.-Marguerite. The church is a perfect site to put a night ambush."

"You heard the orders."

Tactically, our idea made sense. In the confusion, we should have had outposts listening for survivors and for German patrols. Realistically, we had developed the idea because we wanted to fight and knew nothing was going to happen on line. The Germans had humiliated us and we wanted to do something about it. We were good at night work. What we really wanted was to go beyond Ste.-Marguerite and lay an ambush where the road joined the highway. If we had found a German patrol that night, it would have died quickly. Instead, we waited behind the hedgerow all night. The orders were to disperse, but George and I stood together. Ed and Cagle were paired up just down from us. We were all too excited and exhausted to stay awake alone.

I was feeling guilty about playing along the creek. "Ed and I were supposed to be there."

"Aw, Ray was just bitching about not knowing where we were. Westmoreland wasn't going to let them pick up two scouts with no orientation at all. He was over talking with Richards and Button yesterday. They had the map out, and he was probably explaining the patrol."

I felt a little better, "Yeah, I guess so. But it's scary. I wonder who got wounded. That's a bad place for an ambush." I remembered jokes and silly songs I had sung with Richards and Button, help and advice they had given me. Again, as with Dale, the platoon family would not have a funeral.

The next morning we were told to hold our position until I Company replaced us at noon. We got to the reserve area about dark. We had been awake and on alert for thirty-six hours. Tension had kept us awake, but we were all short-tempered. We tried not to cross anyone, not even George. We heard that Westmoreland had been wounded in the foot and Lieutenant Schroeder had a back wound. After the Germans left the ambush area, Westmoreland had found Button's body. A machine gun had ripped diagonally across his chest.

The next morning the remainder of the company assembled for Simmers to give us all the details he had. This was nothing more than what we already knew. Then Colonel Hagerty, the regimental commander, came roaring up in a jeep. He climbed out, assembled us at attention, and began a tirade. He was ashamed to have K Company in his regiment. Third Platoon had been captured by a twenty-man German patrol. Our buddies hadn't even put up a fight—they had just fired a few rounds and surrendered. We stood there shaking with anger. Twenty men meant two machine guns. Westmoreland had counted ten guns. The patrol had fought for five hours with artillery sweeping the area.

Hagerty left us at attention and roared off. Simmers couldn't say anything except, "Dismissed."

As we walked away I was still tense with rage, but George was laughing at me. "Leon, back home they call that 'kicking the cat.' When a man does something stupid and gets caught, he takes his anger out on the animal least able to fight back. Richards was our best scout. He didn't make a mistake unless Devonald forced him to. Third Platoon fought for five hours, and even Westmoreland couldn't break through to them. Whatever went wrong must have been Hagerty's mistake—because he is the one who kicked the cat." He was right, but I still couldn't laugh about it.

A few days later we got a big group of replacements—not forty, but maybe twenty. Captain Simmers decided to spread them over the company and make up a new Third Platoon with a few replacements plus some men from other platoons. First Platoon was to furnish one squad and the platoon sergeant. Monty Staton, our platoon guide, became the new platoon sergeant. He chose Ed and me as the scouts, but left George with First Platoon. Ray had decided to separate me from George because we were together too much. He called us "the Gold Dust Twins."

The next day, Monty Staton—no relation of the jeep driver Hoyt Staton—brought our new lieutenant around. I was on guard, sitting on top of the hedgerow, leaning against a tree, and singing "Elmer's

Tune": "What makes a lady of eighty go out on the loose? / What makes a gander meander in search of a goose?"

Staton said, "This is Standifer, first scout, Second Squad." I jumped down, saluted, and stuck out my hand to shake.

"Can you stand at attention, soldier?" Lieutenant Chilton was short, barrel-chested, and stern. I knew what he saw in me. He was wondering whether a kid like that could soldier. I towered over him like a beanpole. My jacket sleeves were two inches short, and one pants leg was out of my leggings—my pants were too short, but after one leg came out, the other seemed to stay in. I tried to think of something encouraging to say, but what was there? This was me. I *was* a kid.

I wanted to say, "Lieutenant, we aren't fighting with our fists. With an M-1 from one hundred yards, I can place eight rounds in a group small enough for you to cover with your first. That's from a prone position. I could do it standing if I could hold the rifle up." But I didn't.

Staton turned to Ed. "This is Blake, second scout." Ed was no improvement, a skinny boy a little shorter than me, and wearing thick glasses.

I can't give an unbiased account of Chilton. He might have been a good soldier; maybe we didn't give him a fair chance. But we resented this new man who wanted to make us soldier his way. We already knew a better way. He probably arrived with dreams of leading tough combat veterans, only to find that most of us were kids who made a game of war. He was shocked at us, and we would soon feel that way about him.

The reconstituted Third Platoon's first patrol was apparently intended as orientation for Chilton. The skeleton first and second squads totaled only about ten or twelve men. Second Squad included Ed, Gus Amato (the ex-tailor who had fitted my fatigues), and me from First Platoon, plus a buck sergeant and a BAR man from Second. Staton chose Ed and me as point scouts for the patrol, with Nance and Frye serving as flank scouts. Frye had been on the ambushed patrol and had escaped during the confusion of surrender. Nance, Third Platoon's best scout, had been returning from the hospital when the patrol went out. He had missed being on it by about an hour. I knew that Nance could soldier; I thought Frye could when he wanted to, but I trusted him as little as I did Lehrer. Generally, it was a good group of men for a patrol. Now we would find out whether Chilton could soldier.

Chilton's instructions were simple: "Okay, we're going to Locmaria along this route. Move out."

I asked what we were looking for and got a laconic reply: "Germans."

That wasn't enough information if I was to be point scout. I tried again: "Where do we go from there?"

"I'll tell you when we get to Locmaria."

A few hundred yards out, Chilton came up and chewed me out. "Don't be so damned slow. Are you scared of every bush?" Yes, I was scared of every bush, especially since I didn't know what we were looking for. I didn't hurry at all, and he got progressively madder.

At Locmaria, Ed and I passed through the village and set up as security on the far side. About thirty minutes later I went back. Everybody was lying on the ground resting. I asked where the lieutenant was. "He's over in that store liberating some wooden shoes." When I went into the shop, Chilton had a bag full of shoes that he was going to send home. There were no guards anywhere. Ed and I were the entire patrol security.

"Lieutenant, are Blake and I the only lookouts?"

"We don't need any. There aren't any Germans around."

"Lieutenant, I've worked this area five times and missed seeing a German patrol only once." That was impertinent and I shouldn't have said it, but he was risking our lives.

When we left Locmaria, the patrol had new scouts. Ed and I were at the end of the column. We were going through an apple orchard when—*Pe-twanng!*—a bullet ricocheted off the stone wall. I dropped down beside a tree and started looking around. Chilton said nothing. Westmoreland would have been calling to us to see where and how we were.

Ed asked, "Do you see anything, Leon?"

I couldn't see a thing. It wasn't a good ambush site, but somebody had fired on us. There was a hedgerow up on a ridge. One bush was large enough to hide a machine gun. Rifles would be along each side. We were in an apple orchard, and the tree branches would hide our movements to some degree. But when they started calling artillery, the shells would explode in the branches, showering us with shrapnel.

Ed needed a reply.

"The only place for a machine gun is on the high ground," I told him. "Chilton will have us lay down fire on it while we move forward."

But I was wrong. We just lay there getting scared. I thought, "Come on, you crazy cowboy, get us out of here. You gave them time to set this up while you were stealing shoes. If we don't get out of this orchard soon, Mama's going to get our insurance."

Ed said: "Damn this. Do something even if it's wrong." He fired a clip of ammunition at the possible machine gun.

"Cease fire back there! You can't see anything."

No. But I hoped the Germans didn't know it. Nothing more happened. The platoon lay there for about fifteen minutes, got up, and went on to our lines. I don't know why we were fired on or why the Germans didn't follow up. Chilton said there had been only one rifleman, who left after firing on us. What was a lone rifleman doing so far from his lines? German patrols usually consisted of anything from four men to about twenty. My best guess is that a patrol was watching us and one of them fired accidentally. Chilton's initiation into combat showed us how he was going to soldier: lie still and hope something good happens.

Ed and I were both enraged at Chilton for the mess he had made, but Ed was capable of more eloquent fury than I was: "I'm going to find a way to get that stupid, arrogant, incompetent fraud."

I remembered an old expression from Summey in Ninth Company: "Ed, you can't win a pissing contest with a skunk."

"He's too dense to understand the things I'm going to do, but it's for my own satisfaction—not to outpiss him."

While I was on guard one night the sky lit up for about two minutes. It looked like a big explosion behind the German lines, possibly near the airport, but I didn't hear a sound. The same thing happened about an hour later. Still no sound with it. I told Ed about it when he got up for the next shift. He saw two flashes at about the same one-hour intervals.

Those flashes from Lorient were the platoon's subject of gossip the next morning. The most popular explanation was that the Germans were blowing up ammunition in preparation for surrendering. I tried to argue that we should have heard something, but the others said it was too far away. Ed said nothing until he and I were alone. We decided that flares for some sort of practice in night assaults was the more likely cause. Ed thought it strange that most of the platoon wanted to believe the Germans were surrendering. "Within two weeks after a surrender, this division would be fighting in Germany, facing a life expectancy of four to five days. I'm satisfied to be fighting in a quiet sector."

Ed also wondered why nobody had thought of the more colorful explanation: that the Germans had started launching rocket bombs at England. The rockets could be delivered by submarines and fired from the big, bombproof submarine docking facility.

Ed was expanding on this when Chilton came up: "Lieutenant Chilton, could I talk with you privately for a minute?"

Ed came back from the conference with a big grin. His report to Chilton was that as a physics major at MIT, he had studied the construction of rockets such as the buzz bombs that Germany was dropping on London. He had been watching the patterns of light flashes made in Lorient during the night and was sure that the area was being used as a rocket launching site.

Ed and I giggled all that day about what a fool Chilton would make of himself by proposing such an idea to Simmers. The next morning a regimental intelligence officer drove right up to our front lines looking for Pfc Blake. This time Ed had pushed things too far. He was gone all day and I worried all day, but late that afternoon he came back with a bigger smile than ever. He had been driven straight to regimental headquarters for a conference with the artillery commander, General Fortier, along with several other high-ranking artillery officers. Ed's knowledge of artillery operations came entirely from the single afternoon of lecture and demonstration at Benning School for Boys, but he was a quick study. He asked to see aerial photographs of Lorient and for a briefing on the German artillery. Picking up on the jargon the artillery officers used, he asked some leading questions about how they thought Lorient might serve as a rocket launching base. He saw no logic in their ideas—the distances, angles, and fire missions didn't make sense—but he agreed that large rockets could be delivered to Lorient by submarines.

Finally, Professor Blake addressed the group: "Well, let's eat some lunch while I think about this." Regimental headquarters was located around a captured rest camp built for German submarine crews, and the artillerymen ate in the German officers' mess with white tablecloths, napkins, and china dishes. Ed, who had been living on C and K rations, ate steak and savored a cup of freshly brewed coffee, not something made by boiling water in a GI can.

After lunch he agreed with all of their assumptions about the rocket launchers but said that these suspicions should be verified before sending word up to corps headquarters. He gave assignments for one group to record the times at which rockets hit London on a specific night. Another group was to get the times and approximate locations of the light flashes in Lorient. They were also to contact a climatologist for wind velocity at various altitudes. The total of the data would show whether Lorient was the rocket site.

I was impressed. "Ed, if this works you'll be transferred to headquarters—and you may need an assistant."

"Leon, I was feeding them pure garbage. The information they already have says that Lorient isn't a site, and the data will reinforce it. I had no idea my joke would go beyond Simmers or possibly Battalion. Can you imagine such gullible men running this regiment?"

That is all I know about the Lorient rocket launchings. The artillery brass never called Ed back, but they didn't court-martial him either.

The patrols continued to be frightening, but they were generally uneventful. Occasionally we would see a German patrol, call artillery on them, and watch while they retreated with their wounded. Sometimes they would leave a seriously wounded man for us. We could carry him to the nearest road and call for a medical jeep. Badly wounded men were useless to the Germans. We had better hospital facilities and fed them well. But the arrangement had some flaws. On one patrol the flank scout stopped and yelled for me to call Chilton.

The lieutenant came roaring back. "What the hell do you want, Standifer?"

"The scout found something."

"Okay, you and Blake come along to cover me" When we got there, the scout was pointing to a long-dead German. His stomach was bloated, the stench was awful, and flies were crawling out of his mouth. Chilton reached into the man's jacket pocket, pulled out his wallet, took the money for himself, picked up the German rifle, and turned to leave.

I asked, "Lieutenant, what are we going to do with the body?"

"Hell, I don't care, let the Krauts bury him." (To be fair, I must add that Chilton reported the body and Graves Registration picked it up the next day.)

When the patrol stopped for a break, I walked up to see Ed and blow off steam. I was mad about the body, but also because Chilton was taking us too close to the German main defense line. The patrol had gone beyond two German outposts that I had seen when First Platoon had worked the area, and there was a machine-gun position up ahead of us. "Standifer, up front." I went up to where Chilton and Monty Staton were standing.

With no greeting at all, Chilton said: "There's a German on guard up there at about two hundred yards. Can you hit him?"

I looked through the binoculars and said, "Yes, sir, but it's more like three hundred yards. There's a swale in the land that you can't see from here. Why do you want to shoot him? He's sitting beside a machine gun, and they probably have a mortar."

Chilton was getting irritated. "I don't see a gun. Where is it?"

"That brush to the right is dead and isn't growing right. It's a good place for a gun; otherwise, why is he there?" I was playing Sergeant York with him, primarily for fun. I knew that Staton had suggested he call me because I had worked the area with Westmoreland a few weeks earlier. We had swung around to the side, where the swale, the gun, and the mortar were visible.

"Shoot the son of a bitch."

I had known that was coming. "Yes, sir, but we will need to move fast then, before the machine gun finds us." I didn't want to shoot him and didn't intend to. There wasn't any good reason for even wounding him, and I didn't want to stir them up. The smoke from my rifle was going to show for about a minute, which would be long enough for them to find us. But I wanted to shoot: after all we had gone through, I had yet to fire my rifle in combat. I set my elevation for three hundred yards, stretched out, aimed for the helmet sitting between the German and the machine gun, took a deep breath, disconnected my ears, and squeezed the trigger.

Chilton was watching through the binoculars. "Got 'im. Knocked him on his ass."

I knew I hadn't. I might have had the elevation wrong, but laterally I was dead center on the helmet. Both the helmet and the soldier were gone. I started backing off down the hill.

"Where are you going? There might be another one." There was. *Rrripp!* Machine-gun bullets cut the brush around us. Nobody was hit, but we moved out of there quickly.

After the patrol, I sat under my recovery tree and worried. As soon as the machine gunner had opened up, I knew I had goofed. If I had killed or even wounded him, there would have been a delay before anybody got on the gun. I had played the fool simply because I didn't like the lieutenant. Ed came over to deliver his lecture. Nobody else on the patrol knew what I had done, but Ed knew me. He had a standard tirade that I had heard several times. We were all victims caught in a war we didn't want to fight. That unsuspecting Kraut had been defenselesss, but when I scared him he jumped on the machine gun. Ed and I had been defenseless when I walked us up to that tool shed at le Hirgoat. We were all just as innocent and defenseless as the poor women and children who were being bombed.

Ed liked to tease me with: "Blessed are the peacemakers, for they shall be kicked in the ass by both sides." I agreed with him completely and knew I hadn't soldiered as I should have. I wanted to get back under Westmoreland. I would have killed the Kraut for him.

The Chilton conflict steadily worsened. Once, we found a German patrol of about fifteen men, obviously a foraging party, collecting apples, chickens, and a few vegetables. They were headed back toward Lorient. Chilton called artillery on them and ordered us to fire as they tried to retreat carrying their wounded. I saw no way to fake it. He was standing right behind us watching. I fired twice, aiming at legs. One shot was a clean hit: the German fell grabbing his thigh. The other was iffy—I may have missed him—but certainly not a serious wound. I was disgusted with Chilton and wondered what Westmoreland would have ordered. Shooting to kill was wrong, but wounding them made tactical sense.

Eventually, we got some replacements, bringing the platoon up to full strength. I was a little hestitant about the new men. They were probably good, but it would take awhile to learn who was dependable.

The polyglot that we called Second Squad was adequate and nothing more. The squad leader, from Second Platoon, wasn't very bright, but he was willing to follow leads from the rest of us. The BAR man was good, and Amato was dependable. The new men were scared. They didn't know whether we would soldier or why the Krauts had been able to whip our Third Platoon.

I tried to reassure them. "The lieutenant is a little too GI, but he's learning. We're pretty safe behind this hedgerow and back on the road. There isn't a very good line of fire in front of us, so you can walk up-right here where the brush is growing."

"How do you know it's safe?"

"I've been out where a German patrol would come up. You can see a little movement, but not enough to allow a shot."

"How can you sit around relaxed, reading books and singing? Don't you ever get scared?"

I had trouble with that. It was a good question because the right balance of relaxation and fear is fundamental to survival. "Sometimes I get scared," I admitted, "but I try not to. Relax and always be careful. Staying scared won't let you sleep or even rest. The Krauts hit without any warning. If you are tired, you can't react—and that can kill you." I wasn't quite satisfied with my answer. I still got scared on patrol, but I enjoyed the excitement. I finally had learned to be very careful, after having jumped over the snake three times. If I got killed now, it would be from bad luck, not from stupidity.

Betty had sent Ed a clipping from an editorial about workers strik-ing for higher wages in defense plants. The editor was outraged and said that those shirkers should be drafted and immediately sent to the front lines as riflemen. Ed just groaned. "Nothing has changed. Every-body still looks on the infantry as a garbage heap. Does he think that when I'm pinned down by a machine gun I want to have men like Lehrer as my only support?" After two months in combat, Lehrer had done nothing to change our opinion of him. He was still obnoxious, although a lot quieter. Patrols terrified him, probably because he knew that if he got into trouble no one would want to help him out. I re-membered Service again: "Ye would send me the spawn of your gut-ters—Go! take back your spawn again."

Ed was improving a little, both in his attitude toward the army and

*"Straighten those shoulders! How long you been in the army?"*

in his sense of belonging to the squad. During training and early in combat, I had wondered if he would be reliable under fire. We hadn't seen any real combat stress except for occasional rifle fire and light artillery, but Ed was solid. He still hated the army, killing, mud, and incompetence, but he was ready to carry his share of the load. Ed would not have admitted it, but he loved the squad; I had no idea how vulnerable that love made him.

When we were the company reserve platoon, an officer from regiment came down to visit with the troops. He was standing beside the road while the squad moved out for a patrol. He stopped the column and walked up to me. "Soldier, take that German grenade out of your belt. It makes us look like scavengers. Don't you have any hand grenades?"

What? Even Chilton wasn't that bad. I looked at him and thought, You stupid bastard. I'm proud of the way I look and don't care what you think. The Krauts know how we soldier and they are scared to face us. I'm a scout. For two months I've been out there where one mistake can kill me and the entire patrol. We are still alive because I know what I'm doing. You are up here shining your ass in a reserve area because you don't have the guts to go where the fighting is.

But I handed him the grenade and said, "Yes, sir, I've got a grenade in each pocket of my jacket." He could see the bulges but couldn't tell that they were German assault grenades—concussion grenades a little smaller and much lighter than the chunky American fragmentation grenades. Losing the potato masher didn't matter much to me. I would get another one from the next prisoner we took.

When we went back on battalion reserve, things continued as if the Third Platoon fiasco hadn't happened. We ate, slept, and wandered around. I was looking for rabbit skins to replace the blanket liners that I used in my overshoes for guard duty on cold nights. I went to farmhouses asking for skins of *le lapin*. Some of the women smiled at the request, but that didn't bother me. I wanted the skins and had cigarettes to trade for them.

I was walking down the road when I heard a shout. "Eh, Babee!" I hadn't see Emile since I left First Platoon. He had been assigned to a French army unit that our side was organizing. He didn't have a uniform but thought they would give him one soon. "Eh, I got some good wine. I get you tonight and we go to café, drink, eat, play with the girls! You bring some cigarettes." I am writing this as if he spoke broken English by now. Actually, we were speaking my broken French. Emile was speaking slowly and selecting simple words that I could understand.

He came by the camp just before dark. "Emile, you go down the road and wait. I can meet you there as soon as it gets dark." We could wander around during the day but were supposed to stay put after dark. "Ed, I'm going to town with Emile. Cover for me if somebody starts looking." I filled my jacket pockets with cigarettes and drifted off down the road. We went to a café on the edge of Rédéne. There was no one else in it except the waitress.

Emile blustered and bragged. "Yvette, this is Babee, he is good soldier—kills the Boche. Babee lion. Get my wine, we eat." With Emile, "eat" usually meant a loaf of bread, which cost a pack of (my) cigarettes. Yvette brought wine, bread, and bowls of thin soup. "See, we eat." We finished the soup and she brought some kind of dumplings. They tasted good but were a little shy of meat. Still, there was some. It wasn't chicken, must be rabbit.

"Emile, c'est bon. Lapin?" He and Yvette laughed. "Non, non. C'est bon."

Sure it was good, but what was it? "Qu'est-ce que c'est?"

He laughed again. "C'est le bon chat."

I didn't know the word. It sounded like *chan*. *Bonne chance* was "good luck," but that didn't make sense. Emile c'est par lapin?" My French was makeshift and I wasn't sure he understood me.

"Non, non. Yvette, come over and show Babee your lapin." She laughed so hard she just stood there and shook. They had a joke hidden somewhere, but I couldn't see it. Words with double meanings caused problems. I wondered what I had been saying at the farmhouses when I asked the women if they had rabbit skins that I could buy.

It was a good joke after I figured it out. We laughed awhile, and Emile told me how to spell *chat,* but not what it was. We finished our meal, drank the wine, and teased Yvette. Emile was feeling fine. "Eh, Babee, you want to take Yvette upstairs? She's scared of me. Do anything I tell her. If she doesn't, I tell people she used to sleep with the Boche."

Yvette laughed and screamed that she only went to some dances in Plouay.

Take Yvette upstairs. I remembered the sex sermons. Her attraction was pure *erōs*, but it wasn't as if I had nothing to give. She wanted my cigarettes. I decided not to go, but it wasn't like Sir Gawain passing the first test. Maybe my body was the temple of God, but it had taken such a beating lately that a little more abuse wouldn't matter. If I were to go, though, Emile would tell the squad about Babee and Yvette. Emile would do more than that. He would exaggerate and lie. I changed the subject by asking why Yvette went to the Boche dances. It seemed that the Germans had a rest camp there for the submarine crews returning from missions. The camp would round up girls for big dances, which turned into drunken brawls. Yvette said, "You don't go, they shoot you." We joked a little more, finished the wine, and went back to camp. I gave Emile the rest of my cigarettes. We were issued five packs a week, and I only used them for trading.

The next morning I asked Ed what *chat* meant. "I think it means 'cat,' but I'll look it up. Yes, it means cat. Why?"

"Oh, Emile was talking about it last night. Just wait until I tell you what else *lapin* means!"

About the middle of November, a Red Cross officer arranged a prisoner exchange with Lorient. The Germans had seventy-one American prisoners they were having to feed from their own very short rations. Besides the thirty-nine from Third Platoon, there were a few others from our regiment and a scattering of men from the Sixth Armored. With Third Platoon back again, Captain Simmers returned the rest of us to our old platoons, except for Monty Staton. Monty had to stay with the Third because their original platoon sergeant had refused to rejoin the company. The Geneva Convention said that exchanged prisoners could not be required to fight against the same enemy. He could be sent to fight Japanese, but not Germans.

Lieutenant Chilton gave a farewell lecture to those of us returning to our old platoons, saying essentially that he appreciated our help. "And I believe some of you have learned a little more about soldiering." He was looking directly at me and Ed.

I returned his look. "Yes, sir, I know I won't forget what you have taught me." I thought, Though you've belted me and flayed me, by the living God that made me, I'm a better man than you are, Lieutenant Chilton. He would not have recognized the Kipling, but he knew I was glad to get away and he was glad to see me going.

# 12  War's Desolation

During October we gradually came to understand that there would be no assault on Lorient. Brest had surrendered after weeks of intense fighting—and after the Germans had blown up the entire port area. The same thing would happen at Lorient, but we couldn't just walk off and leave 25,000 German soldiers. On the other hand, if they were to surrender, we would be transferred to fight in Germany, where a rifleman's life expectancy was about one week. Scouts and BAR men didn't last nearly that long.

We were being shelled and shot at nearly every day, but with caution and luck I would get through the war without a wound. I was satisfied to stay around Lorient, rather than being fed into the meatgrinder of riflemen fighting at the German border. Still, I could imagine questions in Clinton after the war. Where did you serve, Leon?" "I was first scout in an infantry company." Where? "Playing nursemaid to 25,000 Germans at a lonely submarine base on the Atlantic coast."

"War's desolation" took on a new meaning: wet, cold, isolated, dismal. Lorient is at about the same latitude as Duluth, Minnesota, but the cold weather is moderated by the Gulf Stream. "Moderated" means that when France begins to get cold in November, the moist ocean air turns into cold rain—or from light mist to drizzle to downpour and back to weak lifeless sunlight during the three to four hours of a patrol. We never had frost in the morning, but the low temperatures must have ranged in the thirties and forties. The cold wind cut through wool shirts and long underwear, especially if they were damp, which they were. We had no way to get clothes dry. There was a mobile laundry unit that would wash and dry our clothes while we were taking hot showers, but both the laundry and the hot showers were available only while we were the reserve company. On line we stayed wet, muddy, and smelly. Our feet were always wet and cold. When the replacements had come in, we had envied them for the new "combat boots" with which the army had outfitted them: the rough leather finish would never require polish, and some short leather straps served the purpose of leggings. As it turned out, though, the rough leather sucked up water faster than our smooth finish did, and not having to wear leggings wasn't enough compensation for wetter feet.

My Winchester was clean and had no rust spots, but the beautiful stock was showing stress. I washed it regularly and rubbed in linseed oil as well as I could. The stock had one bad scar where I had dug out a bit of shrapnel; I couldn't remember how it got there. There were scratches from brush, and dents from hitting stones in the hedgerows. The rifle was showing the effects of combat. I didn't look all that good either: scratches and dents—but so far, no shrapnel scars.

Letters from home were beginning to bother me. The Sunday school class had a project of writing a joint letter to one serviceman each week. My turn came about once a month. Because I was the only one in combat, the letters were pretty soupy. "Every day we pray that the Lord will protect you from any harm." Stupid, if the Lord really wanted to help, he would end the war.

My aunts wrote regularly, telling me how worried they were about my health, mental and physical. I could imagine what they were saying to Mother. Atley wrote an occasional pompous letter, building my morale. Bob's letters were good; he knew me. But I was worried for him. When I had gone into combat, he had resigned from flight training and entered gunnery school. Learning to fly took too long; he wanted to fight. I wanted to say, "Bob, stay out of this mess." But maybe air combat wasn't as bad. Shooting a man isn't as much of a shock as seeing the result, a three-day-old corpse.

The best letters were from Charlene Barge. I don't think we had ever dated. She lived in Jackson but occasionally spent the weekend with a friend in Clinton. We were BYPU buddies. Charlene's religion was much more conservative than mine, but she was sharp and defended her concepts well. Her letters to me were really just notes: "I saw this card and thought of you," or, "Hang in there, Leon, we know it's rough!" My letters to her were pretty light too: "Thanks for the note. It's cold and wet here—pretty miserable, but I will make it."

I never really lied to anyone in letters, but there was no way to describe our life: miserable, dull, and terrifying, but not awful—yet.

During October we built log-reinforced dugouts, with small makeshift stoves; these rough shelters were our sleeping quarters, but they leaked and were cramped when four men huddled in them on rainy days. Light for writing letters came from German "assault candles"—small cardboard dishes filled with wax. The wick was supported by a porous ceramic disk. We routinely searched all German prisoners for candles and writing paper. We envied their warm, waterproof boots, which were good for standing guard on cold nights. Two boys in Second Platoon had sent some prisoners back barefooted, but only once. The wrath of Captain Simmers fell heavily upon them.

The only reliable sources for German boots were the dead bodies and seriously wounded men we found on patrol. Standard procedure for dealing with wounded Germans was to bandage their wounds (their bandages, but our sulfa powder because they didn't have any), steal their boots, and tell them, "Doctor come *schnell*." But *schnell* really meant "when word gets back to the regimental medical company and they find a medical jeep to send up." Corpses required special care. Before taking anything from a dead man, it was good to tie a tent rope to his leg and pull, he might be booby-trapped. I had recovered from my shock at robbing dead German bodies. Either we stripped them or Graves Registration would. Nobody was going to waste valuable equipment in a grave. I didn't have any German boots because I couldn't find a Kraut with big feet. It didn't really matter, though: I had lined my overshoes with rabbit skins and wore them at night without shoes.

Even with warm feet, night guard duty was boredom and misery. If I moved my head the wrong way, cold rain would drip down my neck and beneath my raincoat, which didn't fit anyhow—the sleeves were too short and the bottom hit above my knees, dripping water down my pants. To stay awake, I worked hard at remembering poems. *Thanatopsis* didn't fit at all. Nature wasn't lovable; she was cold and wet. Service's tales of the Yukon seemed to work well; from a quarter of the way around the world, Miss Williams looked down her nose at

*"Joe, yestiddy ya saved my life an' I swore I'd pay ya back.*
*Here's my last pair of dry socks."*

me: "Leon, Service's poems are graphic and simple. They offer nothing of lasting value." Well, right now I'm graphic and simple, and I may not last myself. Sometimes I even added my own words to Service's:

Were you ever out in the Great Alone, when the moon was awful clear,
And the icy hedgerows hemmed you in with a silence you most could *hear;*

With only the howl of a hungry dog, and you huddled there in the cold,
A half-dead thing in a stark, dead world, clean mad in this game called war.

Ed and I liked to paraphrase another verse from "The Shooting of Dan McGrew" when one of us crawled back into the warm, friendly dugout after standing guard for two hours in the cold rain:

When out of the night, which was fifty below, and into the din and glare,
There stumbled a rifleman fresh from the line, dog-dirty and mean as a bear.

Everyone laughed at the first few recitations. Then it got a little stale, but Ed and I needed that kind of poetry to break the monotony—and the tension.

The return of Third Platoon gave us a broader picture of the ambush. It had been planned at least a week in advance and was apparently a graduation exercise for a group of German support troops who had been taking infantry training. There was good evidence that an FFI colonel had helped to set it up; gossip said that he was a priest from Quimperlé, but gossip also said that an American officer in battalion had cooperated. The latter was clearly wrong; looking back, I see that the man often used poor judgment, but he was dedicated and loyal. Third Platoon had been told that two hundred Germans wanted to surrender because they were so hungry. The Germans were to be at the foot of the Cap Kerdudal hill. Our patrol, located on high ground, was to fire a few shots and demand a surrender. When they got to Cap Kerdudal, there was nobody to be seen. Lieutenant Devonald radioed back to Battalion G-2:

"There's nobody here. Should we wait?"

"No, they are coming from St.-Michel. Turn left and go up the road to meet them."

The patrol abandoned their high-ground advantage and lined up on the St.-Michel road. Richards was on one side of the road, with Button on the other, when he walked into the machine gun. Then everything was quiet until the medic went up to look at Richards—and all hell broke loose. There were 370 Germans on the hills around them. Some had been hiding in Cap Kerdudal (where Dyer was trapped and killed), others were on the hill behind the patrol, still others on the twin slope in front.

After about thirty minutes the Germans began an assault down the slope from Cap Kerdudal. Third Platoon held its fire until the assault line was about fifty yards away, then each man delivered a full clip— eight rounds—of well-aimed fire. The volley dropped about half of the attackers, and the rest fled in panic. A little later the procedure was repeated by a group wearing the colorful uniforms of Kriegsmarinein- fanterie; they behaved even worse than the first bunch. After one more attempt, the Germans settled in for a siege, using artillery and ma- chine-gun fire to keep Third Platoon pinned down. The platoon fought well, but it was nothing heroic. With their poor position, the first assault would have overwhelmed them if the Germans hadn't pan- icked. The graduation exercise was a complete failure, but persistence paid off: ultimately, Third Platoon ran out of ammunition—and they certainly weren't ready to try using fixed bayonets against machine- gun bullets.

After destroying their radio and weapons, the platoon raised a white handkerchief and quit. Nervous, excited soldiers searched them, taking only cigarettes and K rations. The Krauts were so disorganized that Casey Frye slipped into an empty house and escaped. German medics treated the badly wounded and got litter bearers to take them up the road to St.-Michel, where horse-drawn wagons were waiting. The rest of the platoon walked to the edge of Guidel and were told to halt beside a long, freshly-dug trench. Visions of mass murder sub- sided when they were ordered into the schoolhouse for the night. There were blankets, water, and one apple for each man. Breakfast was a slice of bread and a hot cup of a bitter substance that was called "ersatz coffee." Then the prisoners were marched to Lorient, where clusters of French civilians watched with impassive faces as the Ameri- cans walked along a corridor of ruined buildings. The guards made sure our boys knew that we had destroyed Lorient but had hardly scratched the well-built submarine pens.

Interrogation was simple, individual, and short. Oberleutnant Al- fons Schmitt spoke excellent English because he had a degree from Oxford. "I want only your name, rank, and serial number. You are from the Third Platoon of K Company, 301st Infantry. Your company is holding the area from Cadic to just beyond Kerdudal, but you are the reserve platoon. Your Captain Simmers is known as the best company commander in the regiment. I can't imagine why he would agree to such a stupid patrol. You fought well in a hopeless situation." Occasionally, he would recognize an accent and guess at the home state. He said that food would be a difficult adjustment, but they would be getting the same rations as those of the guards, plus occasional food supplements from the Red Cross. He asked about GI rations on line, and if the prisoner responded, Schmitt would ask about food at home, in camp, and something about training. Individually he got very little information, but collectively he probably learned all he wanted, or all they knew—which wasn't much.

Schmitt was the only reasonable officer they met, and he was probably putting on an act. Under the Geneva Convention, the German command was supposed to furnish the Red Cross with a complete list of prisoners. In fact, the Red Cross representative was only told about the ones who were wounded badly enough to be hospitalized. Those men were given Red Cross food packages and allowed to write to their families. The others simply did not exist. The army was only able to tell their families that they were missing in action and might be prisoners. The unwounded and walking wounded were loaded onto a small boat headed for the Ile de Groix, about five miles off the coast. The sea was rough, and all eight guards became seasick, their rifles lying on the deck while the miserable men hung over the rail. Several Americans were not sick, but no one thought of capturing the boat.

After docking, the prisoners were marched through the town of Groix and up to Fort Surville, a seventeenth-century structure built on the island for protection from British warships. The old cannons had never been fired. Located on the highest point of the island, the fort was being used for some kind of electronic surveillance. The commander had agreed to take the prisoners but would not have his highly trained men serving as guards. That was why the Lorient command had furnished eight guards from a rifle company; it was also why the guards were continually plotting with the prisoners against the local commander. Third Platoon had earned the respect of German combat troops: ambushed and outnumbered nine to one, they had held off massive attacks. The fact that they had killed nearly a hundred German soldiers didn't seem to matter—war is war.

The guards and prisoners were rationed to a slice of bread and a cup of probably "ersatz" cabbage soup per day. The only difference was that the guards got their soup last, because the "cabbage" leaves settled to the bottom. During the day there were minor work details in the fort, but nobody worked very hard. Every night the guards stacked their rifles in the corner of the room and played cards with the prisoners. Once a week they all marched down to Groix to watch a German movie. French civilians would slip bread, fruit, and vegetables to the prisoners, who would hide the food in their trousers. Back at the fort they would all share equally with the guards.

Conversation with the guards was not difficult. Two of them spoke English, and several of the prisoners spoke some German—they had grown up in German American communities. Discussions usually centered on dreams of food back home, but occasionally the men talked war. The dominant German attitude was that the German army was falling back to regroup. Hitler had a new weapon ready to use in a massive counteroffensive. When the counterattack came, the troops in Lorient would break out, heading for fuel depots and POW camps. Within days the American forces would be fragmented and attacked from all sides.

A few of the Germans may have believed that, but the discussions brought out a more realistic point. There was a new German law under which the family of a deserter could be punished for his offense. If a soldier were to surrender under strange circumstances, the commander could contact Germany by radio, and the next day the man's entire family would be in a concentration camp. Did the guards believe in ultimate victory, or were they afraid to sound pessimistic? Regardless of the reasons, it now seemed certain that Lorient was not going to surrender. The Ninety-fourth would be here when the war ended.

When Ed and I returned to First Platoon, we found that George had been moved to first scout and one of the new men had taken his BAR. Westmoreland put me as second scout behind George. My letter home about the move doesn't show any resentment. I had a big ego about my ability as scout, but George was at least as good. We would make a great team, the best pair of bird dogs in the battalion. We didn't pull a single patrol together. One week later the entire battalion was pulled off line and replaced by French troops who had been training nearby. We pulled back twenty-five miles, near regimental headquarters on the edge of Plouay. It was so far back that we could build fires at night. We pulled off our clothes when we slept.

We were given a full day in Quimper, a large city about forty miles away. The army, in its wisdom, decided to let us go in on Monday, the day when virtually every store was closed—in France, Sunday is a religious day, but Monday is the day of rest. Only a few shops and the cafés were open. Maybe the army was right. For three months, the largest town we had seen consisted of eight deserted houses. Did they want to release a rifle company with pockets full of money, cigarettes, and candy on a regular business day? Ed, George, and I walked the streets and tried to sing "The Yellow Rose of Texas" in French, or rather Breton-French. Some French kids were playing basketball at an outdoor court. George wondered if they would let us play. He was remembering his days on the Mount Sterling team that had won the state championship. I ran toward the court calling for them to throw me the ball. I grabbed it, went up for a crip shot, and missed. George came roaring behind me. I passed the ball to him. He shot and missed. Ed came running up, caught the rebound, shot, and missed. The three of us kept running down the street.

Ed decided that we should have crêpes suzette for lunch but didn't know where to find that kind of café. We stopped a man on the street and Ed began asking for directions.

"Young man, you are speaking the best combination of high school French and Breton slang I have heard all day, but let's use English so your friends can understand it." That was a good suggestion because I usually understood about half of Ed's French and George had no ear for language at all. The man had been Standard Oil's regional representative before the war and had recently reestablished the connection—although he hadn't received any pay since the war began. He offered to take us to a good place, and we asked him to join us for lunch.

The small shop was full of Americans, all officers. A light colonel looked as if he felt we were invading the officers' club. Ed threw him a salute and gave a long French greeting, knowing that the man understood not a word of it and would always wonder if (1) he had been insulted, and (2) we were Americans or FFI.

Our French friend (I have no idea what his name was) helped us to order and started a conversation that I now see had been his original purpose for going with us. He had heard that the army was having problems with informants for the Germans; he wanted to explain the French side. Although Brittany was glad to see the war ending and generally liked Americans, our presence wasn't precisely regarded as a liberation. The Germans had brought Brittany out of economic depression by building the big submarine bases and fortifications all along the coast. They paid good wages and were good customers at the restaurants. Lorient had been destroyed by American bombers, not Germans.

"I have no evidence," he said, "but it seems logical that the German army planned for the invasion by scattering French informants over the countryside, and particularly in the FFI. I can't understand why your officers didn't realize that." Ed told him about the Third Platoon ambush and said that he thought the army was beginning to catch on.

The next day word was out that we were going to repay the Germans for the Third Platoon ambush. "Kick ass and take names!" Westmoreland took us into a big tent with a sandbox in the middle of it. It was just like the sandboxes they had at Benning, but this time it meant business. There was the ocean, the bay of the Etel River, and a hill overlooking the bay. Those strange little knobs were fortified bunkers. The big one was going to be ours. It had a large artillery gun pointing into the bay, and a machine gun covering the direction from which we would attack. The engineers would clear a path through the minefield. We would approach along a little path with a stone wall on each side, then wait. At exactly 8:23 A.M. (when it was just getting light) a ten-minute artillery barrage would hit. When it lifted, we would crawl up to the bunker with explosive charges and blow the door. The Germans would then surrender. Ed said, "But the Germans promised to surrender at Cap Kerdudal."

A flare would signal the lifting of the barrage, but we were to stay in position until Westmoreland motioned us up for the assault, because the artillery and machine guns might not stop precisely when the flare went up. After Westmoreland's signal, we would have about thirty minutes to take the bunker, leave some of our people in it, and get off the hill before the German artillery started hitting back. We wondered who knew how long it took the Germans to adjust their artillery and whether they had already registered in the area. We didn't ask because Ed's joke hadn't gone over very well.

After the orientation, Sergeant Monti came by asking if we had seen H. R. He had bought a bottle of something in Quimper and disappeared during the night. "Don't worry about H. R. The French will bring him back." Monti could easily cover up a day's absence by H. R. while we were in reserve, but being absent during an attack was desertion. H. R. didn't turn up, and we never knew what became of him. Brave, loyal H. R. is recorded as the only deserter King Company ever had, but he spoke no French and had no idea where he was.

That afternoon Simmers took a group over to look at the positions we were to attack. I suppose each platoon sent their platoon leader, platoon sergeant, and a scout. Westmoreland, Monti, and George were the First Platoon group. They went to the second floor of a house about two hundred yards from the German position and stood well back from the window. A German sniper fired one shot. The Second Platoon scout slumped to the floor with a bullet hole squarely in his forehead. He couldn't have been spotted accidentally; somehow the Germans had known we were coming. It might have been an easy attack if we had surprise, but not now. If the German commander had any sense at all, he would alert the artillery early every morning (the only time when we could slip up close enough to attack) so that they could start shelling us as soon as our machine guns and artillery began. We would be so close that we could take the bunker in spite of the artillery, but the casualties would be awful.

George and I hadn't discussed death since Holly Springs, but the time had come. We tried to adopt a Shakespearean attitude: by our troths, we cared not—we owed God a death. Well, the debt was there, but I would like to apply for a little extension on the time. "For he today that sheds his blood with me shall be my brother." Phrases that sounded so brave a year ago had become empty. George and I had seen death, and it was ugly. I remembered the dead Kraut with flies crawling out of his mouth, the sick feeling of realizing Dale was gone. I knew the terror of suddenly being fired on and hearing the sharp whine of the bullet as it ricocheted from a stone. The only thought left was Frost: "For I have promises to keep." No matter what happened tomorrow, George and I would soldier. Courage is doing your duty despite fear.

We were to leave on the night of December 7 and attack the next morning. That afternoon we made light combat packs and started checking our equipment. "Mass for Catholics and Communion for

Protestants at 1600." Baptists believed in closed Communion (you can't take it unless you are a member of that congregation), but George wanted to go, so I went with him. There was a short sermon on something like "Yea, though I walk through the valley," then a liturgy on confession of sins: "We have not loved thee as we should, we have not loved our neighbors as ourselves."

But tomorrow we will throw grenades into our neighbors' bunkers, blowing them into shreds of bloody flesh.

Finally, we came to something I knew: partaking of the bread and wine. When the wine hit my mouth I almost choked. In Clinton, the "wine" had always been grape juice.

Communion didn't help me much. Later, God and I had a short prayer. God doesn't deal in bicycles, A's in school, or protection from bullets. "I hope to go through the attack safely but thy will be done. I ask for the courage and strength to do my duty."

Sir Gawain had failed the third test, but I was passing. Maybe. It wasn't that I was refusing the protective talisman. I didn't think it was being offered. I was scared—terrified—but again I told myself that courage meant doing what had to be done despite being afraid. I stripped my rifle down, cleaned and oiled it. I had twenty clips of ammunition, 160 rounds. I dismantled each clip, wiped and oiled every cartridge. I started oiling my bayonet. Leon, what are you doing? Do you think we are going to attack with fixed bayonets? The equipment is ready; quit worrying.

Then I wrote my letter. It had become a ritual for George, Ed, and me to write home before every patrol. Censorship wouldn't let us even hint at what was coming up, and there was only a small possibility that these letters really would be our last. I didn't want to be too emotional but needed to say that I loved my family and my country. I was uncomfortable and frequently scared, but proud to be a line soldier. I wanted them to know that George and Ed were still with me. Problems were easier to face when I could discuss them with friends.

George had to leave just before dark because he had been assigned to follow the engineers as they cleared the minefield. Then he would crawl up close to the bunker and listen. If the noise of our setting up for the attack alerted the Germans, he would come back and warn us. Otherwise, he would return about an hour before daylight and lead us into the assault position. Saying good-bye was awkward. We were going to fight at the same place, but not together. We couldn't hug each other because Ray already suspected we were queer. Finally George said: "Be careful. I'll see you after we take the bunker."

On the way back to our tent I stopped to see Ed, who was sitting alone reading his little *Prophet* book. I knew he needed to talk. I knew he was lonesome and scared. We had been close in Third Platoon, but I had nearly deserted him for George. "A friend is your needs answered." I knew his needs and had no answers. I hadn't been able to help George or myself.

We both sat for awhile before Ed said, "Leon, we are going to get clobbered tomorrow."

He shouldn't look at it that way. "It's going to be rough but we'll take the thing," I told him. "You and I are so lucky we probably won't even get hit. How many times do you suppose the Krauts have shot at us and missed?"

He saw through my argument. "That doesn't make any sense. The Krauts are terrible shots and it wasn't luck, just pure random chance. Anyhow, this is going to be an artillery barrage tomorrow."

Ed was right. Tomorrow we would get clobbered. "We'll make it, Ed. I'll see you after we take the bunker."

But I didn't. I saw him for an instant in the morning and got a letter from him a few months later, but our little talk in the tent was our last personal contact. What would I have said to Ed if I had known we were saying good-bye? He was as close as a brother and I loved him deeply—not despite what I felt were his faults and quirky ways, nor even because of them. I loved the entire man: his sensitivity, integrity, humor, insights, and profound loyalty. "Greater love hath no man than this."

People were gathering around a fire in the company street, and someone was playing a guitar. We began with western songs because that's what the guitarist knew how to play, but we weren't in the proper quiet, lazy mood. For three months we had been under defensive orders, knowing we could outsoldier any Kraut who ever lived. They had humiliated us at Cap Kerdudal, but tomorrow we would get revenge.

Ray and De Rosa began to bellow out, "Praise the Lord and pass the ammunition, / Praise the Lord, we're not a'goin' fishin'."

We rolled into Fort Benning songs: "The infantry, the infantry, with dirt behind their ears, / Can lick their weight in wildcats and drink their weight in beers."

It began to sound very much like a pep rally. I have wondered to what extent Simmers engineered it.

Someone tried to get us into "Remember Pearl Harbor," but it didn't work with me. I remembered Proctor, Button, Richards, and Dyer. I was ready. This was my family. Tomorrow we would fight. Nobody would whip King Company.

At 10 o'clock the cooks served us hot coffee and jam sandwiches. I wouldn't eat again for thirty-six hours. When we loaded on the truck, everybody was still a little nervous. "Ray, is this trip really necessary?" "Aw, shut up, Prado." We started a little parody about being "Graziano's rag-tag band," but it was halfhearted. We had been tense and nervous all day. Now we were tired and went to sleep. I woke up when we started unloading on the edge of the town of Etel at about two in the morning. Everybody else had arrived before the infantry. Cannon Company—the regimental light artillery and heavy machine gun company—had their guns in place. There were heavy machine guns everywhere. Officers were running around as if they were lost. People were stringing communications wires. French civilians were being hustled out of their houses and onto a truck. The noise was awful. How could we surprise the Germans? The idea was to get the noisy things in place, and if that didn't alert the Germans, the infantry would move in. I'm not sure the logic was good, but it worked.

The Queen of Battle sat by the side of the road and leaned against the stone buildings. It was a cold, cloudy night with the moon showing through occasionally and a bitter wind blowing off the Atlantic. We were still a little sleepy, huddling in our overcoats with wool caps pulled over our ears. "Take out your bayonets and move up." I thought, "When you come up, come up a'growlin'." I also remembered, "Fight fiercely, fellows." Surely we weren't going to attack the bunker with fixed bayonets? No. They couldn't find George, and we were going to have to clear our own path over the minefield by probing with bayonets. Lying in the hot, sandy soil of Fort Benning, you learned to push the bayonet at an angle until it hit metal. Don't probe straight down or the mine will detonate. When you find a mine, mark it with a ribbon and move on. Crawling on the wet, cold, sandy soil at Etel, it

*"I can't git no lower, Willie. Me buttons is in th' way."*

wasn't going to be much fun. Then word was passed back to replace
our bayonets. George and the engineers had just come back through
the field.

A column of very quiet men slipped through the minefield, climbed
the stone wall, and crawled up the path. It was so dark that we could
have walked, but Westmoreland was always careful. I don't know
what the others did, but First Platoon crawled. I was calm and careful,

but not frightened or excited. It was an easy operation and we were going to surprise the Krauts. I could hardly see the man in front of me. The wind was cold, my knees were wet, and the rifle wouldn't stay in place on my shoulder. I got to my position, sat with my back against the wall, and waited for daylight. It started getting fairly light around 8 o'clock. We still had twenty minutes, so I pulled my helmet off and peered over the wall. The thing was right at us, maybe twenty yards away, a huge gray monster covered with a camouflage net. The machine gun was pointing down my throat. The big coastal gun was on the other side, overlooking the bay. Standing on top of the bunker was a cold, miserable German soldier. He had his rifle slung, was stamping his feet and swinging his arms to keep warm. His relief was probably inside having a cup of coffee. I wondered how much longer his shift lasted. Obviously, the Germans didn't all have to get on line at daylight.

At eight twenty I pulled off my coat, checked my ammunition, and released the trigger lock. At eight twenty-three the world exploded. Artillery, antitank guns, and heavy machine guns were firing at the bunker. Tracer bullets started coming over my head from both directions. The gunner in the bunker was firing back. Well, he was through drinking his coffee.

Only every fifth bullet in a machine-gun belt is a burning tracer showing the gunner where he is shooting. Somebody lowered his aim a little and the bullets started hitting the stone wall. Tracers were bouncing all around me, with four times as many nontracers whistling among them. I knew it wouldn't be long before some of them found me. I thought, I'm going to die in this wet dismal place. As I began crawling away, a burning sensation hit my right arm, then my leg started burning. I moved beyond the tracers and wasn't in any pain except for a stinging sensation. I could feel warm blood running down my leg.

The flare went up. Another artillery shell or two hit, then most of the noise stopped. "Forward, let's go!" That was Westmoreland. I grabbed my rifle and couldn't hold it. My left leg worked, but not well. Ed passed me and yelled, "Medic! Standifer's down."

Down? I was never up. The medic was just behind Ed. He cut the cloth away and bandaged my leg. "Can I go now?" I asked. He shook his head. "I don't think so. You can't hold a rifle, and I don't think you can walk. We'll pick you and Herrington up on the way down. He has a bad shrapnel wound and may lose his leg." I lay there listening to the fight, hoping we had surprised the Germans, that we could take the bunker in 30 minutes, and that somebody could help me off the hill before the shelling started.

*Whaloom!* The satchel explosive charge had blown the door—I hoped. A couple of hand grenades went off, there was a little rifle fire, and the platoon came back. "Come on, Standifer, let's get out of here." With one man on each side of me, we stumbled down the slope and were crossing the path in the minefield when the German shells started dropping around the bunker we had taken.

# 13  The South's Incarnate Pride

Simmers was waiting by the jeep when we got across the minefield. "Standifer, the Krauts haven't been able to hit you for three months and you let one machine gun take you out. Hell, you need a drink." Boy, did I need a drink! I grabbed the whiskey bottle and began guzzling. It was my first taste of whiskey, but it sure hit the spot.

Simmers laughed. "I said a drink, not the whole bottle."

The jeep took me to an aid station a few miles away. I felt great—maybe a little woozy, but we had hit the Krauts hard. We really showed them how it's done. Nobody could whip King Company. The machine gun hadn't scared me at all. The hospital was going to be great. I needed a rest after three months on line.

George was at the aid station, pale and quiet. He was holding his helmet, which had a big dent in it.

"George, what happened to you?"

"Mortar shell." It had landed near him, hurt his back, and thrown a stone that dented his helmet.

"Man, isn't it great to be wounded?" Not a word from George.

The medics put me on a stretcher and started giving me blood plasma in both arms. "These noisy cases of shock worry me," one of them said. "I prefer the quiet ones." I knew he was talking about me, but he was wrong. I wasn't in shock. I was just happy—maybe a bit drunk. From the aid station I went to a field hospital. They gave me a shot. I passed out and woke up the next morning. I had slept all afternoon and all night. I was sore and hungry and couldn't use my right hand at all. My left leg was bound in splints to keep it straight.

A nurse came by to see if I was ready for breakfast. She said that I had no broken bones, but two bullet fragments were still in my arm. A tracer had shattered when it hit me. They had removed the largest piece, but the others were too deep for easy removal. She laughed when I pointed out that I was tough enough to shatter bullets. The tracer was a ricochet, and the stone wall had already cracked it. The one that hit my leg had made a mess coming out. The hamstring muscle was damaged, but not completely cut. I should be walking in about two weeks and out of the hospital in a month. My parents had been notified by a telegram specifying that I was only slightly wounded.

Captain Simmers came by to visit his wounded. Herrington was in the next tent with a broken leg from that shrapnel wound. Ray had been wounded, but apparently it wasn't bad. Mack had been killed by a nearly direct hit from our artillery. He had jumped up too soon after our signal to lift the barrage. They couldn't find his dogtags, and the body was so badly torn up that Simmers had to identify the pieces to confirm who it was. I asked how George was. I seemed to remember that he had been hit on the head by a mortar shell, but my mind hadn't been working well. It turned out he wasn't really wounded except for being very sore. Simmers said my overcoat had five bullet holes in it. George had counted them because it was his coat. We had gotten coats mixed up before the attack.

Simmers also said he thought one of Cannon Company's machine guns had hit me. The gunner had panicked and frozen on it. I don't know and it doesn't matter.

The next day I was moved to the 127th General Hospital in Rennes. We were using the city hospital, the Hôtel de Merci. The German army had used it before us. The closets still had old propaganda posters in them. One had a picture of a German soldier playing with French children. "Notre Ami, Le Soldat Allemand." When the 127th first took over the place, they were handling wounded from the assault on Brest and Lorient, but that had ended a month ago. The badly wounded had been sent to England and the slightly wounded had returned to duty. Now the facility was serving primarily the Ninety-fourth and rear-echelon troops from central France. I was the only combat casualty in my ward. Herrington was a few wards down, but they were preparing to send him to the States. The ward next to mine consisted entirely of combat casualties—German. They were the badly wounded left over from Brest, but there was no reason to send them to England.

This hospital was much better than the one at Benning. The nurses and doctors were a relaxed, efficient team. They all spoke with a slow Texas drawl. This was the University of Texas Longhorn Hospital. The section heads had been selected from the faculty of UT medical school. Each of them had recruited a staff from their young graduates. They asked the university's School of Nursing to select outstanding nurses from among recent graduates. This group had then volunteered en masse as an army hospital. It seemed strange to me that the army would have enough intelligence to accept such a good team. (I later learned that it was a common practice during both world wars for universities and large city hospitals to send complete units. That wasn't done in Korea or Vietnam. The entire country wasn't at war, so there was no reason to organize hospitals. The television show "M.A.S.H." was about a field hospital rather than one like the 127th, but it illustrated the problems of a mixed draftee unit.)

Was this really the army? My bed had real sheets on it for the first time since I had left the States. In fact, it was my first *bed* since the States, but the sheets were what made it wonderful. My bare skin, rough, cracked, and scaling, was rubbing against something clean and soft.

The nurse said, "All right, we're going to do something about those claws you're using for hands, and this afternoon you get a haircut." She cut my nails, scrubbed my hands, and rubbed lotion on them. Nurse Georgia Yeager was the petite daytime authority of the ward. She put up with no foolishness from anyone. We called her the "Texas Terror." The night nurse was older and quieter; I don't remember her name. Their duty shifts were twelve hours a day, seven days a week. They saw nothing wrong with that. "Line soldiers work a twenty-four-hour day."

Yeager brought in the French barber: "When he first looked in and saw that mop of yours, he tried to break and run," she told me later. The company had a set of barber tools, but none of us knew how to cut hair. We just took scissors and sheared the excess away.

The attention made me vaguely ashamed. I remembered a scene from the movie *Sergeant York* where Gary Cooper says, "I'm not proud of what I did over there." I was no Sergeant York, but "not proud" was an understatement. Out there on the line our lives had seemed reasonable. Within the rules of war, we killed and were killed, maimed and were maimed. We trusted almost no one and stripped equipment from the dead and near-dead. The contrast of that life with the clean, cheerful, caring world of Nurse Yeager made me see that I was dirty and crude. I wasn't her kind of people. She shouldn't have to associate with animals like me. But she did, and actually seemed proud of me. I spent a sheepish, painful day making sense of these jumbled thoughts.

She had volunteered to serve her country, which was at war. For the past three months she had been patching up kids who were shattered physically and emotionally. Surely she knew what we had been doing—and why. I reworded a passage from Stephen Vincent Benét's *John Brown's Body:*

> The Germans were devils, and she could pray
> For devils, no doubt, upon Judgment Day,
> But now in the world, she would hate them still
> And send the gentlemen out to kill.
> The gentlemen killed and the gentlemen died,
> But she was the South's incarnate pride
> That mended the broken gentlemen
> And sent them out to kill again.

"Go get 'em, Infantry! We'll patch you up."

Another wonder of the hospital was that I could listen to Glenn Miller every day. The other boys said that he hadn't been on for several days, but the station still played his records every afternoon.

"This is Sergeant Ray McKinley saying howdy-do, and all the boys in the band saying howdy too.—Now I'll give the drums a little wear and tear. Come on boys, we're on the air!" Who was Ray McKinley? That was Miller's music and Miller's band, but where was Miller? Pretty soon we forgot about it. The band and music were just as good.

At night I slept. No nightmares—those would come in the next hospital. Occasionally I woke up wondering if I had slept through my guard shift. There was one recurring dream: I was scout on the Cap Kerdudal patrol, and by different means (different with each dream) I saved them from the ambush. Usually I was "third" scout behind Richards and Button. The real basis for my dream was that we had gone back to the site a few days after the ambush and done some hard thinking about how we would have handled the patrol. Ed and I felt that Richards was too sharp to have walked into such a trap. We would have insisted that someone check the houses in town—there had been nearly a hundred men hidden there. While the town was being checked, we would have taken a closer look at the far hill—machine guns had been dug in there. Why had Richards let them push him so hard? The place where he walked into the machine gun was an obvious site; he should have taken more time and flanked it. I had been stupid to walk directly into that one at le Hirgoat, but that was long ago, before I understood the facts of life.

In the dream I couldn't stop Richards from walking into the ambush, but when it began I was by a hedgerow gap that led to a heavily overgrown trail. (Both the gap and the trail actually existed.) By taking the trail, I could safely wipe out the three machine-gun positions on that side. In one dream I slipped up behind the entire ambush team and captured the commanding general, who was watching the operation, alone. I always woke up feeling good about my accomplishment, almost certain that it would have happened that way—if only I had been there.

A war correspondent came through the ward, looking for human interest stories. "What did you tangle with, soldier?"

"A machine gun. It won." He wrote down my name and hometown paper. Then he asked how long I had been in combat and what it was like. I said that I had been at it for three months. Combat was about the way they had described it to us at Benning: dull and uncomfortable. We were wet, cold, and hungry most of the time. We patrolled a lot, and on most patrols we saw a few Germans. They were pitiful soldiers who probably wanted to surrender. Patrols were dangerous, but our biggest problems were that regimental intelligence planned stupid missions and that most of the French civilians were spying for the Germans.

That wasn't the sort of human interest story he wanted. The folks back home knew that American soldiers were fighting bravely against a cruel, disciplined, and capable enemy. Our officers were brilliant, and the French were grateful to have been liberated. The correspondent asked for details of my getting wounded. I told him that ricochets from a machine gun had done it. The machine gun could have been German but was probably American.

He started writing on his pad and said: "We need to polish that up a little. How does this sound? You were attacking a German fortification when two of your buddies were pinned down by machine-gun fire. You shot at the gunner, killing him and his assistant, but another machine gun got you in the arm and leg. Then your buddies threw a grenade and knocked it out."

It sounded great, except that it didn't happen. Everybody in the squad would laugh at me. The reporter argued that they would never hear about it. But my mother would save the clipping and show it to everyone. What would I say when I got back home? No, I didn't want that kind of story.

The reporter was disgusted. "Well, think about it, and I'll get back with you. Newspapers won't publish a dull story." But he didn't come back, and I began to worry that he might send the story anyhow. I wrote home (twice) instructing Mother to tell the newspaper it wasn't true. I don't know what became of the story or how common that sort of fabrication was. Obviously, the correspondents were under heavy pressure to produce exciting stories about a miserable war.

One morning a few days before Christmas, there was snow all over the ground. Beautiful, but I was glad to be in a bed and not on line. Then came the news: there was a big German counterattack in Belgium. The reports were sketchy, but bad. In the POW ward a German translated the news, and we heard cheers of "Rundstedt!" I started thinking about German forces that were a lot closer than Belgium. Lorient was about two hours' drive from Rennes, maybe less. The Germans probably had enough fuel to push a tank assault this far if they knew where to capture a fuel depot. If Lorient were ever going to get back in the war, now was the time.

Nurse Yeager came by. "You look worried."

She was so right. "I can't walk or carry a rifle. If the Germans came out of Lorient, we wouldn't have much time to evacuate."

*"Fresh, spirited American troops, flushed with victory, are bring-*
*ing in thousands of hungry, ragged, battle-weary prisoners . . ."*
*(News item)*

Now she was worried too. "How long could the infantry line
hold?"

"We don't have a line—spread so thin you can't see the next outpost. A German attack would go through us like a rabbit through a
briar patch."

"Could the Air Corps stop them?"

"They can't fly in this weather. That's what's wrong in Belgium."

She began to whisper. "Don't say anything about this. I'll see what our evacuation plan is."

The hospital's plan was to hope the Germans didn't try to break out. It worked. Lorient remained quiet. (After the war I read the German commander's report. He had received no notification about the counterattack in Belgium, and in any case would have argued against attempting to break out of Lorient. He felt sure that he could have pushed us back several miles, but his force was not strong enough to hold the newly gained ground.)

Being in the hospital for Christmas was nice. The nurses put up little trees in every ward. The Red Cross furnished a few decorations and the rest was improvised. The hospital had a lot of red ink—all night-duty notes were written in red (day-duty notes were in blue). The nurses painted red stripes on tongue depressors to make candy canes. Fingers from surgical gloves were blown up, painted red, and hung as ornaments. Surgical cotton made snow. Nurse Yeager led us in singing carols and let us tell about Christmas back home. Once I was wheeling past the POW ward and heard them singing "Silent Night" in German. For a moment I was struck by the interesting fact that they had translated it into German. Then I realized that *we* had translated it; we also were putting up Christmas trees, a tradition we had inherited from the Germans. "And they shall call his name Emmanuel, which being interpreted is, God with us." Or Gott Mit Uns, just like the belt buckle.

We had a Christmas service with carols. The chaplain gave an impressive sermon about Christmas presents. "This year you aren't getting any Christmas presents, and you aren't giving any. It hurts until you realize that you are giving a large present to your family, friends, and country, and to France. Your gift this year is yourself, freedom, and peace." It bothered me some that we ended by singing "Silent Night."

A few days later Simmers came by to bring me some clothes from my duffel bag. My shirt, sweater, and pants had been cut off when the medics dressed my wounds. Simmers was also saying good-bye. The division was being transferred to fight in Germany. At the time, he didn't know that the Sixty-sixth Division was replacing us (having lost nearly eight hundred men when a submarine sank their ship crossing the Channel on Christmas Eve). But the Germans knew. Within two days after our division headquarters was notified of the change—and before the companies heard about it—the spy system had reported it to Lorient. The German commander had the nerve to send our general a note saying that he had enjoyed his relationship with us and hoped the Sixty-sixth would be as congenial.

The news of our transfer shocked me. I had been convinced that we would sit out the war in Lorient, and was satisfied with that. Now my platoon was going into harsh fighting and into the cold, which I hated. But if they were going to be in it, I wanted to be with them. So I had to get stronger quickly. I was weak but could walk a little and was taking physical therapy every day.

The doctor examined me on January 10. My right arm was sore, but I could pick things up. The long gash in my leg had healed. The leg was stiff and weak, but I could walk on it.

"You will have to favor that leg for a while. The muscle was cut pretty deeply, and it can't stand much weight yet. There are two bullet fragments in your arm. They will hurt some, but the pain will go away. Plan to leave the day after tomorrow."

I was excited. I hurried back to the ward to tell Nurse Yeager I was well. "Does that idiot know that you are going back to combat in a line company? I wonder if he knows what the weather is like outside. I'm going to talk to him."

I know now that her argument was hopeless for two reasons. First, the German counterattack had drained our replacement pool dry. Eisenhower had ordered all rear-echelon units to send any available men for a one-week course in infantry training. They then became riflemen. The 127th even had to send our ward orderly to become a rifleman. The second reason for getting me out quickly was that the 127th itself was moving to Nancy, where they would be busy treating freshly wounded men again.

Even at the time, I thought Nurse Yeager's argument was foolish. After all, I wasn't going directly into combat. I would have a long train ride across France and spend several days in replacement depots.

On January 11 they brought my clothes and personal gear. The clothes and my jacket had been washed, but the laundry crew couldn't get out the ground-in dirt. My shoes were covered and saturated through with dried mud. They hadn't seen polish since I left England. I had been living like an animal. I washed my shoes, let them dry, and rubbed dubbing into the leather. They still looked awful, and the leggings were splotched with grease and grime. Seeing my gear in that condition reminded me of the shock I had gotten at Benning when I came out of the hospital and saw Ninth Company dragging in from a combat problem.

That night I wrote home saying that I would be discharged from the hospital the next day. It was a difficult letter. I couldn't explain how I felt about leaving. My one-month vacation had let me see how civilized people lived. It was more than being clean: it was living to help people instead of killing and trying to survive. The other side of the problem was that I was homesick for my platoon. They were out there fighting, and that's where I belonged. I was Infantry.

The next morning I put on my uniform: a wrinkled wool shirt and ratty-looking pants, washed too many times and never ironed. I knew how I looked, but I was Infantry again. I went to the nurses' station, came to attention, and saluted Nurse Yeager. "Permission to return to active duty."

She almost cried. "Oh, my God. Give me a hug. I hate this war. Be careful, Standifer."

It embarrassed me. She had joked with the others who left, but I was a skinny little kid headed for a line company.

Looking back, I appreciate Nurse Yeager's love and support, but I realize that she was more nearly typical than unique. Georgia was an army nurse who loved her country and the skinny little boys who were fighting for it. I was never able to thank her for the love. After the war she remained in France, married, and had two children. In the late 1950s she died of cancer.

# 14  Give Me the Mountain

The hospital put me on a truck going to the replacement depot in Paris, where we spent a cold, drab night sleeping on the floor in a department store. Paris was off limits and patrolled by MPs, but they let us go to a bar next door, where we sang and drank beer with some Frenchwomen. It was there that I learned the Parisians don't speak French like the Bretons do. When I tried to order more beer in my perfect French, no one undertood me. I tried again, slowly. The waitress listened closely and said, "Ah, Bretagne." I was enjoying my beer so much that it took some time for me to notice the rapid turnover in "waitresses." Only the downstairs part of this place was a bar. Upstairs they had a different business. But I was clean and decent again—at least for a while.

The next day we were hauled to the railroad and loaded into small French boxcars with their capacity written on the sides: forty men or eight horses. All day and all the next night we were cooped in that cold boxcar with wind blowing through the cracks. It seemed that half the men had colds. The second morning I was coughing and getting a fever. I was disgusted at the group I was thrown with. Women would gather at railroad crossings to wave at us, and some of the boys would yell, "Mademoiselle zigzig?" In K Company, someone would have been in charge of the car and responsible to Westmoreland.

I was sitting in the back of the car with a tech sergeant from Ninetieth Division. "This group is nothing but rabble. You're the ranking noncom. Shouldn't you take over?"

He just shrugged. "I couldn't do a thing. At the replacement depot outside of Paris, an officer tried to get them to stand at attention in formation, and they just laughed at him. They are all casuals [returning casualties], and they don't seem to believe the army can handle them. I think the truth is that they are scared and trying to rebel."

"I hope somebody will shape them up before they get back on line."

We were shuttled through a series of depots before reaching Lucky Replacement Depot. Lucky? "Welcome back to Third Army. I know what discipline has been like until now, but here you will soldier or you will go to the stockade instead of your outfit. I promise that the stockade will make you wish you were in a line company."

Someone began the replacement-center chant of defiance: "Forty-eight, forty-nine—" The procedure was that one man would yell "forty-eight," several more would follow with "forty-nine," and if a much larger number joined in with "fifty," the stage was set for a unison yell of "Some shit."

After "forty-nine," the officer raised his Voice of Command a few decibels. "Men, if only one of you finishes that phrase, you will all sleep in the snow over there in the stockade."

I enjoyed the absolute silence that followed his words. This was my kind of army. People enjoyed cursing old "Our Blood and His Guts" Patton, but he sure knew how to run an army.

After that formation we got some advice from men who had been there a few days. "Don't try to sleep through roll call formation in the morning. If you don't answer your name, you're marked AWOL and will spend ten days in the stockade. You'll repair buildings all day and sleep in the snow at night."

They also told us that the Third Army had a whorehouse in town, one that the Germans had organized. We had simply taken it over and followed their old policies. MPs at the entrance checked passes and explained the rules: no fighting or abuse, and no tips. Pay the standard price and don't waste time, because others are waiting.

The replacement depot had originally been a French military school. The Germans apparently had used it for some kind of cadet training too. The walls were covered with murals and slogans. One showed German submarines shelling New York City, with Roosevelt standing on the shore screaming that all the ships to England were getting through undamaged. The others were largely cartoons of military life and weren't very funny. The English translations were written beneath them, but that didn't help because the German army was so different

"Radio th' ol' man we'll be late on account of a thousand-mile detour."

from ours. The barracks area was good, but cold. Army regulations said that no sleeping quarters would be heated. At formation the next morning the sergeant said, "Anyone who wants to draw more clothing, report to the supply room." I drew another set of long underwear, a size larger to fit over my others, larger pants, and more wool socks. Then my shoes wouldn't go over the socks so I went back, turned them in, and got a larger pair. "You won't need to do that after you get to your division. The line troops are getting shoepacs." The supply sergeant was wearing a pair and they were great. The bottom half was rubber with a thick felt inner liner. They were loose enough to allow for thick wool socks. They were what L. L. Bean now calls the "Maine Hunting Shoe."

"Why can't we draw them now? It's going to be cold while we go up."

"There's only a limited supply, and they're going directly to the line companies." Someone was finally considering the Queen of Battle, but I wondered how the entire supply crew at an army replacement depot had managed to acquire these rarities for themselves.

The next day I went AWOL. Technically, it was probably desertion from a combat assignment and, to quote from the Articles of War, "punishable by death or such other punishment as a court-martial may decide." My desertion occurred in full view of the replacement-center headquarters. I simply stood beside the road until a truck with Ninety-fourth Division markings came along. I flagged it down and asked the driver to wait while I got my gear. Tomorrow the replacement center would send a report to the Ninety-fourth saying that I had been absent from roll call. That would be ignored because I would already have reported for duty.

During combat, the clerk for each company remained with division headquarters, where he kept the records straight and helped to cut red tape for the company. When the truck got to headquarters, I told our clerk that I was going on sick call and wanted some sort of light duty around there until my cold improved. Favors like that were easy to do for men who had good reputations in the company. It wouldn't have worked if I had been known as a gold brick.

Then I got around to the big question: "How is the company doing?"

It was doing badly—awfully. Two days ago K Company had attacked Nennig in bitter cold. They fought all day and finally took a hill on the far side of town. The Company suffered 70 percent casualties, both wounds and frozen feet. First Platoon, with twelve men, was the company's strongest unit.

The clerk said: "You're the only scout in the company. Faber left with concussion from artillery and has frozen feet. Simmers has shrapnel wounds and severe concussion. He probably won't make it. Ray, Cagle, and Ed are out of it, messed up one way or another. Herb was really shot up. He almost died, but now they say he'll pull through." I was nineteen years old, sick, and had lost most of my family, but K Company didn't have any other scout; I was going up.

I was getting a fever and a deep cough. I went to the aid station and got some cough syrup. It was terpine hydrate with codeine, a clear liquid that we called "GI gin." Because it was 40 percent alcohol, it seared my throat and made me shiver, but it stopped the cough. The instructions were to take a dose every two hours, but it worked better to take a swallow every time I coughed. I got two bottles because I didn't know how long I would need it. Then I went to the mess hall for supper. There was Abe Goldstein, clean-shaven and rested, wearing a clean uniform. He was an interpreter for the division POW unit. Abe had originally been assigned to a rifle company, but when the division was alerted for shipment to Europe, he had gone to the regimental personnel officer and pointed out that he was fluent in German. The officer said that the division already had all the interpreters it needed and he was sure that Abe was going to be a valuable soldier in the rifle company. After the division went into combat, someone realized that the MP company was composed entirely of ex-policemen, not one of whom could speak German. So Abe became an interpreter.

I was about ready to cry, both from seeing an old friend and from having lost so many. Abe took me back to his room and we talked until midnight. He spent some time trying to persuade me to report for sick call the next morning and get light duty for a few days. Our clerk and the man at the aid station had made the same argument, but First Platoon needed me. "When duty calls or danger, be never wanting there." Abe knew that my thinking wasn't logical, but he also understood why I had to go. I'm not sure of all the reasons. I wasn't needed badly; the battalion wasn't going to attack until it had replacements. I suppose I had been in the hospital for so long that I wanted to prove I was a soldier. Maybe I was ashamed of not having been there when they needed me.

Abe started trying to reassure me about the fighting. "You know that none of them was killed. They're in the hospital like you were.

The fighting up there is bad and the weather is awful. But it's your time to fight, and you aren't going to back away from it. You'll get wounded pretty soon, but you won't get killed. Only about 8 percent die." I'll always be grateful to Abe. He gave me strength, courage, and confidence. He had very little to work with. I was sick and going into a bad situation. "'Are ye able?' said the Master."

The next morning I went to the Headquarters Company supply room. "I'm from K Company, 301st. Can I draw some clothing?"

"Sure, come on in. Were you are Nennig?"

"No, I was wounded at Etel. I'm just going up."

"Man, K Company beat the hell out of the Krauts up there. Last week the 302d got hurt bad and lost most of the town. Captain Simmers wasn't going to take any crap from the Krauts."

"Yeah, King Company is good, but it must be rough up there." The small talk was necessary because I wasn't really entitled to draw supplies from him. At the replacement depot they had given me the new leather-palmed gloves, but I wanted the older wool knit ones— they were warmer, and I could cut a slit in the thumb and trigger finger to make it easier to operate the rifle. I also wanted a handful of condoms for my personal protection: I used them over the muzzle of my rifle to keep out rain, snow, or mud. If I had time to aim before firing, I could take the condom off; otherwise, I could just shoot through it.

Then I asked for some shoepacs. "Sorry, we don't have any. They're supposed to go straight to the line companies, but nobody in the division is getting any. It's all screwed up. Rear echelon has them, but not the combat men."

"Well, let me have an old blanket." In Brittany, before I got the rabbit pelts, I had padded my overshoes with strips from German blankets. Also, I wanted to make a big wool muffler for my neck and face. The supply man offered me some more heavy socks. By careful packing we worked the socks into the gap above my helmet liner, where I also kept toilet paper. He gave me a handful of D rations— tightly compressed chocolate bars. He had me try on a new hood that was supposed to be warm, but I liked the wool knit cap. The visit gave me a comfortable feeling. That man had never seen me before, but he treated me like a brother because I was his Infantry.

Then I went to the ration depot to look for transportation. One man from I Company and two from L were waiting to ride the ration truck to Nennig. I crawled on top of some ration boxes in the rear. Boy, it was cold! A few days earlier the temperature had dropped to five below zero, Fahrenheit. It had warmed a little since then, but not much. I huddled in my warm clothes and tried to work up my courage. I remembered the song from my last church service in Clinton, "How Firm a Foundation." In it, the Lord makes a promise to the faithful:

> "In every condition, in sickness, in health,
> In poverty's vale, or abounding in wealth;
> At home and abroad, on the land, on the sea,
> As your days may demand, shall your strength ever be.

> "When through fiery trials thy pathway shall lie,
> My grace, all sufficient, shall be thy supply;
> The flame shall not hurt thee; I only design
> Thy dross to consume, and thy gold to refine."

It wasn't working. I was scared. George, Ed, Ray, and Cagle had all gone through this. But they had been together. I was going up alone.

Nennig was a small town, only a little larger than the French farming villages. There seemed to be two main roads. One went down to our company command post (CP). The other forked to the left. A side road led to a small castle, the Berg Schloss. The town had been fought over four times and had been shelled to rubble. The weather was bitterly cold and snow covered everything. The company's forward CP stood at the end of the road in a building that was nearly rubble, although the basement was sound. As I walked down the road I realized those snow-covered mounds were bodies.

They were Germans who had been killed attacking Third Battalion of the 302d on the night of January 21 and the following day. That had been almost a week ago. The ones killed by K Company on the twenty-seventh hadn't been snowed on as much. The American bodies had been hand-carried to the forward ration depot; from there, trucks could take them back for burial. It would have been hard on morale for us to see the frozen bodies of American soldiers. I understood that, but the logic slipped away when I saw a blank, frozen expression on the face of a German soldier who had died for his country. Maybe it was because I had seen so many of them alive in Brittany—alive, scared, hungry, and incompetent.

At the house across from the CP the bodies had been stacked in two neat piles. Well, not very neat—the outstretched arms and legs were frozen that way. What a sad, miserable place. I went into the CP house. The basement had a small headquarters room, a kitchen that always had hot food, and warm-up room with a pile of dry clothes. Leave your rifle outside or moisture would condense on it from the humid air. When you went back out the moisture would freeze in the mechanism.

There were always eight or ten people sleeping in the warm-up room. Every twenty-four hours we each were allowed two or three hours there to get a hot meal, change clothes, and sleep. I reported to Sergeant Angley, who was dirty, tired, and unshaven. "Henry, take Standifer up to First Platoon." Bill Henry was platoon runner now—dirty and exhausted, with the glazed eyes that everyone seemed to have. "Welcome back. I got your Winchester after you were wounded. I meant to give it back, but yesterday artillery cut the stock off while I was in the CP."

I grinned. "Don't worry, I believe this one will work. Maybe I'll use this stock and put the Winchester mechanism in it. Is it still under the snow out there?"

The question didn't even register on him. "Maybe. Let's go."

As we walked to the edge of town, I asked about the attack but got nothing. Bill was so emotionally exhausted that he couldn't work out complex sentences. After the war I was able to piece together a reasonably accurate story of the fighting. George had gone down in a preliminary attack the day before. An artillery explosion had knocked him, unconscious, into an antitank ditch. When the medics picked him up later and carried him to the aid station, they found that he had badly frozen feet. That same day—the twenty-sixth—the platoon was briefed for the main attack, and given time to write letters home. Ed wrote his wife about how lonely he felt with both Leon and George gone; he had no one to talk with. That night they sneaked up into some houses on the south edge of town. It was so cold that nobody

*"I'm depending on you old men to be a steadying influence for the replacements."*

could sleep, and they couldn't move around to keep warm. At dawn Bill took some felt-padded boots from a dead German and wore them with four pairs of socks. Ed was trying to get the boots from another German and found that half the body was gone—a pig had been gnawing it.

The attack went well at first. They had to knock out a tank, and after that were able to push through town to a flat area leading to a steep ridge. Heavy machine-gun and rifle fire began to pour down on them, so they pulled back and rolled artillery along the ridge. Then they charged up the ridge and into an orchard on the flat plateau. Germans were lying behind nearly every tree, but most of them had been hit by shrapnel. A few had been killed outright; many were slowly dying from exposure, trauma, and blood loss.

At the far end of the orchard the Germans had dug machine-gun and rifle positions. Cagle dropped his rifle in order to take over the BAR from a wounded man. Ed ran out of rifle ammunition and picked up a burp gun. When the platoon reached its objective, they seemed to be in good shape, having lost only ten men from the original thirty-five. As they regrouped, however, Westmoreland started sending back those with wounds and frozen feet. That's when he found that the platoon only had twelve able men. Cagle was bleeding from shrapnel in his back, but his frozen feet were the biggest problem. He could barely hobble along. Ed, who hadn't been hit, sat beside a tree and started crying. When Westmoreland went over to help, Ed hugged him and started crying harder. He finally calmed down enough to help carry wounded to town. The aid station sent back word that they were diverting him to the hospital.

When we got to a trail leading up the ridge, Bill said, "That Kraut up there is dead." It was eerie. The German soldier was lying beside a tree, aiming his rifle directly at us. His eyes were open and he had a calm expression on his face.

"Bill, these dead Krauts are spooky. I wish somebody would move them."

"It was more than spooky when they were screaming for help and we had to keep moving on or die." The dull voice of this old friend gave a vivid picture of what he had gone through.

We stopped at the edge of the orchard. Frozen bodies were scattered everywhere. The one closest to me lay with his legs spread, his bloodless hands clawing at the snow. A knife was sticking out of his boot. Bootknives weren't standard issue, but I had seen some in Brittany. This one was a long slim knife of Solingen steel with a sheath that clipped onto the boot. I might need that knife; the German certainly didn't. I pulled it out and slipped it onto my overshoe.

We had to cross the orchard to our position on the far side, but the area was under German artillery and mortar observation. That was going to be interesting. Everywhere, I saw the pockets made by exploding mortar shells. Before leaving the CP, Bill had given me a white tablecloth to use as camouflage. It covered my head and reached a little below my waist. Bill was wearing white coveralls he had taken from a dead German. I was frightened at walking in the open so badly exposed. But nothing happened.

We trudged toward the far end of the orchard, where I could see snow-covered mounds and a few people walking around. Twelve cold, exhausted men were left from the proud platoon that had marched past the cheering Red Cross girls in September. "Go get 'em, Infantry."

Lieutenant Westmoreland came over, pulled off his glove, and shook my hand, trying to welcome me to this mess. My neat, trim, alert platoon leader was dirty, tired, and expressionless. He had taken a piece of shrapnel through his nose, and the wound bled occasionally. He said I would have to patrol that night, but to start digging my hole now. The ground was frozen to about six inches. I adjusted the entrenching tool so it was like a hoe, closed my eyes, and chopped away. (If I had left my eyes open, frozen dirt might have chipped into them.) After I broke through the frozen zone, the digging was easy. I dug to about five feet, piling the dirt in a mound around the hole. Then Ignetz, a buddy I remembered from Second Squad, helped me saw some logs to put on top. We left enough open space to climb into and to shoot from. Then we heaped dirt on the logs for protection from artillery. We lined the hole with blankets. Every German soldier had been carrying one blanket in his pack.

I crawled into my hole, took off my leggings, and threw them away. I pulled off my shoes and both pairs of socks. Then I rubbed my feet until I could feel them, and put on the socks from my helmet liner. I tucked the wet socks back in my liner, trying to keep them away from the toilet paper. I ate a K ration and part of a chocolate bar, and sat. We took turns on guard, which simply meant sticking your head out of the hole to watch. The work had driven away my panic. I was here, and nothing much was happening. I was still coughing and developing a fever, but you had to have a temperature of 102 to get off the line. What a miserable place to be. The encouraging thing was that the Germans were just as bad off as we were. They had better winter gear, but they were losing the war. Why didn't they surrender and stop this useless killing? "Shall the sword devour forever? Knowest thou not that it will be bitterness in the end?"

We were facing an infantry unit of the Eleventh Panzer Division. They had been pulled from the Russian front for the December attack but hadn't been used. The upper level officers were experienced, but the riflemen were mostly old men and kids.

I had been a kid at Benning.

The Eleventh Panzer was supposed to have the new König Tiger tanks but had only used the smaller Panthers. A few SS troops had shown up, but we didn't know what that meant. All in all, there wasn't much reason to expect an attack, but I was going to have to see what I could find tonight. My ramblings stopped when we started taking some artillery. It sounded like harassment but could have been working up an attack. I wasn't on guard, so I just huddled in my hole. Then the guard yelled: "Get up! They're coming!" I grabbed my rifle and came up out of the hole. I realized I wasn't shouting—I was growling like an animal. "Come up a'growlin'." I was Infantry again. It wasn't an attack, just a little movement in the German lines. It took me a while to calm down. I was cold, mad, and scared.

At ten o'clock that night I went back to the warm-up room. My clothes were already wet and smelling. I pulled them off and looked through the pile for something that might fit. It didn't even have to fit—I just needed something to cover my skinny frame. Then I ate pancakes and jam with hot coffee.

I believe that was the night I patrolled (I was probably too sick the next night). During the afternoon Westmoreland had taken me back to the company CP—not the warm-up room, which was the forward CP, but the rear CP at the far end of the town. He and a battalion officer briefed me. Westmoreland introduced me as a sergeant. I was a squad leader with no squad. Briefing was simple. The Germans had been beaten so badly that it seemed unlikely they could attack without reinforcements. They had some light tanks back beyond Sinz, but the only serious threat was that they might move infantry up during the night for a dawn attack. Companies I and K had each sent out scouts the night before. The one from I Company had reported no activity, but our man had not returned. I was to leave our line at two in the morning, go to the edge of Sinz, and be back by five.

I'm not sure of all the details surrounding this patrol. My memories of it are out of focus and mingled with strange nightmares I had about Nennig in the hospital. Jim Westmoreland helped me to reconstruct the events when we visited at a reunion. He said that the company probably sent out a one-man patrol at around 10 P.M., and I took over after 2 A.M.

Two o'clock on a cold black night was a good time for a patrol. The enemy guards would be groggy; I would be alert and careful. Someone woke me at about one to start getting ready. There wasn't much to prepare: knit cap with no helmet, bootknife in my overshoe, and the white tablecloth for camouflage. I remember thinking of Sergeant Cohen: "Surely you wouldn't send a sweet little kid out on a night like this? I could catch my death!" I thought of Abe's "Now it's your time to fight." And that long-ago preacher's "Caleb, now there was a real man—give me the mountain!" And there was always, "I will fear no evil, for thou art with me." But I did fear evil and I wasn't sure I wanted the Lord to even know where I was.

I didn't try to use a compass. I sighted on a tree beyond the Sinz-Bubingen road and kept back-sighting on a tree in the orchard. At the edge of the road I sighted along a tree near Sinz. Now what? Should I crawl along the ditch, get on the road, or stay in the woods? I wished Richards were there to tell me how to do it. Richards was dead, but I could feel him beside me, and I already knew how he would do it. Take the edge of the woods and go slowly. "Let's go, let's go! Goddamnit, let's go!"

Westmoreland had shown me the locations of two machine guns and some mortars. I slipped along behind one of the guns and heard the Germans talking, just like the night problem at Benning. It sounded to me as if they were cold and complaining about the rotten position they had. I wished for a hand grenade. I could end the misery for those damned Krauts. If they would surrender, the war would be over. Why did the bastards keep fighting?

I realized I couldn't use a grenade even if I had one. It would wake everybody up, and I wouldn't get out alive. Keep moving. There isn't any way to kill those bastards. When I got almost to Sinz, I slipped up on another group talking and shivering. Nothing was happening. They were cold and miserable, but they certainly weren't preparing an attack. That was my mission: work up close to Sinz and see what was going on. Nothing was going on.

I started back, skirting farther into the woods to miss the machine gun. I was squatting beside a tree deciding whether it was time to turn back toward the road when I felt a tap on my shoulder. I looked back and saw a German helmet outlined against the sky. I braced my feet and reached for the knife in my boot. I rose up like the wrath of God, stepped to the side, pushed his shoulder, grabbed his chin, threw my knee in his back, and slid the knife across his throat. Sergeant Schmidt had been wrong. If you cut smoothly there isn't even the gurgle of blood. But the blood gushes all over your glove. I reached in the German's jacket for his wallet, and I took his belt buckle. Then I squatted there to calm down. I remember no emotion at all. There had been no decision to kill. I wasn't going to be captured in this cold, stinking place. I didn't wonder why he had been standing too close to use a rifle. My response had been instinct and training. The enemy was there, so I killed him.

I had a more critical problem to consider now. The night had started out bitterly cold, but while I was on patrol a drizzling rain had begun. I was wet, shivering, and miserable. I still had to get past a machine gun, and I had to keep my mind on landmarks. This was not a good place to get lost. Stand fast, Standifer.

"Why he left his home in the South to fight in Europe, God only knows."

Move slowly; stay low; don't try to slip up on American positions; go between them. I finally got to the warm-up room, reported on the little I had seen, and turned over the wallet. The belt buckle said, Meine Ehre heisst Treue, Loyalty Is the Foundation of My Honor. I had finally met the SS, man-to-man in liberating strife. I went to the kitchen and got a cup of split pea soup. I sat there breathing in the warm vapors and shaking, both because I was still cold and because the tension of patrol was wearing off. I put on dry clothes and went back to the line.

The next day my warm-up time came at noon. Westmoreland took a look at me and said, "Go by the aid station and see if you are sick enough to go to the hospital." I plodded across the apple orchard, holding my tablecloth around me. It wasn't such a good camouflage anymore: the weather was breaking and the snow was melting. More bodies were being exposed. When I reached the edge of the orchard, I stopped to rest. I started to sit on a log and realized it wasn't a log. The thawing body gave a bit and let out an ooze of gas. I took a deep breath and drew in the stench of cordite from the artillery mixed with that of decaying of bodies. If the world were to end now, the Lord would find me here. "No; there's a cross for every one, and there's a cross for me."

But I had carried it long enough. First Platoon was gone. We had only Ignetz and Wendler, plus a handful of replacements. Bill Henry wasn't really a rifleman anymore. I've got to get out of here. Courage is doing what must be done in spite of conditions. To hell with courage. I've got to leave this God-forsaken place. If I don't get sick enough to leave by the time of the next attack, I'm going to find a way to get wounded.

I went to the aid station but wasn't sick enough to leave. I returned to the warm-up room, changed clothes, ate, and slept. Then back to the hole. With the thaw, it was nearly full of water. Now we sat on logs under the trees. I wondered whether I would go into the hole if artillery started.

The thaw was worse than the cold. Just before dark, Germans started coming in to surrender—the weather was getting to them, too. They were all saying, "Nicht Deutsch. Polski." Ignetz started questioning them in Polish. He said that some spoke excellent Polish; others knew only a few words. It was a long, cold night. Each of us got to go to the CP to warm up once more. It was hard to find the way back in the dark. With the snow gone, you couldn't see the trail. I plodded along, aiming toward a tree. I stopped for a strange sound. It was far away, but I couldn't recognize it or pick up the direction. I took off my helmet and pulled the knit cap from my ears. Then I turned slowly to pick up the sound. I got the direction but realized I didn't know whether it was toward our line or the German lines.

I was sick and wasn't thinking very clearly. In turning around, I had gotten lost. Neither we nor the Germans had solid lines; there were only scattered strong points. If I chose the wrong direction, I could end up back with the German artillery, and then in a prison camp. Or I could get lost in a minefield. I sat on my helmet to wait for daylight. Then I heard voices of two men walking toward me. As they came nearer, I heard that they were speaking English. I wasn't going to take a chance by frightening two tired riflemen on a dark night. They were either going toward Nennig or back to their position, but at least they weren't lost. I followed them quietly to the edge of Nennig. They went past the company warm-up house, so they must have been from I Company.

I pushed the blackout curtains aside and went into the bright, warm, stinking room. A few men sat at the table, eating and talking.

> When out of the night, which was fifty below,
>     and into the din and glare,
> There stumbled a rifleman fresh from the line,
>     dog-dirty and mean as a bear.
> He looked like a man with a foot in the grave
>     and scarcely the strength of a louse. . . .

The poem had been funny when we used it in Brittany, but that was long ago. Now it fitted too well. I got a cup of coffee and some pancakes with jam on them, sat at the table, and said nothing. Some of the men were old friends, but I was exhausted—scarcely the strength of a louse. I changed clothes before eating my food. Then I slept. Someone woke me about daylight and told me to go to the aid station. This time my fever was high enough. "Okay, soldier, you're going to the hospital. Do you want to go back and get any gear?" What gear? I had it with me: a toothbrush, Bible, wallet, and an address book.

"Can I take this bootknife and belt buckle?"

"Sure. That's a fine knife. Don't let anybody steal it." But the knife was stolen by some medic before I reached the hospital.

I was leaving Nennig. It was a strange feeling. I didn't have the strength to go back and say good-bye. Westmoreland knew I was leaving, or at least thought so: he had given the word for them not to wake me until daylight, and then to send me to the aid station.

I was leaving weak, exhausted men who needed me, but even they were glad I was getting out of it. And I was glad to be leaving the nightmare. Replacements would be coming in. They hadn't trained or fought together. They were just soldiers, potentially good, but not a team. The sweet little children were all gone now. They were scattered in hospitals all over France. They would trickle back to fight and get wounded again. The team, King Company, had trained together for two years and lasted through nearly one day of hard combat. Heavily outnumbered, we had taken the high ground and held it. The traditions Simmers had built would be continued by Captain Warren. At the war's end, the company would have taken every objective, never lost a foot of ground, and paid the price of 400 percent casualties.

> Furl that banner! True, 'tis gory,
> Yet 'tis wreathed around with glory
> and 'twill live in song and story.

# 15  Forgive Our Foolish Ways

From Nennig I went to the battalion aid station, where they took my temperature and sent me to regimental aid, where they took my temperature again and sent me to a field hospital. I was still wearing my muddy clothes that smelled of cordite and decaying bodies. As I was carried in, a nurse with her back to me said, "God, I'm sick of Nennig. The kids all smell the same and look alike: scared, sick, skinny, and pale." That hospital knew the smell of Nennig well. They cleaned me up, gave me some medicine, and sent me to the 145th General Hospital at Verdun. I had pneumonia and frozen feet. I had expected pneumonia, but why did I have frozen feet? I could remember rubbing my feet and putting on dry socks the first day. I probably did the same thing in the warm-up room. I couldn't remember even thinking about my feet during the last day. Maybe I had wanted frozen feet for the same reason I had wanted to get a higher fever, or maybe I was just too tired to care.

They put me in the frostbite ward, which they kept cool—the treatment for frozen feet was simply to keep them uncovered and cool. They put a salve on the bad cases. Mine weren't really very bad. The boy next to me had a bad case. They took him off to an examination room and brought him back from surgery, unconscious. Everyone else in the ward knew what that meant, but I was new. As he came to, he looked down and said: "Where are my feet? They're gone! My feet are gone!" What a way to treat a nineteen-year-old kid. They probably had told him that amputation was preferable to dying of gangrene, but he was physically and emotionally exhausted—maybe he had agreed, and maybe he forgot. The usual procedure was to have a chaplain there when an amputee woke up, but there had been some sort of mix-up.

Stories of amputations and near-amputations will remain as long as the war is remembered. Casey Frye, from Third Platoon, was evacuated with frozen feet, but he quickly learned about procedures. When they took him in for examination, he demanded to know what they planned.

"We'll probably have to amputate. If gangrene sets in, you will die."

"No, you won't. I am not going to live with two stubs for feet. If I die of gangrene, at least I will die honorably."

Frye recovered and returned to full duty. Maybe he was just lucky: maybe the gangrene hazard was as bad as the doctors said it was; people who accepted the risk and died aren't around to tell about it.

After a few days I was moved to a warmer ward because of my pneumonia. The hospital had once been a concentration camp. More precisely, it had been the barracks area for Russian women who were used as labor in a nearby factory. It was a fairly nice building. The nurses said it had been filthy and infested with lice when they got there. They had scrubbed and painted for two weeks. It wasn't as well equipped as the Rennes hospital but was just as warm and friendly. At night I would wake up hearing someone moaning or crying. The nurse would sit beside him and give him some quiet conversation, a glass of water, and a blue 88. The name referred to the 88-mm artillery piece the Germans used with terrifying accuracy. A blue 88 was amobarbital, used as a strong sedative for men with combat fatigue.

This nurse was Italian, with jet black hair and an overflowing concern for her boys. I can bring up her visual image, but no name. She wasn't as pretty or witty as Nurse Yeager, but was equally caring and capable. Other nurses would come around during the day to visit and listen to us talk about combat or home. I didn't want to talk about either. I could hardly remember home, and I got sick thinking about Nennig.

Nennig became a series of nightmares. In one of them I was walking through the orchard and the German bodies were still alive, moaning and begging for help. When I stopped to help, Lieutenant Chilton would appear, telling me to hurry, hurry, the war was still going on. In another vivid dream, I found a dead German with big felt boots. As

I started pulling at a boot, his entire foot came off. Then I looked at his face and saw that it was George, in a German uniform.

Apparently I made no sounds during the dreams, because I would wake up alone in the quiet ward—but the smell of putrefying men remained. I knew the smell was only a memory, but it was difficult to erase. The nurse said that we could mask nightmares by bringing up pleasant thoughts. My pleasant thoughts were of George, Ed, Dale, and Cagle—but that was a circular path taking me back to Nennig.

I tried to work out some kind of logic during the day. I was ashamed of being a part of the obscenity. I was also ashamed of my failure. My country, community, and platoon had expected that I would soldier at Nennig. Well, I had. I had held the line. I had pulled the patrol and fulfilled the mission. I had killed a man. He could have killed me with a shot or the rifle butt. He decided to capture me because I wasn't armed. He had been a fool. Never trust anyone in combat and never look on the enemy as human. I had done what I was taught. But I wasn't taught to kill helpless men. I could hear Bob Souder saying: "But will I be able to kill? God, I hope not!"

Maybe I hadn't killed anyone. Maybe it was just another nightmare. I was a reconnaissance scout. I had gone to Sinz, seen no activity, and come back. But where did I get the SS belt buckle? I couldn't remember. On the other hand, I thought I had brought a bootknife to the hospital, but I didn't have one now. I hadn't really soldiered. I hadn't been able to take the shock of pale, frozen, expressionless bodies, and the smell of those bodies when the thaw came.

I remembered a sermon to the effect that in difficult situations, the primary question should not be whether you live or die, but what is right and wrong. But had right existed at Nennig? All of the options I saw seemed to be wrong. "Oh beautiful for heroes proved in liberating strife,/Who more than self their country loved, and mercy more than life."

"On my honor I will do my best to do my duty to God and my Country."

This muddle of thoughts made very little sense to me. God, Country, and Community were part of the same concept. Bob, Mother, Charlene, and even Atley were proud of me. There could be no conflict in where my duty lay. But why did I feel so awful? I was ashamed of having been glad I was sick enough to get out. If I hadn't been sick, would I have tried to desert? I didn't think so. There were stories of boys who had shot themselves in a foot to get out. I wouldn't have considered risking the shame of a court-martial for that. In the next attack I would have been very brave and gotten wounded. Is it courage to hate your duty so deeply that you would risk serious injury or death?

I couldn't discuss those thoughts with anyone: nurses, friends, or the chaplain. I prayed over it, but wasn't sure God was listening to me anymore.

As patients improved, they were assigned routine housekeeping duties. Newcomers began with sweeping and carrying food trays. I advanced to giving penicillin shots and alcohol back-rubs. Attending to bedpans and P-38s was the duty of a Hispanic wardboy named Jésus. The P-38 was a German army pistol, and inevitably the term became our nickname for the hospital urinals. That was a fun joke, but calling for "Jesus" to collect bedpans gave me trouble.

I got a very strange letter from Ed. Mother had heard from Betty that Ed had received a psychiatric discharge and seemed to have improved a little but spent a lot of time gazing into space. Mother sent my hospital address and suggested that he try writing to me. Because Ed didn't realize that I knew his situation, he was trying to sound cheerful. The fighting in Germany hadn't been bad, but it was so cold that he froze his feet. At the medical clearing station, an officer began asking strange questions. Ed recognized them as psychological screening for combat fatigue. He realized that by giving the right answers, he would get a trip home—and it worked. The sense of his letter was that he was sorry I was in the hospital but wanted me to know he had no mental problems. He said he still felt rather tired and lazy but thought he would start back to college soon.

After a month I was much better. A deep cough showed I wasn't quite ready for combat, but regulations wouldn't let them keep me in that hospital longer than a month. Knowing the army, I thought I would be sent to the front anyway; this time I was wrong. They shipped me back to England for convalescence in a hospital that had been built for the army near Hereford. I had become an authority on hospital care, and this one wasn't as good as the others. It was almost as strict as the one at Benning. One of the nurses told me that it was a matter of staffing levels. The hospitals receiving men directly from combat were overstaffed with nurses as a sort of cushion against the stress. In England patients got the care they needed and nothing more. The nurse doing the talking had been at a hospital in France and preferred it to this, but the army tried to rotate nurses because there was emotional stress on them too.

Those of us in the convalescence wards were checked by a doctor daily, but we wore uniforms and ate in the mess hall. We were on call day and night to be stretcher-bearers for badly wounded patients flown from France. It was a pain to roll out of bed at two in the morning to unload ambulances of moaning, smelly men. These soldiers didn't smell the way I had. There was a stench of decaying flesh and blood from under the plaster casts. One painful part was that I couldn't feel sorry for myself. These men were miserable and needed help.

I liked the group of boys I was with, except that every night they wanted to go out and get drunk. Paratrooper Goode had stolen a bottle of blue 88s when he visited his friend in the psycho ward. If you took one pill, a single glass of beer would get you roaring drunk. After one night out with the boys, I decided that I wanted different entertainment. Once a week the Red Cross held a dance for us and the patients from a British army hospital. That's where I met Teddy—Corporal Edwina Davies of the ATS (Army Transport Service), a military unit composed entirely of women who were trained as drivers.

Teddy was tall, slender, and reserved—shy. I thought she looked a lot like Princess Elizabeth, but that was partly because they wore the same uniform. Her Royal Highness was also serving in the ATS. Teddy was from Bebington, a suburb of Liverpool. She was probably not as aristocratic as I believed, just very British and conventional. I remember trying to explain the Southern Baptist church to her and listening in turn to her accounts about the Church of England. The discussion wasn't very interesting, and I wondered if we had much in common; we kept dating because her roommate thought we were good for each other.

Although I called Teddy a lorry driver, she was actually a dispatcher and had varied duty hours. I was on a standard eight-hour-day training schedule, but discipline was so loose that I could leave easily. When she had an afternoon off, we enjoyed walking along the Wye

River, which ran through the center of town and had a beautiful park along its bank. We would sit on the grass, joke, and talk with the kids. British children loved American chewing gum, but their parents thought it was a repulsive habit. Most of the children would run up with their stock phrase, "Any gum, chum?" Others would walk up very quietly and say, "My parents say that it's rude to ask Americans for gum, so I don't." That always worked with me.

One afternoon as we were sitting in the grass on the river bank, I decided to try telling Teddy about Nennig. I no longer knew exactly what had happened at Nennig, but I wanted to talk about the smell, the bodies, and my memories of maybe having killed a man. It took me a while to tell it all: I had trouble separating fact from nightmare, and occasionally I had to stop and control my emotions.

"Leon, that's what war is about. We are going to keep killing Germans until they quit fighting. I'm just a lorry driver, but I do it so men like you can be out there killing Jerry. My only regret is that they won't let me do it with you. I wish *I* could remember having German blood on my hands."

I had seen this attitude in some overenthusiastic soldiers who couldn't quite understand what was happening, but in gentle Teddy it shocked me. I didn't want to argue, to point out that most of us were innocent victims of a brutal war. I had known the Germans in Brittany. The average German soldier had been sold a God and Country message by his family and Führer. Or maybe he simply fought to protect his family from a concentration camp. Either way, he was a victim. I could show that if I actually had killed the SS kid (I wasn't sure it had happened), it was because he had made the fatal mistake of believing that someone far behind German lines must be a friend. But those points didn't matter; it was Teddy's hatred that shocked me. Regardless of what the newspaper reporters were saying, hatred is a liability in combat; it makes soldiers take foolish risks and leads to careless mistakes, just as an overexcited football team can't play well. At best, killing is horrible, but the motives should arise from loyalty, discipline, and sometimes self-preservation.

Maybe I didn't really understand. Through most of her teenage life, Teddy had known bombings, destruction, and awful frustration. She was a quiet, conventional lady, except for her capacity for hate.

At night we usually went to a quiet little pub with some of her friends who were dating British and Canadian soldiers. I had learned to drink beer in Chippenham, but Hereford was apple country: awful beer, excellent cider. We couldn't afford much entertainment. I was the rich man, drawing five pounds—twenty dollars—a month (my actual salary was higher, but that was my hospital allowance). The Canadians were getting three pounds, and the British made a little over two. The British soldiers had a saying that the trouble with GIs was that they were "overpaid, oversexed, and over here." That applied more to the Air Corps than to those of us who more closely resembled Bill Mauldin's Willie and Joe. Five pounds a month is not overpayment.

We talked a lot and drank slowly. The two Canadians had been wounded in combat, but none of us wanted to discuss war. The talk covered mainly jokes, problems at work, and hometown tales—wondering at the why's of our cultural differences. When Roosevelt died, the girls were shocked that the American army did nothing more than fly the flag at half-mast. At the very least we should have postponed the dance until after his funeral. I tried to explain that Roosevelt wasn't a symbol to us in the way the king and Churchill were to them. The Canadians agreed with me; they didn't really worship King and Country themselves.

I was comfortable with this group. These were my kind of people, and they weren't even Americans. Most of the boys in K Company weren't my kind of people. Clinton had contained a lot of slobs, too. I no longer tried to justify everything K Company or Clinton did. I only had to answer for my personal actions, and wasn't sure I could do that very well.

At first I had felt awkward taking a nice girl like Teddy to a pub, but she gradually convinced me that it was like going to the Owl Cafe in Clinton. People never sang songs like that at the Owl, though. I never really got used to singing "Roll Me Over" with proper British girls. "But, Leon, it's not a men's song: 'Roll me over, lay me down, and do it again.'" Well, I suppose she was right. We would sing the verses and girls would come in strong on the chorus. "I've Got Sixpence" was British, but we always ended it with "Happy is the day when the Yankee gets his pay, and we all roll 'im, roll 'im home." "Pistol Packin' Mama" had been popular in England, so we sang it some. They didn't know any of my Baptist songs. I taught them: "I've got the peace that passes understanding / Down in my heart, down in my heart to stay." They thought it was strange to sing a funny, light-hearted religious song. It meant more to me. I was beginning to make peace with myself. I could still smell the decaying men and remember blood seeping through my gloves. I had wavered and bent at Nennig, but I had kept the promises; I did my best to find my duty. I hadn't killed anyone—by now I had convinced myself of it—except indirectly, by calling artillery. I was still ashamed of the way we had left bodies to putrefy, but I hadn't really promised to do my duty, only to do my best. I wasn't running the war. "Dear God and Father of mankind, forgive our foolish ways."

Toward the end of the night we would move into: "There'll always be an England, and England will be free. / If England means as much to you as England means to me." It was a lonely, tearful song for us all. The war was almost over, but it had been long and hard.

After six weeks in Hereford I really was well. I got a one-week leave. I had wanted to visit London but couldn't afford the high prices, so went to Edinburgh instead. I walked the battlements of the old castle and visited again with Dale. He and I looked out over the Highlands, dreaming of Merlin, Lancelot, and Sir Gawain. I walked through the military museum and read tributes to past heroes. After a week in the Highlands, I reported to the replacement center at Southampton. We were issued full combat gear: rifles, steel helmets, leggings, gas masks. I felt like a new recruit but knew that I could turn in the gas mask and leggings at division headquarters. Real soldiers were wearing the new combat boots now; since warm weather had come, the boots no longer would cause frozen feet.

That night we boarded a ship, and woke up entering the harbor at Le Havre. It was a tricky spot because the Germans had sunk an ammunition ship at the mouth. There was enough room to edge past, but we hoped the skipper was a careful man. Safely docked, we walked down the gangplank, assembled in a column of fours, and started toward our camp at the edge of town. Quartermaster and other rear-echelon troops lined the streets to jeer at us. "Here comes the army of occupation!" This rankled some of the boys more than it did me. The standard answer to such remarks was, "Kid, I've worn out more rifles

*"I see Comp'ny E got th' new-style gas masks."*

than you have GI socks." Or, "I've spent more time in combat than you have in the army." But it was useless to yell things like that, and it didn't really matter. So what if they wanted to believe we were raw and scared? I enjoyed remembering the same thing on Utah Beach: "Look sharp, Infantry." But now looks didn't count. We *were* sharp. We were Willie and Joe, the combat infantrymen who had whipped the Krauts.

The next day rumors were flying about the end of the war, but we loaded on boxcars and headed east. When we pulled into the depot of a small town in Belgium, people were dancing and screaming, "La guerre est finie." We poured out of our boxcars and joined them. So did the occupants of a westbound train on a siding. They were French soldiers who had been captured during the 1939 blitzkrieg: 1,869 days as prisoners.

We had a wonderful party. It seemed like half the women in town had come to dance, laugh, hug, sing, and drink—and a few slipped off for other adventures. The polyglot of dialects was a laugh. Most of the GIs had fought somewhere in France and had picked up a few phrases, but we had learned them in different provinces. My French was still fairly serviceable, but distinctly Breton. The women spoke French with a strong Flemish flavor. One of the ex-POWs had a small accordion that he played while we sang or hummed, depending on whether we knew the song. He knew a lot of English and American songs from having listened (secretly) to the BBC. Everyone knew at least a few words of "Der Führer's Face" because the BBC had enjoyed beaming the Spike Jones version toward Germany: "Not to love Der Führer is a great disgrace, / So we *heil, heil,* right in Der Führer's face!"

We all laughed, cried, and sang for about an hour. As the pace began to slow a bit, the engineer on our train let go with three whistle blasts, and we climbed back into our boxcars.

I sat in the doorway and watched the spring countryside. The war was over and I had lived. Dale and Richards were dead, both better soldiers than I could ever have been. As for George and Ed, I had been told that George might lose his feet, and I sensed that Ed had lost even more. What had I done for the platoon? I had fired my rifle once—no, three times. One shot was a deliberate miss, and two were probable leg wounds. I had been a good scout. I had saved us from an ambush at le Hirgoat, and maybe a few other times. All I did at Etel was get wounded. I had pulled that patrol at Nennig. Although I couldn't remember it very clearly, I knew it had been awful—but I had done it. I never backed away from an assignment. "When duty calls or danger, be never wanting there." I was there. I had been First Scout in the Infantry.

# 16 Blackberries, Chickens, and Courage

There is a basic formula for every good sermon:

1. Tell them what you are going to tell them.
2. Tell them.
3. Tell them what you told them.

This chapter is step three, something between a summary and an analysis. It is my attempt at going back to the problems of a nineteen-year-old rifleman, but with the advantages of more experience and of having read accounts of what was happening beyond my own narrow field of view. In the final chapter I will attempt to make some sense of the original issue: why we fought.

After the war I suffered from what is now called "postcombat trauma syndrome," but it was never very serious. During my first year in college (at Mississippi State) I had trouble sleeping; the Veterans Administration hospital gave me a big bottle of blue 88s. Amobarbital is extremely addictive, but I was lucky. Bob Canzoneri and I talked about combat, a little. He remembers my story of sitting on a dead German. He also remembers that I was moody and quick-tempered. But it all faded. In graduate school—about 1956—I was drinking beer with George Keitt (my friends all seem to be named Bob or George) and mentioned the shock of cutting a man's throat.

He was appalled. "Do you mean that literally?"

With the help of those few beers, I dug back into the past. "I think so. No. I don't know. But I used to dream about having blood all over my hands."

It faded again. In graduate school I met Marie and convinced her that I was much better than I am or ever have been. We married, and I graduated and found a job. In 1961 we were able to go through Europe on the way home from working in Africa. We visited friends in Bavaria, did some shopping, made some professional contacts, and visited Nennig. Marie knew all of my war stories and the degree to which the current versions differed from the earlier ones. We read a brochure of tourist attractions in the Perl governmental district and were surprised to find that Nennig had the ruins of a 105 B.C. Roman villa. The villa's floor mosaics were among the best examples in Germany, but we weren't going to Nennig to study mosaics. I hoped that seeing the town rebuilt and peaceful would help to soothe the old scars. Some friends had said that it might not work, that such a visit could revive dormant ghosts.

We spent the first night of our battlefield visit at Trier, toward which the Ninety-fourth Division had been driving when I was there; the division finally captured it later. The next morning we drove to Nennig. In a little under an hour we covered the distance that had taken the division two months and many lives. I knew exactly where to go in Nennig. The Berg Schloss was to the left, I remembered, up a hill. To the right, down beyond *Gemeinschaftplatz* (it simply means "Community Square," but during the Nazi era that innocent-sounding name had heavy racial overtones), the town ended. To the left stood the house where our men had piled the dead German soldiers. Across the street the forward command post had occupied the basement of a nearly demolished house. You took off your wet, muddy, stinking clothes and searched through the freshly washed pile until you found something that almost fit. There was always hot food—I remembered the split pea soup—and some blankets to sleep on. Past the warm-up house there had been a trail. You followed it to a little draw, turned left, and went up to the apple orchard where we had dug holes in the frozen ground. Beyond that had been the road to Sinz, the shivering Germans, and their machine guns.

It wasn't quite that easy when we got there. The Schloss (castle) was actually in the town of Berg, a couple of hundred yards away. Gemeinschaftplatz had been renamed Marketplatz, and two streets went off to the right; I should have asked directions but was afraid. "I helped destroy your town, and we left the bodies of your dead brothers lying around until they rotted. Would you mind helping me to find where I did those things?" (In 1986 I established correspondence with Waldemar Bach, who has written an excellent history of Nennig. He said that actually, Marie and I would have been welcomed by almost anyone in town. Nennig had lost sixty of its young men fighting in the war, and our repeated assaults had destroyed the town's physical structure, but there was no strong resentment against Americans, because we had represented the only possible means of defeating Nazism. The ruins of the Roman villa had come through unscathed, lying under the flat field where machine guns ripped through K Company.)

The street on the extreme right seemed a good bet, so we followed it to the edge of town, where a sign read Nach Butzdorf. This was the right place, but in 1945 the sign there had said Mines Cleared to This Point—Go Farther at Your Own Risk. The warm-up basement had been in the last house on the right, but with everything rebuilt I couldn't distinguish old houses from new. I couldn't bring myself to knock on a door and say: "I used to sleep in your basement. Could I see it again?" Somewhere across the street had been the two piles of German bodies. When the Germans had recaptured Nennig from the 302d Regiment, they had found similar piles of their earlier dead. The division was then condemned in German radio broadcasts about the "atrocities of Nennig." Axis Sally—good old Midge—used the accounts of bodies stacked like cordwood to blast the Ninety-fourth for slaughter of prisoners; she said we were not soldiers but bloody butchers. I never understood the logic; our desecration of German bodies was obscene, but why did stacking them make it worse?

I followed the Butzdorf road to where a trail led past a trash dump and up to the plateau we had called "Nennig Mountain." Nennig is on the flood plain of the Mosel River and this "mountain" appears to be a first terrace. Over to the right the dead German had lain with his rifle pointed directly at me. The machine guns that swept Nennig had been farther to the left.

At the top I faced a flat field. Our artillery had destroyed the orchard, and the trees had been pulled out and replaced with annual crops. Somewhere along here I had sat on a decaying body and heard gas wheeze out. Ed had charged across there giving the last full measure of devotion—to what? In combat, God and Country is only a distant abstraction. You fight for friends, pride, and survival. But Ed had had no friends left. George, Cagle, Leon, and Dale were gone.

Four months of combat had taught Ed how to survive, physically and emotionally. Hold back and work toward the flank, firing occasionally but not enough to attract attention: take cover often. But he hadn't done that. He had fired his entire 160 rounds of M-1 ammunition, then picked up a Schmeisser and nearly burned it out. That isn't survival procedure. Ed had soldiered; he was too shrewd to simply get caught up in the emotion of an attack. Maybe he was trying to get a quick wound. Maybe he—I don't know what; Ed gave until he was empty.

Standing at the lonely edge of that field I began to smell decaying bodies. My fingers became warm and sticky, my feet were numb, I was cold and frightened. I simply couldn't go any farther. There were ghosts everywhere. Marie held my hand and comforted me while we walked back to the car. I couldn't go over to the Roman villa. I had expected to stop at the bierstube and raise a cool beer in memory of King Company, but couldn't.

After I calmed a bit we drove to Serrig, the small town where K Company had crossed the Saar, taking heavy casualties. I stood on the bank and looked over the peaceful river where my brothers had crossed in fog and smoke with machine guns firing blindly at them, bullets tearing through the plywood boats and into frightened boys. In this quiet, peaceful place, shrapnel had ripped through Jim Westmoreland's lungs and torn the muscles of his back. The cement fortifications on the other side had been painted to look like farmhouses; the faded paint still showed. Giving Patton his due, the German general reported that resistance would have been much better if the "enemy hadn't moved so rapidly"; as it was, the Germans were able to get only half their troops over the river and had no time to prepare the defense. If Serrig had any ghosts, they didn't bother me, but I had seen enough of the war. We drove up the Mosel and had wine, bread, and cheese in a peaceful inn near Bernkastel-Kues.

In the summer of 1984 we went to England on a six-month leave from Louisiana State University for me to study at the University of Reading and Marie to work at Kew Gardens. We landed at Heathrow Airport on August 13. Forty years earlier to the day, I had gone through Reading on a troop train headed for Chippenham. This time we caught a bus to Reading and went to the hotel for a short rest. The laboratory where I was to work was located in an old World War II hospital. The structure and design were exactly that of the hospital in Hereford. Walking through the old ward was like going back in time. (Part of the dazed feeling probably lay in the fact that my body was still on Louisiana time. It took me three weeks to get my clock reset.) I spent most of the time at Reading studying, but over coffee and tea I learned about Britain. Coffee was the morning break, tea the afternoon. I was the only one who could talk firsthand about wartime Britain. Among the other members of the lab, even the older ones had been young children during the war and remembered only what their parents had told them.

"In October I want to go over to Brittany to see where I won the war. Forty years ago I was stationed at Chippenham. I was a rifleman in the President's Own Ninety-fourth Light Infantry." I talked confidently but was still worried. I knew I wasn't ever going back to Nennig again, but in Brittany I had been a kid and war had been a game. I would enjoy a holiday in Brittany. I had been living in south Louisiana for twenty years, and I could speak Cajun French well enough to get along. I had once known Breton French pretty well, and it would come back to me quickly. The problem was that I wasn't sure I could find the areas where we had fought. I knew nothing of Lorient. I knew a little of the area around Quimperlé. We had patrolled nearly to Gestel, but that was a long way from Lorient.

Once after the war I had written Francis Peramont, the fourteen-year-old boy who had practiced his English on us. I knew that he had attended the Collège Moderne at Quimperlé; with that information I was able to get his current address in Vannes—where he was teaching English. He telephoned saying for us to hurry down before the rains started. I had no trouble remembering the cold rains of November. Marie and I flew to Nantes, where Francis and Hélène were to meet us. I vaguely remembered the fourteen-year-old boy of forty years ago. He remembered a skinny nineteen-year-old. I was fifty pounds heavier and he had a thick, graying beard. Fortunately, it was a small airport and our wives had no outdated images. They brought us together because each was obviously searching for someone.

After the war, Francis had finished school and moved to Lorient, where he worked helping to rebuild the city. He began teaching after that and met Hélène, who was also a teacher. They had no children— or rather, they had a thousand children at the school. Francis taught all morning and had the afternoons off. They could both be off all day Wednesday. This schedule determined our program. Because Etel was close by, we decided to go there the first afternoon (Monday). Marie had a slight cold and Hélène had to teach, so only Francis and I went.

Etel had been a fishing village on a small bay where the Etel River ran into the Atlantic. After the war, Lorient's rebuilt harbor had facilities to handle fishing boats that were larger and could work over a greater area than before. This advance was partly the legacy of the German navy, which had improved the port. Etel was one victim of the change: its smaller boats could no longer compete economically, although even today a few older fishermen continue to work out of Etel, mainly because they enjoy it. Maybe *victim* isn't the word for Etel's fate; the place died as a fishing village but became a summer resort. The bay is small and peaceful, with good sport fishing. There is always a nice breeze coming off the Atlantic. As the fishermen retired, their homes were converted into rental houses; most of the renters are Parisian families who want to get away from the city.

We drove to the almost-deserted dock. The vacation season was over, and only two men were there working on their boats.

"Do you know where the Americans assaulted the fortifications?"

"Les Américains? Ici? Mais non."

We found an older man who said his brother had been there with the FFI. "They came along that road and unloaded at the end by those two houses. After the attack they carried the wounded out on jeeps." Francis had to translate all of this to me; the words sounded nothing like the French we used in Louisiana, and were spoken much more rapidly. Francis drove us along the indicated road and stopped at the end. That's where the Queen of Battle had sat alongside the houses, forty years ago. The cold wind had cut us while we waited to move up. At the bend in the road, a walkway led into a small, wet pasture where a few cows were grazing. The meadow had stone walls and the layout of a Celtic field. It was the old minefield. That cold December night in 1944, we had gone the length of it, which was only about thirty-five yards but had seemed like a hundred. The whole area had been a series of narrow fields leading to a trail lined on both sides by a stone wall.

Francis and I walked across the old minefield. I remembered how we had drawn bayonets to probe for mines when Simmers at first couldn't find the path cleared by the engineers. After the attack the engineers discovered that the path wasn't necessary because salt water had corroded and rusted the mine mechanisms. The only vegetation in the soggy field was sedges and marsh grasses. We went through the gap and took the trail. Ahead on the left, a housing development was under construction; that night we had gone to the right, our objective the big bunker overlooking the bay. It was eerie to walk here warm and dry and standing upright. I didn't recognize anything: I was working from a forty-year-old memory of a crawl in the dark. Then the bunker loomed up. From this side it was about six feet high, with a few artillery scars and many rusty hooks on which the camouflage nets had been tied. I had sat about here and looked over the wall at first light. That's where the guard had stood, stamping his feet to keep warm. I had felt sorry for him, knowing that within a few minutes he was going to die from machine-gun bullets or a massive artillery barrage.

Moving closer I could see the slit for the German machine gun. Now it had a small glass window in it. The trail ended where a new asphalt road came up from Etel going to the housing development. The front of the bunker had a fence around it. A sign on the gate gave the telephone number of a rental agency. I had to laugh. For rent: Vacation cottage with picture window overlooking beautiful Etel bay. Window is tall but narrow because constructed to house coastal gun. Original metal security door removed after unfortunate explosion just before original owners decided to move.

I would have enjoyed a tour of the house, but the rental agency was closed for the season. Throughout that area, most of the old German bunkers had been renovated into houses and shops. After the war, the French government had decided that it owned the bunkers. If a citizen had one on his land and wanted to use it, he could buy it from the government; there was no charge for not using it. We took some pictures and went back down the trail. I stopped and looked for bullet scars along the stone wall. That was hopeless; it had happened too long ago, and I had no precise location. But this was the drab gray wall where I had almost died. If I had followed orders and stayed put, I probably would have died. If I had crawled away sooner, I might not have been wounded. Would I then have frozen my feet like George or broken mentally along with Ed in the Nennig attack?

Somewhere near here an artillery shell had mangled poor loyal Mack almost beyond recognition when he forgot to wait for Westmoreland's signal and jumped up as soon as he saw the cease-fire flare. His IQ had been only a little higher than H.R.'s.

We went back across the minefield to the place where Dick Simmers had met me with a bottle of whiskey. "Francis, ask that old woman if she lived in the house when we fought."

"No, hardly anyone stayed when the Germans were here. It was too dangerous and you couldn't fish."

That was it. And all in all it had gone well—much better than Nennig. The place had ghosts, but only of loyal young men trying to serve to the best of their ability. Well, Lehrer had been there, terrified. He had been running away when he got to me, and I had chewed his butt, saying that if he kept running I would shoot him in the back. He turned around and ran to Westmoreland with the word that Standifer, Mack, and Blake were dead. Maybe I should have shot him anyhow. But then he would have gotten a Purple Heart and been one of the Etel heroes.

The Etel visit could have gone badly, but with Francis' friendship and support, it had been peaceful, quiet, and pleasant. I was beginning to get excited about Lorient. The four of us started early Wednesday morning on the fifty- to sixty-kilometer trip. Soon we moved out of the flat country into rolling hills like those around Quimperlé. The walls of the old stone houses were the same, but the thatched roofs had been replaced with neat gray slate. (Thatched roofs are pretty and insulate well, but the fire insurance on them is prohibitive.) The farmyards were clean and well-kept instead of the dirty quagmires I remembered, but they weren't working farms anymore. The suburban trend was to renovate an old farmhouse and commute to Lorient. There were still a few apple trees here and there, but they looked awful. Marie had grown up on an apple farm in Michigan, and I had told her about the beautiful apple orchards of Brittany.

"Francis, what happened to the apple trees?" He didn't know what I meant. It turns out that Brittany isn't nearly the apple country that Normandy is. Cider production is only a cottage industry and no one has ever taken care of the trees. They looked as good as they had ever looked. To a boy from Mississippi, any apple orchard had been beautiful.

I was glad to see that the old farmhouses were still in use, and I mentioned the one at Tréoual with the date 1528 carved over the doorway. I recalled being impressed that a house built virtually in medieval times was not a museum.

Francis laughed. "All three of the houses at Tréoual were built in 1914. The stonemasons liked old buildings, so they carved early dates on them."

We were coming to the outskirts of Lorient. There were large condominiums with nice shopping areas, all built after the war. Lorient itself is only about three hundred years old. The French East India Company (Compagnie des Indes Orientales) established it as a port to avoid the municipal laws of St.-Nazaire. It was named L'Orient because the company traded with India and China. Old Lorient is virtually gone. As we reached the city's prewar edge we saw a few old houses, then a mix of new buildings and older ones. All of the old structures showed scars from the bombing. Closer to the town center there were no old buildings at all—everything had been destroyed by the bombs. The little narrow streets had been replaced by wide clean boulevards.

We drove to the city hall, which had a fortieth-anniversary exhibit: "Bombs over Lorient: The Agony of a City." The entrance to the exhibit had a rusty B-17 engine on one side and a rusty American .50-caliber machine gun on the other. Francis asked, "Do you remember the .50 looking down the road to Cadic?" Francis had seen the seven dead Germans before they were taken off for burial—"That gun sure makes a mess." Did I really want to go back to see that little road? Would the ghosts be there?

The exhibit fascinated me. I looked over a mass of posters and leaflets telling civilians what to do during an enemy air attack. The enemy planes shown were British Wellingtons and American Flying Fortresses. The enemy was us. The Germans never bombed Lorient. A big collection of photographs showed picturesque scenes of the old town center. Parts of Vannes still look that way. Then there were pictures of the same spots after bombing—almost completely rubble. I had passed through Nuremburg after the war, and the area around the station had been absolute rubble. Except for an occasional lamppost, you couldn't tell where streets had been. Lorient wasn't quite that bad, but both were terrible, and degrees of terrible don't mean much. Does it matter that Nuremburg was an enemy town? Innocent people bled and died in both places.

There were pictures of the submarine base, first when it was under construction, then after having survived the air raids. You could see the heavy antiaircraft protection. There were mannequins of British and American airmen and of a German submarine commander. Why not something to show that the American infantry had fought here for nine months? Because we had not been part of the bombing or the liberation.

When the Germans started building the submarine base, a French engineer, Jacques Strosskopf, was in charge of construction. In 1941 he passed copies of the plans to the British to show them what the installation would grow into if it weren't bombed. The French underground didn't realize that as yet the British couldn't do much bombing. It had been frustrating to see the construction progressing so rapidly. After the base became operational, the Allies began bombing, but the bombs barely scratched the thick concrete structures. The entire center of the town was destroyed with no effect on the base.

The exhibit included a series of charts showing the numbers of supply ships sunk each year by U-boats. As the submarines were destroyed, the shipping rose. Finally it became possible to ship enough men and supplies to support the D-Day invasion. The theme was that the destruction of Lorient was necessary before the invasion and liberation were possible. It looked reasonable, but in fact the submarines were destroyed in the Atlantic after sonar was perfected. The destruction of Lorient amounted to harassment.

We left the exhibit and went to the submarine base at Keroman, which was no longer a distinct town but part of urban Lorient. The base was not open to the public because it was still an operational naval station. We stood at the quay where the submarines had come in after their two-month missions. In his book *Iron Coffins*, Herbert Werner describes the U-557 coming into this spot after it had sunk 37,000 tons of shipping. Submarines from here had lain in wait at the mouth of the Mississippi to sink freighters coming out from New Orleans. We hadn't known how successful they were because of censorship. I had a cousin in the merchant marine working out of New Orleans, but the family worried more about my safety because I was in combat. Lothar-Günther Buchheim's *Das Boot* was written with Lorient as its primary base. In the movie, the sub pens are those of La Rochelle because the French navy wouldn't allow the film makers to use the active base at Lorient.

A German band playing just where we were standing had welcomed each returning submarine crew. A chain then pulled the sub along tracks and into the repair bunker. During the air raid period, the Germans could get a sub out of the water and into the bunker in two minutes. There had been a square in front of the old prefecture building. Admiral Doenitz would come from Kernvel and review the crews returning from missions. I wondered if the officers said, "Submariners, pass in review," and the band played Sousa-style marches.

We wanted to take Francis and Hélène to lunch at one of Lorient's fine restaurants—provided that Francis chose the restaurant and ordered for us. He suggested a seafood restaurant well known for a local specialty he thought we would like, although he would have to show us how to eat it. "I'm not sure what it would be called in English, but it is very popular here." We started with wine, a wonderful bread, and salad. Then the waiter hefted in a large steaming platter of crawfish! I realized how close I was to home: crawfish is a favorite of French Louisiana, too. I enjoyed the contentment of sitting in a restaurant overlooking the submarine base we had tried to capture and eating boiled crawfish. The local crawfish were a bit larger than ours—I realize now that they were probably small lobsters—and the seasoning was subtler than the fiery "crab boil" that everyone uses in south Louisiana.

After lunch we started for Quimperlé. *Quimper* is a Celtic word meaning "river junction." The *lé* refers to the town's being at a junction of the river Ellé with another stream. Quimper, where George, Ed, and I once had crêpes suzette, is a larger city also located on a river junction. I was beginning to understand how much of Celtic Britain remained in Brittany. We passed the airport that Lorient had planned before the war but hadn't been able to build because the farmers weren't willing to give up their land. The Germans had looked at the plans, cut the red tape, and built it.

Then we went through Gestel. I remembered some combat advice: "If you get cut off on a patrol, stay away from Gestel. Those innocent little houses are full of German troops." Francis said it was a common billeting method for Germans. If they built barracks, we would bomb them so they billeted with French families. Hélène had lived near St.-Nazaire at that time. Three German officers were billeted in her home. She didn't remember it as a bad situation. The family usually had more food than others did. The officers were never harsh. In fact, the main conflict she remembered was her mother scolding the Germans about not keeping their rooms clean. I used to think of Gestel while I stood guard in the cold rain. My German counterpart was sleeping in a warm bed in Gestel. That wasn't precisely true. I had seen Germans standing guard when we patrolled in the cold rain. But when they weren't on line, they lived in Gestel.

Francis broke into my thoughts: "Locmaria is over that way. The remains of Cap Kerdudal are right down there. They didn't rebuild it after the war." Cap Kerdudual was the high place where Richards had walked into the machine gun.

We turned off the highway and drove down a small asphalt road to a little two-farm village with a small chapel. This was Ste.-Marguerite. It had been far out beyond our lines, a spot where, about forty-five minutes or an hour into the patrol, we would take a break. I would sit on a stone, lean back against the chapel, and shake a bit. The stone was there and I sat on it again.

We drove about two hundred yards to the next town. Francis said: "This is Cadic. My house was right over there beside the railroad." This didn't sink in very well; I remembered his house as being a long way from Ste.-Marguerite.

We took some pictures and drove another couple of hundred yards. "This is the position where you had the .50-caliber machine gun." I knew he was wrong because I could look back and see Ste.-Marguerite not a quarter-mile away. The hedgerows and brush were all gone, but Strongpoint Graziano should still have been identifiable; it had stood on a steep hill, looking down a narrow sunken road. Francis and I argued about the gun's location, while Marie and Hélène laughed at us.

Slowly, I saw how things had been. Westmoreland had made a good decision in placing a daytime position here. It looked strange now because Strongpoint Graziano was the front yard of a modern home. The point where the gun had waited was no longer a hedgerow, but a small fence. A flood of memories hit me. For the first six weeks this had been the focal point of my war. It was home when we came in from patrol. Most of the time it was a dull place where George and I would sit all day and discuss the meaning of life. At nineteen you can come very close to eternal truths.

We doubled back to the night position. A hedgerow still surrounded the small field, but the brush was so thick that we couldn't get in. From the road I could see the tree where George, Ed, and I had shared the guard post. I remembered the hours of solitude I had spent there thinking of war, courage, fear, and patriotism. We had sung songs to the Germans: "We must be vigilant" and "They'll be drivin' Tiger tanks when they come!" and, of course, "Drinkin' Beer." Where that brush now grew we had spent thirty-six hours on alert and in shock when Third Platoon had been captured; as I looked the place over I was glad Ray hadn't let us go way out beyond Ste.-Marguerite to set up an ambush.

Tréoual was down the road to the left. The road was now paved, but the improvement stopped at Tréoual. Beyond there, it was still the kind of sunken road I remembered; narrow and muddy, with hedgerows and brush on each side—an easy place to walk, but bad if you got ambushed. That was what the road to Cadic had looked like.

Tréoual was still a one-family farmstead with a house, two stone storage buildings, and a barn at the end. Ed had been standing near the road close to the main house. I had been chasing the rooster toward him from back near the barn. I suppose the rooster ducked between the two storage buildings when he saw Ed. The scene was much smaller and simpler than I remembered it. The buildings were very close together; I had remembered the space as being a small side street. I think the German must have been hiding back there, waiting for us to leave. He may even have been trying to surrender. But when the rooster turned and ran, I did too.

The farmer came out to see what we were doing in his barnyard. He recognized Francis from school days. They spoke in French about old times. I could catch a few words but not enough to follow the conversation. When Francis introduced me, I tried my Cajun French, but the farmer understood nothing of it, so Francis translated while I apologized for stealing the man's chickens. It turned out that the couple who owned the chickens had died long ago, and their children had sold the land to this man. He worked in Lorient and farmed as a hobby, but we weren't looking at some quaintly remodeled farm-house—the place was a dirty, muddy farm with a few cows and a few chickens.

I asked the man where he had lived when the Boche were here. He said he had lived in Quimperlé when les Allemands were here. I began to realize that only I was calling them "Boche." It had become a dirty word. The Germans had occupied this area during a war long ago. The war was over and the Germans were welcome as tourists. Most of the household appliances in the homes were German. The older people remembered that some German soldiers had been mean, but others had been nice. Building the submarine base had provided work for a lot of the men.

After we walked back to Strongpoint Graziano, the others gave me a little time alone to think, to be nineteen, proud and brave. *The thoughts of youth are long, long thoughts.* I looked over the rolling hills and thought of Dale. *I am Proctor who followed the gleam.* I had dreamed of charging a machine gun, giving the Rebel yell, capturing the gun, and earning a Silver Star. I had thought that courage was an absolute: you were brave or a coward. But courage is a sometimes thing. If things go well, you can be confident and brave, but sometimes nothing goes well; you make awful decisions and can hardly stave off terror. Even an all-American quarterback has days on which he can do nothing right. Loyalty, love, and integrity are absolutes, but sometimes they aren't enough. My war wasn't very rough; I was never really tested. At Nennig I had wavered a little, but that was because all my friends were gone. Most of the studies on the psychology of combat conclude that fighting for God and Country is much less important than fighting for George and Ed; you fight for the group. I agree, but the psychologists should remember that we joined the army be-

cause the community endorsed the war. In contrast, the Vietnam draft
was a disaster.

We got in the car, drove back a little way, turned left, and started
down a short slope. "Wait, we have to stop here. That's the famous
creek. I was about here behind that wall. No, I had slipped to this side
and was picking blackberries."

Willi had been right down there when he scared me with his burp
gun. I wanted a picture of me picking blackberries. As we walked
down to the creek, I looked up at the banks and realized that Willi *had*
been trying to kill me, but missed. Burp gun slugs are heavy, with a
short range. I had been about thirty yards away, but because of the
slope he had overestimated and aimed too high. Why hadn't I shot
him? It was probably buck fever. I had a good firing position and had
seen movement. The M-1 had more power than burp-gun slugs; eight
rapid-fire rounds would have hit him or come very close. The creek
wasn't nearly as large as I remembered, three or four feet across and
maybe a foot deep. George, Ed, and I had been washing up right here
when Third Platoon went out on patrol.

A little farther down, we passed a farmhouse cluster I recognized.
The pretty French girl had lived there. Francis knew the family, but
they didn't have a daughter. "Now, I remember. For a while they kept
a refugee from some bombed city. She was friendly and pleasant, but
no one knew much about her. She wasn't a very good worker."

I tried to remember more. The house had been just behind the
Third Platoon position; some of those boys were always around her. I
remembered that she hadn't been able to learn any English at all. We
would try to teach her names for objects: apple, bread, canteen. She
could repeat the names but couldn't remember them. Francis hadn't
known this; he said she must not have tried very hard, because learning GI terms had been a popular pastime in the farm families.

What Francis said came back strongly two years later when I read
Wilhelm Fahrmbacher's account of the siege of Lorient. The former
German commandant praised the French for their help and coopera-
tion throughout the siege, and said that he had paid them a total of
seventy million francs for goods and services. That pretty girl had
moved into the area during July or August, and had left when the
French soldiers took over the area. Is it possible that behind her blank

smile she understood every word we were saying? She could have carried information to the Germans very easily. French people often passed through our lines to visit relatives. It seems unlikely that her reports could have been the Germans' only source of information from our sector. In planning the Third Platoon ambush, they certainly needed more than a girl listening to some GIs.

We turned down a lane crossing an open field, and Francis laughed. "You were here with the crazy officer we called the 'Chicago gangster.'"

"Yeah. That was Chilton. We had a hard time teaching him to soldier." Francis remembered that Chilton was always chasing him off, saying that all the French were spies.

I had to defend Chilton on that. "Remember that he was brought in because our patrol had been sent into a planned ambush. Francis, were there really a lot of spies around here?"

"No, there weren't any. Well, I don't know. I was just fourteen, and I only heard people talking about liberation. After Lorient surrendered, the collaborators there were all punished. Women who had dated or even worked for the Germans had their hair cut off and were publicly humiliated. Some of them had actually been informants for the FFI, working in bars or dating Germans to get information. Since the war, it hasn't been popular to admit to spying for the enemy. I suppose there were spies around here; maybe some were punished. I was really too young to know such things."

I couldn't get my bearings at all in the big field. We had built our dugout somewhere out there, but the hedgerows had been cleared. Francis kept reminding me that the hedgerows were properly called "talus," because of the rocks; Normandy had hedgerows. The two-family village that had stood in front of K Company's position was being remodeled. Francis and I went down and saw the old well. On those cold fall nights someone used to get up and draw water. The chain rattled as the bucket fell into the water with a splash; then came the creak of cranking it up. I remembered hearing it the night we took a patrol out to ambush the Germans. The ambush field had been somewhere over near Kervalze, probably close to the old highway, but we couldn't locate it now.

Francis was a patient host. "Do you want to go to Cap Kerdudal and Locmaria?" No. I had seen enough. Now Marie and I wanted to visit the coastal area where Gauguin had painted. It was across the river and down through a beautiful forested area. The coastline was wonderful; large granite boulders with the waves washing over them, and occasional sandy beaches. We stopped at a little restaurant overlooking the coast, had coffee and sandwiches, and talked about the old days.

The trip back to Vannes was warm and comfortable. I had seen the war and it was over. "Francis, what were the Germans like?"

He thought for a minute. "I don't know. We didn't see them much." He remembered a patrol that inspected the railroad tracks every day, but they didn't stay around. The bakery in town had a contract to furnish bread once a week. The soldier driving the bread-wagon would usually shove a loaf off when he saw some kids, so they looked forward to his coming. The submarine crews had a rest camp at Plouay, and some of the girls went to dances there. The crews would get drunk and occasionally cause trouble, but in general the Germans were orderly.

Until the Americans came, Francis hadn't seen the Germans in combat. They were always dressed neatly and looked sharp with their black boots, leather belts, and big belt buckles. The American soldiers looked sloppy. "You wore faded cotton uniforms that were dirty and baggy. Instead of leather, you had canvas rifle belts, unpolished shoes, and canvas leggings. You joked, sang songs, lay around, and got drunk whenever possible. It was hard to believe you were beating the Germans."

I laughed because his description was absolutely right. "Yeah, I suppose we didn't look like an army, but we fought well."

The Germans had an extremely good image-army. Even now TV producers enjoy using the polished black leather, the imposing helmet, Stuka dive bombers with shrieking air sirens, and the stark, bold form of the swastika for creating images of evil, efficient invincibility. German infantry wore caps on patrol because the helmet blocked their hearing, but its shape was so impressive that Steven Spielberg adopted it for Darth Vader. The old Teutonic form of the swastika was not nearly as striking as the new block form that Hitler-the-artist selected.

This image, with hard work and creative tactics, frightened the entire world; yet we still do not know how the German army of 1939 and 1940 would have fared against a well-trained, confident force that could not be bluffed. In any case, Hitler (meaning his entire leadership group) did not develop uniforms, flags, and trappings to frighten the world. He began with a defeated, fragmented, and diverse group of cultures and molded them into a confident national community, the *Volksgemeinschaft*. His flags, posters, and uniforms reinforced his hypnotic speeches. There were many components in the Wehrmacht's confidence and pride, but certainly the uniform played a part. Earl F. Ziemke's report on the attitudes of Germans toward occupying troops emphasizes that the Americans seemed to have no pride in the uniform they wore.

Image is a key to confidence in every army. Our image was as carefully cultivated and as misleading as that of the Nazi-designed army. We were sons of the pioneers, railsplitters, mountainmen, cowboys, rednecks, and lumberjacks. Our image was, and still is, pragmatism. We were massive power, competence, and ingenuity in the face of hardship. The hero of Mauldin's cartoons in *Up Front* was the sloppy, undisciplined, pragmatic American soldier. It was an open secret that when necessary, that slouching, unshaven GI could be strongly disciplined and dedicated to the needs of his unit. The infantry, with dirt behind their ears, could lick their weight in wildcats and drink their weight in beers.

But pragmatism means getting the job done even though that may require the sacrifice of ethics, honor, and integrity. The Iran-Contra arms deal was pragmatism. In World War II, we pragmatically put loyal Japanese Americans in prison camps. At a much lower level, my regiment left German bodies to rot, not from malice, but because it was practical. Our medical officers used the term *objective-mindedness* instead of pragmatism. Patton epitomized objective-mindedness when he drove his combat troops to near-exhaustion during the Battle of the Bulge; the British were shocked and the Germans amazed. Perhaps Patton saved more combat casualties than he lost to frozen feet, pneumonia, and combat fatigue; or maybe he was just feeding his ego. Pragmatically, he may have been right in slapping that private. It defined his standards of military conduct. After the war he turned civil control over to any Germans who were able to do the job, regardless of their political history. That pragmatism cost him the command of his Third Army.

Charles B. MacDonald, in his book *Company Commander*, has a section on his concern over men in his company killing prisoners simply because it was more convenient than taking them to the collection point. He was permitting a flagrant violation of the Geneva convention, but rationalized it on the grounds that it would become an atrocity only if we lost. There must be a place for ethical pragmatism even in combat, but I'm not sure where.

Marie and I stayed a few more days for sightseeing. Francis and Hélène took us to Carnac to see the great stone monuments, built before Stonehenge. Dale had talked about these structures and wanted to see them. Nothing is known about the builders. What drove them to so much work? Was it a religious effort?

The visits to Nennig and Lorient had brought me some peace but had stirred up several disturbing questions. "I know because I was there" is not an absolute. I knew only what a young rifleman had seen. But Dick Simmers and Jim Westmoreland understood more of what was happening, which leads me to another thread of this story.

Sometime in the early 1950s, I got a letter from Dick Simmers saying that his head injury was such that he could only work for short periods, but that he was helping a group of men to organize a divisional veterans group. He was particularly interested in contacting all the men of the original K Company who had gone overseas together. I had a few addresses and suggestions, and I offered to search some telephone directories for him. His final list, which he sent to each of us, was impressive. The division began having annual reunions, and I heard that K Company invariably was the most heavily represented.

I had researched the addresses out of respect for Dick, but I didn't want to attend a reunion. Why should we dig up pain, fear, and shame? For years I avoided the gatherings. Then, finally, in the summer of 1978, I was in Denver on business at the same time the division was having its reunion there. Okay, I would stop by to see who showed up. Ray Monti, our platoon sergeant, recognized me immediately and started introducing me around. A lot of the K Company boys were replacements I didn't know. I bumped into Monty Staton, my Third Platoon sergeant. We talked awhile about Chilton. Staton hadn't known him well, but remembered him as an aggressive man trying to break into a very close-knit group. He also pointed out that Blake and I had been pretty harsh on Chilton.

In a sense, Staton was right. Ed was a master at subtle harassment, I was a good student, and we both had inflated egos. But we also knew that a frustrated officer could make mistakes that would kill us all. Still, there is a limit to what you should expect of nineteen-year-old kids with no authority and a tremendous amount of responsibility, and the officers should have solved the problem. Either Simmers or Westmoreland could have sat on us and put an end to the harassment. More important, Simmers should have shown Chilton how to handle troops. I don't know whether Simmers tried. When I asked about Chilton at a reunion, Dick changed the subject. I think Westmoreland must at least have protested to Chilton. Jim always considered that Ed and I were just on loan until things settled down. When I asked him about Chilton at a later reunion, he laughed and said, "No comment."

Staton did have comments. "Standifer, you made at least as many mistakes as Chilton." I asked if he had known I didn't shoot the machine gunner. No, he said—but he saw how mad Blake got, and guessed I had made a fool of myself again.

I ate lunch with Jim and Jo Westmoreland. Jo was a gentle, beautiful wife for Jim. While he was visiting with someone else I was able to tell her how deeply I admired her husband and that I had often built decisions around the question, "What would Westmoreland have done?"

When the division met in New Orleans, Marie and I spent two days visiting with the Simmerses, Westmorelands, and Montis. The local newspaper printed an extensive story on the reunion, explaining that we had been the spearhead division for Patton's asssault on the Siegfried Line. Our divisional paper reported that somebody was listening to a couple of bellboys discussing the article: "You mean that these pot-bellied old men were General Patton's assault troops?"

I made a trip to Brittany in 1984 and reported my experiences in a letter to the platoon. By 1986, my report had produced many questions on which I needed help. The division's reunion that year was scheduled to be near Detroit, where Marie had grown up and where most of her relatives lived. We decided to go up for a visit and to let me see the platoon again, but the gathering was pretty slim. Dick Simmers and Monty Staton were too sick to travel, and Ray Monti had died of a heart attack. Jim and Jo Westmoreland were there but spent the day sightseeing. Marie and I did get to sit with them on the night of a banquet. Jim and I talked so much that the women couldn't hear the entertainment. We had to retreat into a hallway for serious discussion.

My primary concern was about what had actually happened at Nennig. "Jim, I think I killed a man with a knife, but I'm not sure it wasn't a nightmare."

It wasn't. The next day, the battalion intelligence officer had contacted Jim to say that one of Jim's scouts was close to the breaking point. I had made the patrol and given a reasonable report, but I was covered with blood and my nerves were tightly strung. Jim already knew that I was under stress, so he went to the battalion aid station to request that I be pulled off the line for a few days' rest, because of both my cold and my nerves. A few days earlier, however, General Patton had chewed out our division commander about the large numbers of "noncombat casualties." I suppose that meant frozen feet, exhaustion, pneumonia, and combat fatigue. As a result, the aid station had orders to impose higher standards for admissions. Jim had known the medical officer since Camp McCain, and tried to argue that a few days' rest was better than pneumonia or a nervous breakdown. The man had either no imagination or no courage, which is why Jim had to keep sending me to the aid station.

We tried to piece together Ed Blake's story, but with only a little success. Understandably, Jim had blocked out a lot of that day. He rebuilt fragments for me, but it was painful even after forty years. The platoon had fought well against heavy opposition and in bitter cold. Everyone was shocked by the moaning and screaming German wounded. Jim thought he remembered Ed running out of ammunition and picking up a German burp gun. Beyond that, he had only flashes of wounded men stumbling through the snow, firing at their tormentors. After the battle he realized how much the platoon had given. Nearly everyone was wounded. Jim had three shrapnel wounds that he couldn't remember getting. He remembered Ed hugging him and crying something about "the pigs." Jim had thought he was talking about the Germans, but I remembered Ed's finding the pig-

gnawed corpse. It doesn't really matter what happened. Ed's circuits
simply overloaded. But sharp, bitter, cynical Ed had carried his load.
He collapsed, but only after the game was over.

Jim and I talked a little about Brittany. He had been lonely there.
He couldn't speak French and wasn't free to slip off as we kids did. I
asked what he remembered about our aborted night ambush. Both he
and Dick had been furious with the man at Battalion G-2. Dick should
have refused to send us out, but he was a loyal soldier. Jim remembered very little more than I did about the Third Platoon ambush.
Dick had chosen Richards and Button as point scouts—he had more
confidence in them than in Ed and me. Jim had discussed the planned
route with them and pointed out the problem at Cap Kerdudal. Richards had said that he planned to hold the patrol in the town (on high
ground) while he and Button checked the far hill. That didn't happen.
Did Richards change his mind, or was he overruled? Either answer is
plausible. Neither Jim nor Dick had known that there would be no
backup force and that the reserve company would be taking showers
in Quimperlé. Those decisions were made by the same man who
planned our night ambush. I can't present his side of the story because
he was killed in Korea.

I asked Jim about the tradition of Westmorelands fighting as infantry. He laughed. "You got that from Dick Simmers." The tradition
existed but wasn't rigid. Jim had taken ROTC at Wofford College and
planned to enter flight school. Because the demand for new pilots was
decreasing, flight school was flunking out increasing numbers of trainees. Jim had chosen infantry not entirely out of tradition, but partly
because his chances of success were better. I noticed that his only two
choices were combat-oriented. Then I asked the final question for this
role model of my youth, my gentle, strong, intelligent, considerate
platoon leader: "Jim, why did we fight?" There was almost no hesita-
tion. "Our country was at war." Loyalty to the community that
raised, fed, loved, protected, and taught us was inviolate. I believe Jim
Westmoreland would have fought honorably and bravely in Vietnam.
I admire his love, loyalty, and courage. I think I would have refused to
go—out of love, loyalty, and courage. Loyalty and honor are individual, often painful, decisions.

# 17 The Country for Which It Stands

Now I am back to trying to explain why we fought, wondering why I attempted such a broad question. I can only give a few ideas on why I fought. It was long ago, but wars don't really change, nor do the reasons for fighting them. Here is my list of reasons, or categories; you can probably think of others.

1. Combat is fascinating, if you can ignore the possible consequences.
2. We seemed to be fighting for a just cause.
3. It was the honorable and ethical thing to do.
4. The country was at war.

The first reason is not as shallow as it might seem. In *Gone with the Wind*, Margaret Mitchell describes a scene in which the men discuss Fort Sumter and the likelihood of civil war. The young southerners are full of excitement, but old man McCrae knows better: "You fire-eating young bucks, listen to me. You don't want to fight. I fought and I know. . . . You all don't know what war is. You think it's riding a pretty horse and having the girls throw flowers at you and coming home a hero. Well, it ain't. No, sir! It's going hungry, and getting the measles and pneumonia from sleeping in the wet. And if it ain't measles and pneumonia, it's your bowels. Yes sir, what war does to a man's bowels—dysentery and things like that."

Old McCrae was wrong. His little speech is like saying football is sleet, mud, broken teeth, pulled muscles, and shattered knees. Football is losing yourself in a community. The whole is greater than the sum of its parts. At high school reunions, the football team sits in a corner and relives the big game they won—or lost, it doesn't really matter. What matters is that for a few hours the individual had no needs or problems; everyone gave the last full measure of devotion. Even defeat was exciting because everyone gave his all.

For excitement, football can't hold a candle to combat. There is the exhilaration of a roller coaster, the challenge of drag racing, and the danger of the Indy 500. Combat is a many-faceted experience. The excitement comes from facing fear, looking it directly in the face, and surviving. It is intensified because you have committed yourself to the group, which is in danger. No sane person would take such risks, but you will do it for the community.

Ninety percent of the combat time is boring. War movies are unrealistic because they can't show the boredom, which seems to act in counterpoint to the excitement. The experience can be enhanced by a vivid imagination, but without the long, dull days with nothing to do but wait, the explosions of activity would lose much of their impact. The noise and dangers of combat are both terrifying and thrilling; the total experience develops into pride. The team effort was satisfying even if you lost.

But excitement and a sense of team effort are not sufficient reasons for risking your life. Regardless of similarities, war is not a football game. What, then, about the second motivation on my list—the justice of the cause? Certainly there is honor in fighting for right and freedom. But war is an obscene activity, war is a mistake made by the country as a whole and fought by its youth. We, or our leaders, try to sanitize it into a just war. The Crusaders used "God wills it!" The German phrase was "God with us." We preferred "In God we trust." If we are right and God is on our side, the enemy becomes the devil incarnate. The noble crusade degenerates into a vicious war because the enemy deserves awful punishment. But the enemy is the other country, and they or their leaders made mistakes. They, too, are fighting a just war and invoking God's patronage to help drive off an enemy who wants to destroy their way of life. In Old Testament times, people at war usually believed that God wanted them to kill every man, woman, and child of the enemy. Sometimes the women could be saved, and occasionally the victors only smote through the loins of the conquered men.

Maybe a parable will illustrate my point. If your house is burning, the fire department tries to put it out. They break down doors and pour water on the new living room carpet, but those actions are not "just" or "ethical" or "moral." Such terms have nothing to do with fire fighting because the fire must be extinguished. While it is burning, no one argues over who started it—although later there may be calls for tighter fire codes.

War is like that, but not precisely. During the Vietnam era, many people believed that the war was a fire that we had started and that it would quit burning if we stopped pouring napalm on it. Before the Persian Gulf War began, Congress argued—often with eloquence— about how we got into the situation and whether to give sanctions more time. When the majority agreed that it was time to fight, politics became irrelevant. The military took control and did a spectacular job of putting out the fire. The cost in Iraqi and Kuwaiti lives was tragic and enormous, but our military losses were small.

At this point, I must say that I do not understand why countries wage war. During the Gulf War, I listened to child psychologists as they tried to help parents explain to their children why we were at war. The children knew that if two of *them* got into an argument and began fighting at school, they would be sent to the principal's office, where—despite claims of "He did it!" and "Did not!"—both would be punished. Maybe children already understand war.

Hitler was an evil man, or maybe he was a marvelous leader who became evil during the war. Hitler plunged the world into war, or maybe he was a bit actor in a war that became inevitable. Historians are still arguing over the causes of World War II, but no one says that either side was blameless. Maybe the verdicts on the Persian Gulf War will come out clearer, but I doubt it.

I grew up in a culture that tried to justify the War for Southern Independence. True, that war was about slavery, which was both morally and economically wrong. But it was also about how slavery should be abolished and what would happen to wealthy slave-owners who were national leaders. The southern soldiers were patriotic and valiant; they committed awful atrocities and had the worst desertion record of any American army. The southern veterans nursed emotional scars until the last man died. Why did they do such awful things, and why did they fight?

This brings me to my third point, the matter of honor. The Confederacy's soldiers fought, as we did, because of what they had been taught about ethics, honor, and duty—because they believed it was possible to serve their society honorably in a just war. But again, war is always obscene. It is an activity in which young men blow holes in stomachs, cut throats, and get blood on their hands. Combat soldiers face the scriptural text that there is a time to die, a time to kill, and a time to hate. The time is now. How can they hate and kill in the name of the Lord? I do not have an answer beyond, "On my honor I will do my best to do my duty."

The final point is, I believe, the strongest. To borrow from Hitler's oratory, we were (and are) a national community of farmers, manufacturers, parents, girl friends, and skinny little kids. We might try to blame the president or Congress for mistakes, but we elected them, and they did what they thought we wanted (or, at least, what they thought would get them reelected). War is a community problem, and we all share in the debt that riflemen must pay.

That simplistic formulation doesn't help the soldier, airman, sailor, or marine who must live with the trauma of what he or his unit did. He was imprinted with a simple and stern ethic, "Thou shalt not kill," which the military community tried to override for wartime. It doesn't matter whether he actually committed the atrocity; the artillery man fired the rounds that the truck driver delivered. The nurses and club-mobile girls saw the effects of war and knew that they, too, were part of it. All of this has been true since the early tribal days of mankind. Countries make mistakes and youths sacrifice their futures, bodies, and lives for God and Country. At first, the soldier tries to maintain his personal ethics, knowing that combat is not an unbridled license to kill. But he has a deeper problem that Shakespeare's "to thine own self be true" cannot answer. A soldier can define his personal ethics, but he is not a lone eagle; he is not Sir Gawain. He is a unit in his platoon, which is a unit of the company, and so on and on. He wears the uniform of his country and is a part of what it does. He can stand above individual obscenities but cannot affect the action of his company or regiment. The military chain of command produces collective guilt. The helpless soldier can only watch. The news releases won't report the brutal truth, and the country won't know until much later. In Vietnam some of the truth was reported, which made the problem worse.

Censorship was tighter during the Persian Gulf War, but we saw enough to know what was happening. Many of us at home grieved daily about the obscenity of war, and this time we shared the blame with pilots and riflemen.

Somewhere in this discussion is my answer to the graduate student who asked why we fought. We fought because of what we had been taught about ethics, honor, and duty—because we believed that we would be able to serve honorably. I am afraid we all found that that is impossible. War is obscene. Even if we succeed at the level of individual ethics, we discover that the army, country, and mankind are flawed. All communities, divisions, and countries have sinned and fallen short of the glory of God. Occasionally, we were misled by evil, stupid people. More often, the leaders were good, intelligent people who made mistakes. Our youth usually had to pay for the larger mistakes, but the guilt belonged to the community. We, the community, served to the best of our abilities, making mistakes and working within guidelines drawn by flawed leaders. But we all sinned.

On a more personal level, how does my list of reasons for fighting conform with my own experience of war? The first reason does not fit my situation well. I did not go to war for the excitement or fascination of combat. In fact, I selected an area in which there seemed to be no possibility of having to fight. But, once I found myself in combat, I enjoyed the fear and excitement of it. The second reason more clearly applies to me. I joined the army believing that our war was just and that Hitler was a personification of Satan. Those perceptions gradually changed as I matured and as I came to see that the German soldiers were ordinary young men. As for honor and ethics, I believed very firmly that I could fight a war while retaining my personal ethical integrity. I had some modest successes and some serious failures. I think the most traumatic blow was the realization that First Platoon, King Company, could not be ethical while remaining loyal to the battalion and regiment.

Loyalty to the group is fundamental—and that brings me back to the fourth reason for fighting. Certainly, I went to war for my country, my community. But going to war and going into combat are two different things, and the motivations behind them differ as well. Psychologists are firm in saying that a rifleman fights for his group of friends rather than for God and Country. (The German soldiers had a saying: "Patriotism dies five kilometers from the front lines.") I fought for my community, but as we got closer to actual combat, that community became less and less the United States of America, and more and more First Squad of First Platoon, flawed but loving and reliable. I was still concerned about God, Clinton, and Country, but when I walked into that machine gun at le Hirgoat it was for the approval of my squad. I wanted them to know that I was reliable because within a few minutes I might be badly wounded and needing their help.

Combat defies description; every football game is different and every player sees it from his own position and background. Perhaps the most fundamental distillation of typical combat would involve a frightened boy being assigned as replacement to a rifle company and being wounded two days later. He remembers the terror and horror, but with little sense of accomplishment because he was never really part of the squad. As combat goes, First Platoon didn't have a very rough time. We were a close, nearly snobbish unit because we had trained together. The group mixed bright, confident kids and more stable, experienced men. We had a reliable platoon leader and a good company commander. Also, we were allowed to ease into combat slowly. I was lucky to survive the childish mistakes I made while I learned to soldier.

We never fought against a very capable enemy. Jim Westmoreland said the quality of the German troops we faced varied from very poor to good, but they were never our equal. Ironically, our superiority created a psychological disadvantage for us because, particularly in Brittany, we tended to see the enemy as blundering and ineffectual—in short, as human. We captured frightened, wounded boys who hurt badly and needed help. But some of their frightened boys killed some of ours.

Our Brittany situation was unusual in that we were able to fight as a unit for three months without substantial casualties. The attack at Nennig was more typical of infantry combat. Riflemen don't last long in heavy fighting. Being well trained and careful helps, but the statistics are against you. There is a Bill Mauldin cartoon in which the rifleman says, "I feel like a fugitive from the law of averages." We all knew we were going to get wounded, either through stupidity or bad luck. We knew about the noise, confusion, and fear. We didn't know that Ed would see a body gnawed by a pig. We didn't realize that we would watch the bodies of brave men freeze, thaw, and decompose. The kids at My Lai didn't know they would have to murder a village.

The SS motto was Meine Ehre heisst Treue—Loyalty Is the Foundation of My Honor. Loyalty is an elusive term. In the 1930s, Lew Ayres starred in the classic antiwar movie *All Quiet on the Western Front,* which emphasizes the brotherhood of man and the obscenity of war. When World War II came, Ayres registered as a conscientious objector, knowing that it would ruin his postwar acting career. Throughout the war he worked as a hospital orderly. Ronald Reagan volunteered for service in the army and was assigned to make training films. Henry Fonda chose the navy and protested strongly when he was given a public relations job. By using political clout, he was able to get a combat assignment, and he came very close to losing his life. Because Fonda was an excellent actor, he could have probably played the title role in *Mr. Roberts* without combat experience, but his record did help the image. At a tribute to his acting career not long before his death, the Naval Academy choral group sang for him; the performance ended with each member stepping forward, saluting, and saying "Thank you, Mr. Roberts." Although I have a conflicting personal opinion, I admit the possibility that all three of these men loved their country deeply and served it loyally.

Love and loyalty do not require that we all fight in the same way. During Vietnam, many brave, loving men fought and died for their country. Some of them were in Vietnam, and others were on college campuses. A similar point was clear during the Persian Gulf War: brave statesmen stood in Congress and said that they felt we should give sanctions more time but would support the community at war. Local communities formed support groups to help families who were paying a higher price than that most of us had to pay. We knew that the entire country was at war.

But if hand-to-hand combat is not the only way to show love of country, why do we veterans brag about it? I think we do it to remember the sensation, to call back the echoes praising the rifleman. Combat is fascinating, frightening, degrading, and exciting. It is a rare opportunity to demonstrate courage and loyalty to your fellow man.

"Greater love hath no man than this." Most of the time, combat is physically no worse than a football game: fatigue, mud, cold, and fear. Psychologically, however, combat is horrible because it scars your soul in the service of God and Country. Veterans come home with intense feelings of both pride and shame; the community can never really understand the depth of the shame, but it helps if they share the pride.

Those of us from World War II came home to honor and respect, which is better than having the community condemn you for the obscenity of war. The scar remains, but we can cover it with medals, bluster, and glory: "Stars and Stripes Forever." The tragedy of Vietnam was not that we were wrong—wars are always the result of mistakes—but that we sent young men and women into combat and ignored the price they paid. We condemned some for the horrors, but we also condemned our children who fought bravely on campus and in the streets, and they were the ones who ended the war. Did we really lose in Vietnam? Did we win in the Persian Gulf? It may not be possible to win a war, but at least this time we will be able to show veterans that there is room for pride.

One of the books about the ASTP trainees' being sent into combat says it was a shame that such bright, promising young men had to be used as cannon fodder. It is a shame that anyone must be used as cannon fodder, but we ASTP men owed a large debt to the country: for loving communities and excellent educations. Ethically, it seems that we *should* have been the ones to pay the higher price. Pragmatically, however, it was an unusual situation. Why are the less-privileged and poorly educated always overrepresented in the more dangerous combat arms? Although the army has an excellent record in implementing social change, its primary mission is to win wars. Soldiers are placed where they are most needed at that time. Dale and Ed could have been excellent electronics technicians, but the army was ready to invade France and needed riflemen.

Dale's and Ed's assignments would have been different if they had been drafted a year earlier. Mack and H. R. would have been riflemen under any circumstances. Mack's weakness was a poor education, but H. R. was simply not qualified to be a soldier. He would have been useful and proud of his contribution if he had been placed in a sheltered workshop producing war-related goods. Have things changed for the new, technological army? The M-1 is no longer a rifle; it is an electronic marvel of a tank. I would have loved having an infrared, see-in-the-dark scope on my rifle during those long nights on guard duty. Shoulder-fired, heat-seeking antitank rockets would have been wonderful at Nennig. How many of us would have been able to use them? Mack and H. R. would not have made useful soldiers in the new army, but that doesn't mean that the brightest and best will now do the fighting. Combat is still boring and terrifying, and riflemen are still called "grunts."

In 1944 the country was at war, and we served where we were put, to the best of our abilities. I am proud to have served as an infantry scout in King Company. But the truth is that I was drafted and put in the infantry, and wanted a transfer to the Signal Corps or anywhere else. Realistically the entire country—men, women, and children, literate and illiterate—fought in the war to the best of our abilities. We can be justly proud of the victories and profoundly ashamed of the things that had to be done.

I suppose I am still a soldier at heart. I still have my old Eisenhower jacket with 9/4 shoulder patch, Pfc. stripe, and combat badge on it. The fabric has shrunken badly through the shoulders and particularly around the waist. The cap with blue braid still fits. Because I am an American, I was also part of the army in Vietnam, which shames me. I think we blundered into the Persian Gulf War, but I helped in the blunders and suffered during the combat there. And I am part of many other communities. I am very much a child of God, and a Christian, but no longer part of the current Baptist church; I am one with them in the Priesthood of Believers. I am grateful both to Clinton and to King Company for love, protection, and training, although I don't agree with all of either one's methods. I still talk like Mis'Sippi and, through loyalty, refuse to change. I am a rhetorical southerner, Celtic, redneck, Good Ole Boy. I get goosebumps when I hear "Stars and Stripes Forever." I love to make a joyful noise singing old revival songs. Praise the Lord and Erin go Bragh.

In England after returning from Brittany, I pondered my old and new questions and looked for reasonable answers. Our chidren flew over to be with us for the Christmas holidays. We stood in the crowd at Heathrow, waiting for them to walk through customs. Beth came out first—Elizabeth Moore Standifer. Tom Moore would be proud of her. She is a missionary in the modern manner. Beth is planning to go into social work. Now she works with Amnesty International and a battered women's program. Then Scott Standifer—how Celtic can you get? Scott is tall, proud, and brave—real BYPU courage. The Vietnam war was over when he turned eighteen, but he registered for the draft because it was the law. He then wrote that he was a conscientious objector and would refuse to fight or to take a job which would relieve someone else to fight. He would not have fled to Canada. These are my beloved children in whom I am well pleased.

We spent a day wandering in London and another day dreaming in the Romano-Celtic ruins at Silchester, quiet and peaceful on the outskirts of Reading. We followed the worn stones of the guards' pathway along the collapsing old walls, and looked over barren fields that still bear the impressions of the ancient streets and foundations of buildings. Camelot, wherever it is, must look like this. Camelot, like First Platoon, existed primarily in the mind; but perception is the base on which reality rests. Individually, Dale, George, Ed, and Jim were not heroic. They became Gawain, Lancelot, Merlin, and Arthur only to the extent that we all believed, loved, and trusted. The whole was much stronger than the sum of its parts.

We went to Scotland to see the Highlands. Scott and I looked in telephone books for Standifers. By now we realized that the root name Standiever is Germanic rather than Gaelic, but in my opinion and experience, race is more cultural than it is genetic. We are Celtic to the core. We spent a day in Edinburgh and went up to the castle that I had visited when I got out of the hospital. There was a large room with memorials to men who had died in the world wars. "When you go home, tell them of us, and say, 'For your tomorrows, we gave our todays.'" That was in memory of a British infantry battalion that had defeated a reinforced Japanese division, and in doing so had been almost annihilated.

We got back to Reading for Christmas, then Beth and Scott went to Holland to spend New Year's with friends. Marie and I had planned to go to a party on New Year's Eve, but decided to stay home because we heard that the Scots went all out for the celebration and we wanted to watch the BBC telecast of the festivities, live from Edinburgh. The celebration wasn't quite up to New Year's Eve in Times Square. The Scots had some dances, told jokes, and made small talk. But we were really waiting for the midnight celebration—to hear "Auld Lang Syne" sung the proper way. At the first stroke of midnight the camera focused on a solitary bagpiper in the kilts of the Black Watch standing on the gray stone wall of the castle battlements. To our surprise, the haunting notes of "Amazing Grace" came floating over the Highlands. I thrilled at it. The war was over. I had gotten rid of the ghosts, the moonlit nights, and the misty mornings. I was heroic Lancelot and glorious Merlin.

> Amazing grace! how sweet the sound
> That saved a wretch like me!
> I once was lost, but now am found,
> Was blind, but now I see.
>
> . . . . . . . . . . . .
>
> 'Twas grace that taught my heart to fear,
> And grace my fears relieved;
> How precious did that grace appear
> The hour I first believed!
>
> Through many dangers, toils and snares,
> I have already come;
> 'Tis grace hath brought me safe thus far,
> And grace will lead me home.

I hate war, and love the warriors.

# Appendix 1  Morning Report: King Company, 1991

*Simmers, Richard, Captain, Company Commander*
Dick was evacuated from Nennig after a shell exploded very near him. He had a few wounds from shell fragments, but the primary problem was concussion damage to his inner ear. Also, his frozen-foot injury was so severe that the surgeon in England advised amputation. Dick refused and was sent home from rehabilitation. He worked briefly as chief of security at Frankford Arsenal but had to retire, suffering from nausea and severe headaches. After that he devoted full time to working with the Ninety-fourth Division Association. He has located and contacted more than 5,000 members whose addresses had been unknown. Dick and his wife, Helen, had attended every reunion until his death in 1987.

*Warren, William C., Captain, Company Commander*
Bill Warren graduated from West Point in 1942 and was immediately assigned to the newly activated 301st Infantry Regiment. He went overseas as company commander of the Third Battalion Headquarters Company. He took over command of K Company after Simmers was wounded at Nennig. Bill retired from the Army in 1963 and worked for the New York Highway Department until his second retirement in 1980. He lives in Delmar, New York, and is active with the Red Cross.

# First Platoon

*Westmoreland, James, Lieutenant, Platoon Leader*

Jim was wounded on four occasions, most severely on February 22, when the company was preparing to cross the Saar River. Shell fragments tore muscles in his back, and some of the metal cut into his lungs. He was sent to a naval hospital in Memphis and underwent therapy for nearly a year. His physical activity was limited through the rest of his life, but he went to Yale for a master's degree in architecture before setting up practice in his hometown of Spartanburg, South Carolina. He retired in 1986 and died a year later of complications arising primarily from his back injuries.

*Monti, Raymond, Technical Sergeant, Platoon Sergeant*

Ray was slightly wounded at Nennig but returned about a week before the Saar crossing. On the morning of that action, he was ordered to send a scout across the river to report back on progress. He sent one who failed to return, then another, and another. He decided that he couldn't continue sending men to apparent death. Ray wrote a short letter to his wife saying that he loved her and might not make it back. As he was preparing to cross the river, one of the scouts returned and reported that a foothold was established. Ray was badly wounded later that day and returned home for discharge. He worked in California as manager for a wholesale dairy products company and retired in about 1976. He died of a heart condition in about 1986. Ray was an extremely good soldier and a dedicated platoon sergeant. We often felt that he watched over us like a mother hen, but that watchfulness reflected dedication and love.

*Staton, Monty, Staff Sergeant, Platoon Guide*

Staton acted as Ray Monti's assistant until after the Third Platoon ambush. He was made platoon sergeant of the new Third Platoon and continued to serve until he was wounded at the Saar crossing. I didn't ever get to know him well, but boys who served under him in the Nennig area were very proud of him. Staton returned to North Carolina, where he operated a farm until his death in 1981.

First Squad

*Graziano, Raymond, Staff Sergeant, Squad Leader*

Ray was slightly wounded at Etel and was transferred to Third Platoon when he returned, which is why I did not see him at Nennig. Ray survived the rest of the war without frozen feet or wounds. He was promoted to platoon sergeant when Staton was wounded. After the war Ray was in the home heating and air conditioning business until his death in 1987. Despite all our kidding about Ray, I enjoyed serving with him and felt that he was a pretty good soldier. He made some mistakes in combat, but so did we all. He was loyal, brave, and considerate—especially of wild young kids.

*Standifer, Leon, Pfc, Scout*

I returned to the company in May, 1945. A few weeks later we were sent to Czechoslovakia to serve on the line between Russian-held and American-held territory. In October those men with enough discharge points were shipped home with the company. I had missed getting a battle star (five points) during my stay in the hospital, so was transferred to guard duty at a POW discharge center near Munich. After the war, I studied soils chemistry at Mississippi State College and worked with a commercial firm for a few years. I learned that the business world was not for me and returned to graduate school, studying plant physiology. In 1961, I came to Louisiana State University, where I stayed until my retirement in 1990.

*Blake, Edward, Pfc, Scout*

I got a Christmas card from Ed after the war, and then no replies to my letters. In the 1970s, I wrote that I was scheduled to attend a meeting in his hometown and would like to stop for a visit. There was no response; the telephone directory listed his home phone and his business, an electrical engineering consulting firm. I was tempted to call, but decided that he had chosen not to aggravate the scars. While writing this manuscript, I have missed Ed and needed his help. At times (maybe five times) I got desperate and wrote asking if he would help and if I could use his name; I got no answer and shouldn't have written.

*Faber, George E., Pfc, BAR*

The day before the attack on Nennig, George was sent on a scouting mission to study the terrain. An artillery shell exploded beside him, knocking him unconscious but with no wounds. After recovering, he crawled back to our positions, and a medic took him to the aid station. They found no serious problems from the explosion, but his feet were badly frozen. George was kept in a Paris hospital for three weeks and given a shot of whiskey every day to make his feet feel better. He was then sent to a hospital near London, where he stayed until after the war ended. He rejoined the company just after I had returned, and we were together until October, when he was shipped home with the division. He attended Ohio State and received a degree in chemical engineering before going to work for the 3-M Company. He retired as plant manager several years ago and now lives in Brea, California. Using his experience as the best poker player in King Company, George occasionally serves as duplicate bridge director on cruise ships. It doesn't pay very well, but he and Sherlie get to travel free. We have kept in Christmas letter contact since the war. I am still grateful for the young man who was my anchor and best friend.

*Cagle, Hubert, Pfc, Sniper*

Cagle traded in his sniper rifle after a few weeks on line; there was no need in shooting people so far away. He got badly frozen feet at Nennig and was discharged the next summer. Cagle returned to his job with J. C. Penney at Knoxville, Tennessee; he later moved to nearby Oak Ridge. I got this information about his civilian life from his widow just after his death in 1985.

*Adams, Herbert, Pfc, Rifleman*

At Nennig, Herb received twenty-one serious wounds from an artillery tree burst. The medic's triage decision was that Herb was so near death that others should be treated first. But Herb was tough; he lived. He was discharged with 80 percent disability: severe head injury, left lung destroyed, and one leg two inches shorter than the other. He returned to his hometown of Brodhead, Kentucky, where he remained until his death in 1979.

*Henry, William, Pfc, Rifleman*

Bill is the man who went through the entire war without a wound—officially, that is; a few months after the war ended, a sore spot developed on his back and a small shell fragment worked itself out. I think Bill became platoon runner when the regular runner was wounded at Nennig; the job was to take messages to wherever he was sent. Bill was with the company when it was sent home in October, 1945. He attended the University of Wisconsin, where he envisioned the commercial potential of computers. Back when you had to persuade people that computers would work, Bill established a consulting firm to help companies develop computerized bookkeeping procedures. He still has the firm, working out of Reedsburg, Wisconsin.

*Prado, Julius, Pfc, Rifleman*

I know very little of what happened to Prado. He was with the platoon when George left, and gone when I got to Nennig. He returned to the company after the war. Dick Simmers obtained a Gary, Indiana, address for him, but there is no Julius Prado now listed in the Gary telephone directory.

*Budny, Walter (Peewee), Pfc, Rifleman*

Again, I have little information. Apparently Peewee was wounded at Nennig and sent home for discharge. At the time he lived in East St. Louis, Illinois, but Simmers was not able to find an address.

*Lehrer, William, Private, Rifleman*

The man whom I call Lehrer was badly wounded during an attack while he was arguing with another GI over possession of a German officer's pistol. I saw him once in England and loaned him five pounds. I knew I wouldn't get it back and that he didn't deserve it, but he was still family. I know that he attended one reunion and have heard that he died of a heart condition in the early 1970s.

*Wendler, Herman, Pfc, Rifleman*

Wendler was one of the good, reliable, sturdy soldiers. Quiet, brave, and capable, he was one of the men who carried me off the hill at Etel. He was discharged with badly frozen feet and works in his old hometown of Morris, Wisconsin.

## Third Squad

*DeRosa, Frank, Staff Sergeant, Squad Leader*

Sometime before the attack on Nennig, Frank was transferred to Second Platoon, then to Third Platoon, and was wounded soon afterward. Frank returned to the company near the end of the war and went home with it in October. He is still active at division reunions.

*Richards, Thomas, Pfc, Scout*

Richards was killed in the Third Platoon ambush. The Germans gave him and the other dead Americans a military burial with full honors, including the firing of rifles over the graves. His body later was reinterred at an American military cemetery not far from Mont-St.-Michel, France. After the war, Jim Westmoreland tried without success to locate Richards' relatives.

*Button, Jack, Pfc, Scout*

Although there is some question about it, Button was probably killed by a member of the Third Platoon patrol. The French FFI officer who was on the patrol panicked and began firing at random when the ambush began. Button had run back to the patrol and was climbing the hedgerow when he was hit. Button, too, was buried in Lorient with military honors, but after the war his body was returned home to southern Michigan. During the war, Dick Simmers received an inquiry from Button's sister, his next of kin, asking for more details. Dick worried over it for several days and decided not to mention the French officer.

*Proctor, Dale, Pfc, BAR*

Dale was from a very poor and hard-working farm family. His high school had three major fields available: commercial training, general, and college prep. Dale chose college prep, hoping that he might somehow be able to afford a higher education. A football scholarship was the answer to that dream. Dale was on the freshman team in the year that Nebraska played Stanford in the Rose Bowl. He is buried in the same cemetery as Richards, just a few rows away. His family decided against having the body returned.

*Herrington, George, Pfc, Rifleman*

At Etel, George had his thigh bone broken by shell fragments. Throughout his life he suffered from various complications of the injury, and finally had a hip replacement in the early 1980s. Infection of the bone caused more problems, and he died in 1988.

*H. R., Private, Rifleman*

There is very little more I can say about H. R. (the initials are pseudononymous; they belong to a friend I like to needle). According to Jim Westmoreland, H. R. was one of the four men in the platoon whose AGCT scores—roughly equivalent to IQ—were around 60. He was a warm, sensitive, caring man, but very child-like. My best guess is that he got into trouble while drunk, and someone killed him, stripped him of his clothes, and threw him into the river. There was a heavy demand for good, warm clothes at the time, and dead bodies in the river were common.

## Third Platoon

*Devonald, David, Lieutenant, Platoon Leader*
At age nineteen, Dave was the youngest officer in the division. He turned twenty a week before the ambush. The officer's bar painted on Dave's helmet made him a prime target; a German rifleman had been assigned to shoot him in the first blast of the ambush. The shot went through the helmet, grazing his head and rendering his entire left side paralyzed. Leaning against the hedgerow, Dave called artillery for the entire five hours. He was taken to a hospital in Lorient, where he received very good treatment and was visited every day by Oberleutnant Schmitt, the intelligence officer. It was through Schmitt's efforts that the prisoner exchange was made. Dave was sent to the States immediately. After six months, he recovered full use of his muscles. Dave taught at a private military school until his retirement in 1986. He died a year later of a heart attack.

*Chilton, D., Lieutenant, Platoon Leader*
The man whom I call Chilton in the text left the company at or before the Nennig attack. He returned to the company just after the war ended and stayed for only a short time. The company still has many Chilton stories, but no one seems actually to remember him personally. Apparently, he was a loner during the entire stay with us. He returned to his hometown, and I understand that he is practicing law there. When the division association wrote asking him to attend a reunion, he replied that he had lost too many friends in the war and didn't want to remember it. I considered writing him to get his side of the story, but decided that he deserved the privacy.

## Enemy Personnel

*Schmitt, Alfons, Oberleutnant, Intelligence Officer*

Before the war Schmitt had been teaching German and English in a Rennes high school. Dave Devonald felt that Schmitt had been placed there as a spy, but I don't think the Germans planned ahead that well. Schmitt was commissioned into the German army to act as translator during the construction of the Lorient Base. Apparently, he was used later to interrogate captured French saboteurs, and then downed American pilots. Schmitt interrogated most of the Third Platoon men in a friendly manner, although he did lose patience with some of them. He had photographs taken of the funeral ceremonies for our dead, brought copies to Dave in the hospital, and said, "When you get home, I hope you will show the Americans that we were not all barbarians."

When the war ended, Schmitt apparently was convicted of war crimes. He was discharged from prison in 1957 and returned to Germany to stay with his next of kin, a nephew. The nephew wrote me that Schmitt had been in extremely poor physical condition because of abuse by guards and died a year later. The nephew was very cooperative but knew nothing about the Lorient period; Schmitt simply did not want to talk about it.

*Gillars, Mildred, Radio Personality*

Midge was originally from Portland, Maine, but graduated from high school in Conneaut, Ohio, and attended Ohio Wesleyan College. Her major interest was drama, but the faculty at Wesleyan remembered her as "completely undisciplined and noticeably eccentric." She went to Europe and had various jobs acting, teaching English, and doing translations. When World War II began, she was broadcasting news in English for the German government. She was also in love with a German Foreign Service officer who kept promising that he would get a divorce and marry her. After Pearl Harbor, the American embassy tried to persuade her to go home, but she decided to remain in Berlin and take German citizenship. She claimed to have renounced American citizenship, but that the records of the action burned in an air raid.

When the Americans invaded North Africa, Midge developed a

news, music, and propaganda program called "Smiling Through." The theme was that Americans couldn't possibly defeat the German army, so it would be much better to surrender and sit out the war in a safe POW camp. (That theme may have sounded more convincing back in those early days than it did by the time we were in France; it was futile to try convincing us that the Germans were winning.) Sometime during this early period she became known as Axis Sally. I don't know why "Sally."

After the war Midge was convicted of treason and served twelve years in a federal prison. If she could have proved German citizenship, there would have been no valid charges against her. After prison she went to Columbus, Ohio, where she taught music at a kindergarten. She died in 1988 at the age of eighty-seven. She lived a quiet life in Columbus and never granted interviews. Her neighbors said that she was very intelligent and had a wide range of interests. I was surprised to find that Midge had been forty-four when she was entertaining us with the seductive voice of a girl in her early twenties.

# Appendix 2  The Ninety-fourth Infantry Division

The Ninety-fourth does not possess the long, proud traditions of many regular army and National Guard divisions. It was activated in 1942 to fight the war, and inactivated in 1946. We were in combat for a total of about six months, but the fighting was bitter for only two months, from mid-January to mid-March of 1945. During that time, we destroyed one of Germany's best panzer divisions, a strong infantry division plus fragments of two more, and two smaller SS mountain divisions.

In September, 1944, the division was assigned to relieve the Sixth Armored Division in Brittany so that the latter could be used in the Third Army's drive across France. At no time during our stay in the vicinity of Lorient and St.-Nazaire was there any consideration of our attempting to take either port. The Channel ports were closer to the combat area and thus constituted much better points of supply. Our division commander was promised repeatedly that we would be relieved and sent to the heavy fighting in Germany, only to be disappointed (the commander was disappointed, not the riflemen). On Christmas Eve, 1944, a ship carrying two regiments of the Sixty-sixth Infantry Division was torpedoed and sunk with the loss of 798 men. This disaster weakened the division so badly that they were given our soft assignment, while we went to the Third Army.

We were assigned a defensive mission on a particularly strong part of the German Siegfried line. (We called this section the "Siegfried Switch"; the Germans called it the "Orsholz Oblique Defense.") The division was allowed to probe at the defenses, but only in battalion-sized units. On January 14 and 15, units of our 376th Regiment made highly successful attacks. There was a counterattack, but things looked pretty good until January 17, when the Germans brought up the Eleventh Panzer Division. Called the "Ghost Division," this outfit had been one of the best in the war against Russia. It had been brought over and refitted to spearhead a drive on Metz after the (anticipated) initial success in the Battle of the Bulge. Because that success quickly faded, the Eleventh was sitting back at Trier, waiting to hit someone—like us.

The two divisions stood like boxers slugging it out, infantry against armor. The weather was bitterly cold, and we were up against men who had learned to fight in a Russian winter. Our frostbite and exposure casualties were so bad that Patton came up personally to chew out our commanding general for having so many "noncombat casualties." (I am rather proud that our medical people evacuated men with feet frozen so badly that amputation was sometimes required, and particularly glad that they evacuated young men with pneumonia and a fever of 102.) But Patton also visited Nennig and other towns and saw how brutal the battles had been. He gave us a unit of the Eighth Armored Division—plus a lot of artillery—and told us to tear the Ghost Division up. After two weeks the Eleventh Panzer no longer existed as an effective unit; it was "extracted" and replaced by more infantry plus two Austrian SS mountain divisions. By mid-March, organized German resistance in front of the Ninety-fourth had collapsed. During those two months, K Company incurred roughly 400 percent casualties, and other rifle companies had it even worse. The division as a whole suffered approximately 11,000 casualties during the war.

People often say: "Ninety-fourth Infantry? I never heard of it." True, we fought hard for only about two months, but when we did fight, we fought very well. The division was officially inactivated, unit by unit, during late January and early February, 1946, at Camp Kilmer, New Jersey. It is now an Organized Reserve unit, the Ninety-fourth ARCOM. It has infantry brigades instead of regiments, so King Company of the 301st Infantry no longer exists.

# Note on Sources

Any book of this kind necessarily relies on the personal and often highly subjective recollections of a number of people, including the author. I was gratified when, after completing my version of the Third Platoon ambush, I sent a copy to Dave Devonald for his comments: along with a few minor adjustments, he expressed his amazement at my fantastic memory. In truth, I have trouble remembering where I parked the car; memory is a strange process. When I began writing this, I could remember only some flashes of emotion from combat: exhilaration, cold fear, despair, and the comfort of being with friends. As I wrote those early fragments, a few details came back, but not nearly enough to tell a story. Historians helped me in finding good reference books. George Faber, Bill Henry, and George Herrington helped me by contributing what they remembered. At that point the process was much like working a jigsaw puzzle, all the while realizing that some pieces might be misshapen from flawed memory or might even belong in another puzzle.

I wrote the city clerk at David City for more information on Dale Proctor. Through her, I met Dale's brother, Don. The National Association of Retired Army Nurses located Lieutenant Colonel Barbara Cullom, who had been in the 127th General Hospital with Lieutenant Yeager. A career officer, Barbara was able to give me a comprehensive view of the combat fatigue and frozen-foot problems. The American Red Cross located Rosemary Norwalk, who had been in charge of the clubmobile operations when we left Southampton. I received a lot of help from Jim Westmoreland, Bob Feitig, Dick Simmers, Bill Warren (who replaced Dick as company commander), and our battalion commander, Colonel William McNulty.

In writing this I realize how many people helped, and that I cannot name them all. Some of the help was critical in nature: "I don't think it happened this way" or "Your facts seem sound, but I don't think they mean what you say they mean." I appreciate all of it, even where I decided to stick with my original recollection. This is what I saw, or seem to remember seeing.

A number of published references helped me to see the broader picture of which K Company was a small part. The army did an excellent job of documenting its actions in World War II. During the early stages it assigned professional historians to the various branches with instructions to study and record the operations so as to be able to write detailed accounts after the end of the war. This material has been published as a series: U.S. Department of the Army, Office of the Chief of Miltary History, *The U.S. Army in World War II* (99 vols. projected; ongoing). Most of the volumes are well written and documented in great detail. Several were especially helpful to me: The formation, purposes, and fate of the ASTP are described in Robert R. Palmer, Bell I. Wiley, and William R. Keast, *The Procurement and Training of Ground Combat Troops* (Washington, D.C., 1948). Operations in Brittany are discussed in Martin Blumenson, *Breakout and Pursuit* (Washington, D.C., 1961). The operations around Nennig are recounted in Charles B. MacDonald, *The Last Offensive* (Washington, D.C., 1973). Information about the footwear supply problems came from William F. Ross and Charles F. Romanus, *The Quartermaster Corps: Operations in the War Against Germany* (Washington, D.C., 1965).

I relied on Laurence G. Byrnes, ed., *History of the 94th Infantry Division in World War II* (Washington, D.C., 1948), for some details of the division's operations and history.

When the war ended, the army ordered all captured German commanders to write detailed accounts of their experiences, including descriptions of the difficulties they encountered and evaluations of both German and American troop effectiveness. Microfiche copies of these reports, which carry the prefix MS, are available at a nominal cost from the National Archives, Washington, D.C. My reference for German views of the fighting in Brittany is MS B-731, the report of General Wilhelm Fahrmbacher, commander of an Army Group that fought in Normandy and later in Brittany. He took command of the Lorient garrison on August 16, 1944, and remained in command until the end of the war. Fahrmbacher has a dry, straightforward writing style, but his accounts seem honest and reasonable. I used two other manuscripts to a lesser extent. MS B-066 is a report by Ludwig Graf von Ingelheim about the activity of his Eighty-second Corps in the Nennig area. He tends to be wordy, but the account is interesting. Of his three divisions, he considered two to be very good. He has no comments on the effectiveness of the American forces other than that we were very wasteful in the use of artillery and that we moved into new openings with unexpected speed; the latter appraisal probably means that Patton pushed us much harder than von Ingelheim would have done in the same situation. (Fahrmbacher had the same observation about our reliance on artillery. Apparently the German army did not have the luxury of expending massive amounts of artillery to save the lives of riflemen.) MS B-417 is the report of Werd von Wietersheim on the experiences of his Eleventh Panzer Division. It is quite short and says very little except that he was at a disadvantage because of the terrain and our overwhelming artillery usage.

In 1956, Fahrmbacher co-wrote a book that elaborates on his account: Wilhelm Fahrmbacher and Walter Matthine, *Lorient: Entstehung und Verteidigung des Marine-Stutzpuntes, 1940/1945* (Weissenburg, West Germany, 1956).

Many of my thoughts on why we fought were drawn from three published studies. The standard reference to why men fight is S. L. A. Marshall, *Men Against Fire: The Problem of Battle Command in Future War* (New York, 1947). Marshall was a psychologist assigned by the army to study this aspect of combat. The most frequently quoted statement is his estimate that only about 20 to 25 percent of the American riflemen ever fired their rifles in combat. The attention given this estimate is unfortunate because the book addresses much more. I believe that the estimate is sound, but I feel that Marshall looked too closely at the individual and too little at group influences. In my opinion, the better reference is Samuel A. Stouffer *et al.*, *The American Soldier: Combat and Its Aftermath* (Princeton, 1949), Vol. II of Stouffer *et al.*, *Studies in Social Psychology in World War II*, 4 vols. Stouffer headed a research team of sociologists who looked at several aspects of combat effects on soldiers. In contrast with Marshall's study of the individual, Stouffer's group looked on the squad, platoon, or company as communities to which the soldier belonged. Their work shows very clearly that the response of a rifleman in combat rests with his sense of loyalty to the unit. During the confusion of the Battle of the Bulge, commanders often picked up small groups of soldiers who had become lost from their units. The consensus was that units of four or five men who had fought together before also performed well in later combat. By contrast, men picked up as solitary soldiers were seldom of any real value until they had come to know other soldiers in the new unit. Essentially, Stouffer's group concluded that courage in combat springs from loyalty to the group. That conclusion supports the assertion that soldiers fight for their friends rather than for God and Country. Separated from their group, they are poor combat troops. Unfortunately, the same is true of replacements who do not have time to become part of the squad. This point is covered very well in a mimeographed publication, Leonard S. Lerwill, *World War II* (Washington, D.C., 1953), Vol. II of U.S. Department of the Army, Office of the Chief of Military History, *The Personnel Replacement System in the United States Army,* 2 vols.

J. Glenn Gray, *The Warriors: Reflections on Men in Battle* (New York, 1959), was very helpful in the problems of ethics and combat. Gray, as a new philosophy Ph.D., was assigned to the headquarters of an infantry division fighting in France. Because of his fluency in French and German, he was assigned to interrogate French civilians for information on the actions of German troops. During that time, he kept a personal journal of his thoughts on the destruction and ethical aspects of combat. About fifteen years later, he wrote *The Warriors* as commentary on those thoughts from the perspective of a philosopher. The book is interesting because Gray had the advantage of reading other reports and was not addressing a broad problem, but simply developing his thoughts about combat. Gray promotes the concept that because soldiers act as units, the individual soldier has very little control over his ethical standards.

I know of three interesting books about the fate of former ASTP soldiers after the program was disbanded. The most comprehensive is

Louis E. Keefer, *Scholars in Foxholes: The Story of the Army Specialized Training Program in World War II* (Jefferson, N.C., 1988). Keefer sent a questionnaire to former ASTP soldiers and received 250 replies. He reports that the college training program was so accelerated that many good students were close to failing. Others were saved only by the army's concept of a standard curriculum for all students; they were repeating courses which they had taken as civilians. That group had a wonderful social life while in the ASTP. Keefer points out that although most of the ASTP soldiers were assigned to the infantry, others went into more interesting jobs. Gore Vidal wrote that he used political influence to get assigned to a transportation unit. A boy in my company at Benning was sent to Special Services because he had been a lead singer in the movie *Best Foot Forward.* Henry Kissinger was put into Military Intelligence because of his German background.

William Wharton, *A Midnight Clear* (New York, 1982), is a novel about former ASTP soldiers fighting as riflemen during the winter of 1944–1945. No unit is identified, but it appears to be the 106th Division in late December. The story is fascinating and chilling, but I think that Wharton overdoes his point concerning intelligent young soldiers and the injustice of their having to fight.

Frank F. Mathias, *G.I. Jive: An Army Bandsman in World War II* (Lexington, Ky., 1982), is another interesting account of the program. Mathias, a member of the ASTP band at Fort Benning, was assigned to a rifle company of the Thirty-seventh Division, fighting in the Philippines. While Mathias was waiting for transportation to the front, a clerk noticed that he played a saxophone, and remembered that the division band needed such a player. The book is largely an account of the duties of a bandsman during combat. The life was slightly safer than the life of a rifleman, but not much.

The revival songs are so deeply imprinted that they were easy to recall, but the words that I remembered varied from those in the song book. I used the 1940 edition of *The Broadman Hymnal* (Nashville, Tenn., 1940). My Bible quotations are entirely from the King James Version that we used in Clinton. I was occasionally tempted to use different, more exact translations but decided it would add to the confusion. At best, the Old Testament is difficult to understand.